AF254793

Landscape
COLLAGE TECHNIQUES

Impressionistic collage paintings, step-by-step

ELIZABETH ST. HILAIRE

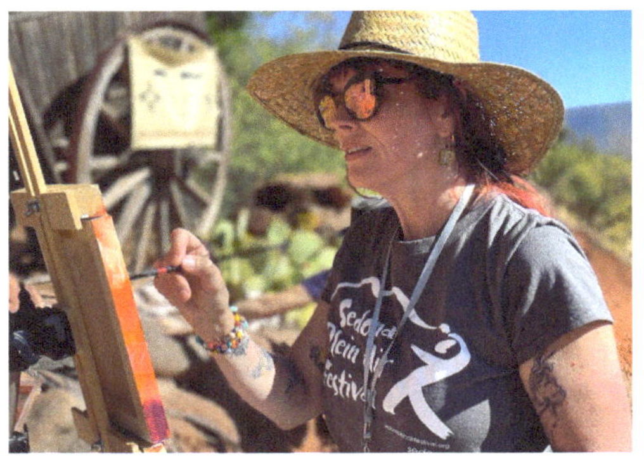

For Emilie and Connor

*Thank you for loving me for who I am,
for supporting me in what I do, and for
understanding both.*

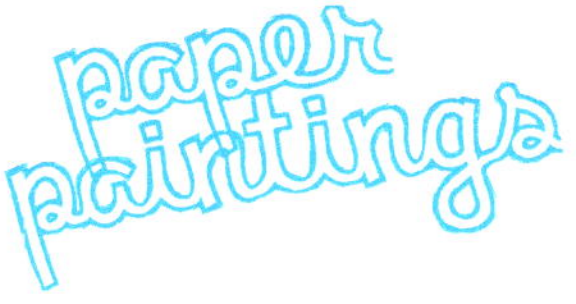

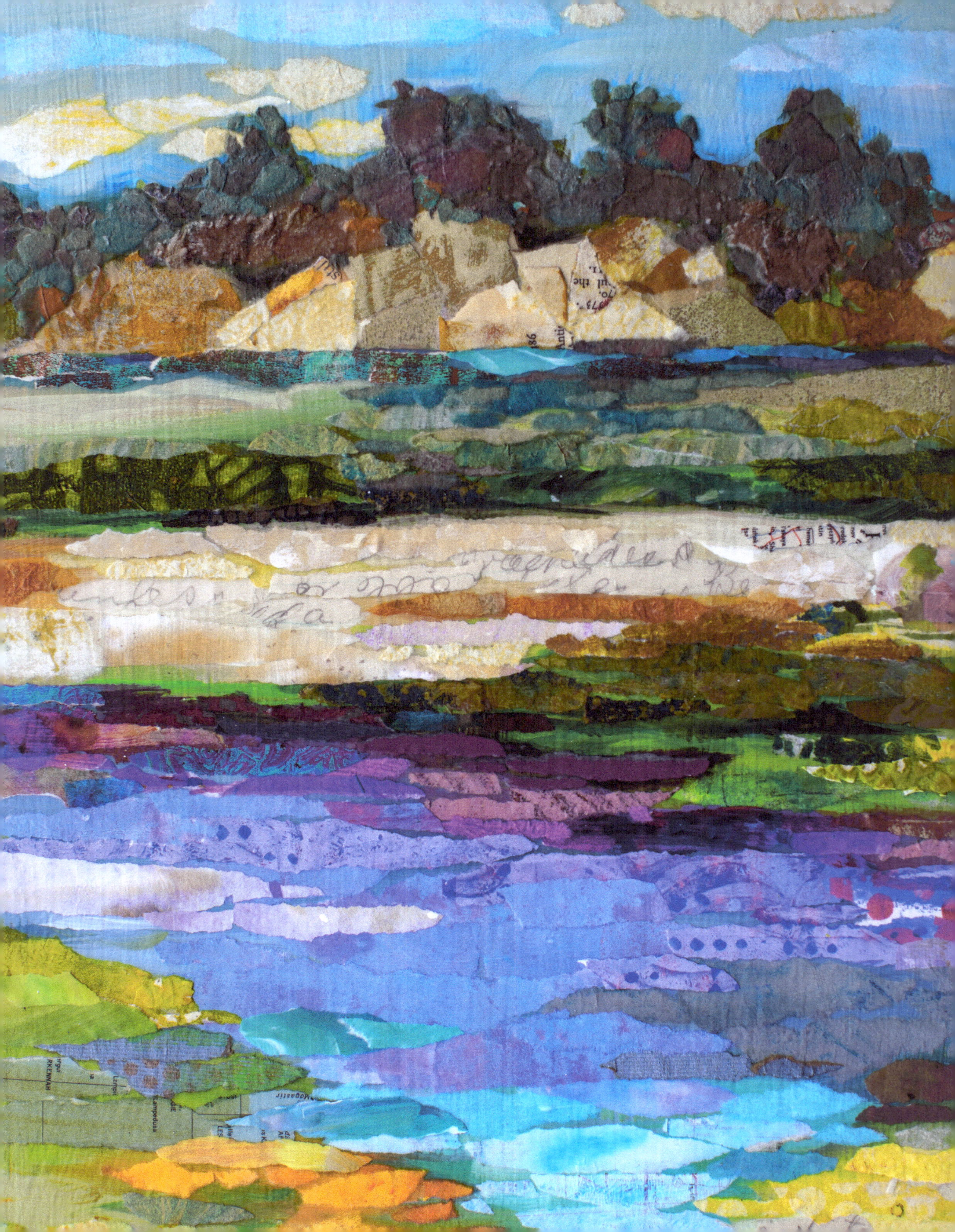

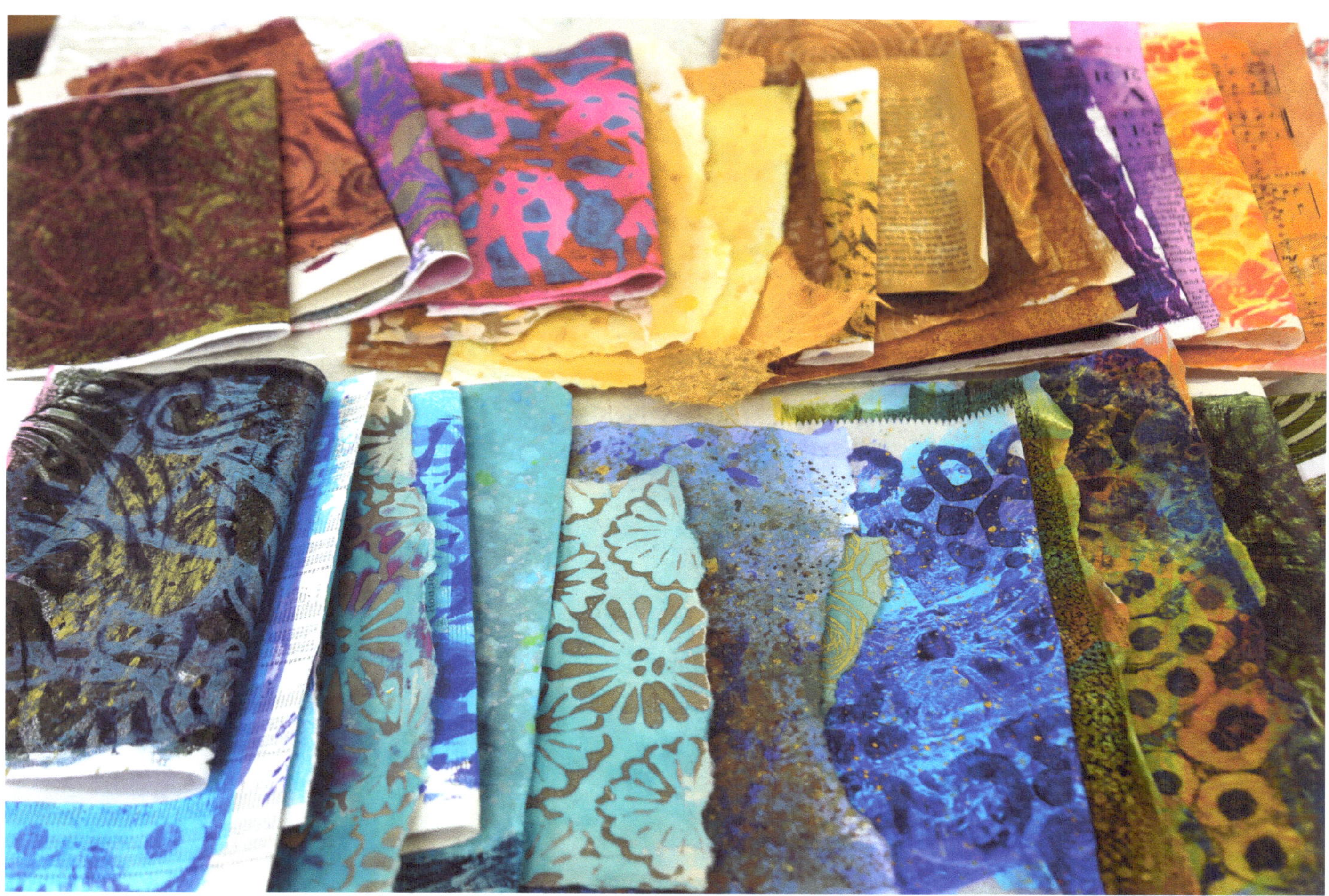

what is a paper painting?

A figurative, painterly collage is created by adhering hand-painted, hand-made, and found papers over an acrylic under painting on wood panel.

The overall impressionistic feeling of the work is achieved by treating every bit of torn (not cut) paper like an brush stroke, keeping details loose, and using a variety of texture and shades of paper in every color field.

Creating your own papers for collage offers a custom paper palette with every shade of every color that appeals to you, offering variety and inspiration.

Utilizing the same techniques that apply to painting with acrylic or oil, the success of the work depends on a firm understanding of shading—light, dark, and medium values coupled with "brush marks" that follow the form.

Often times, the viewer will be totally surprised that this artwork is not a painting, but rather a mixed media collage. Even up close, people will still ask, *"You mean it's not a painting?"* This is the a-ha moment that I love.

Landscape Collage TECHNIQUES

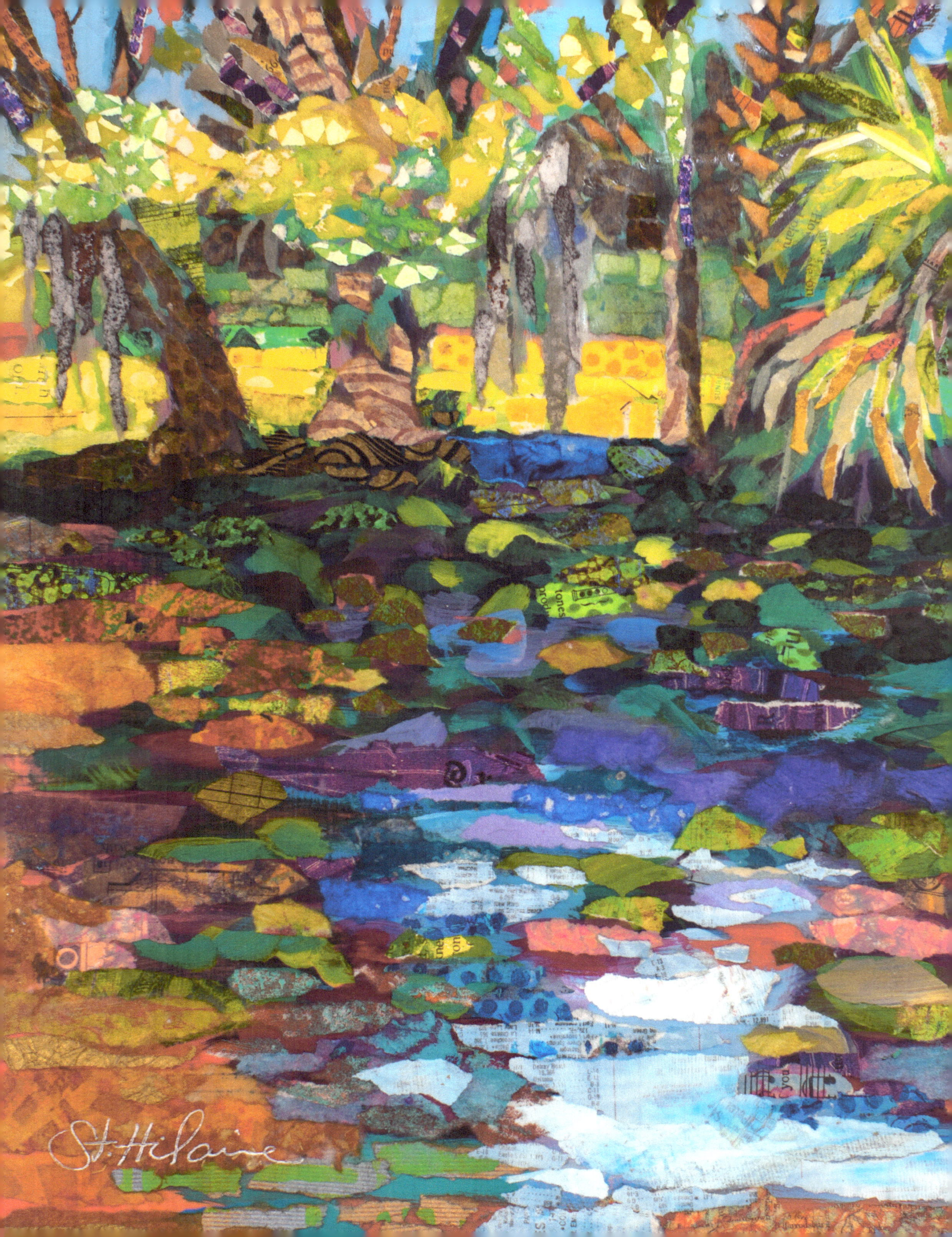
St. Hilaire

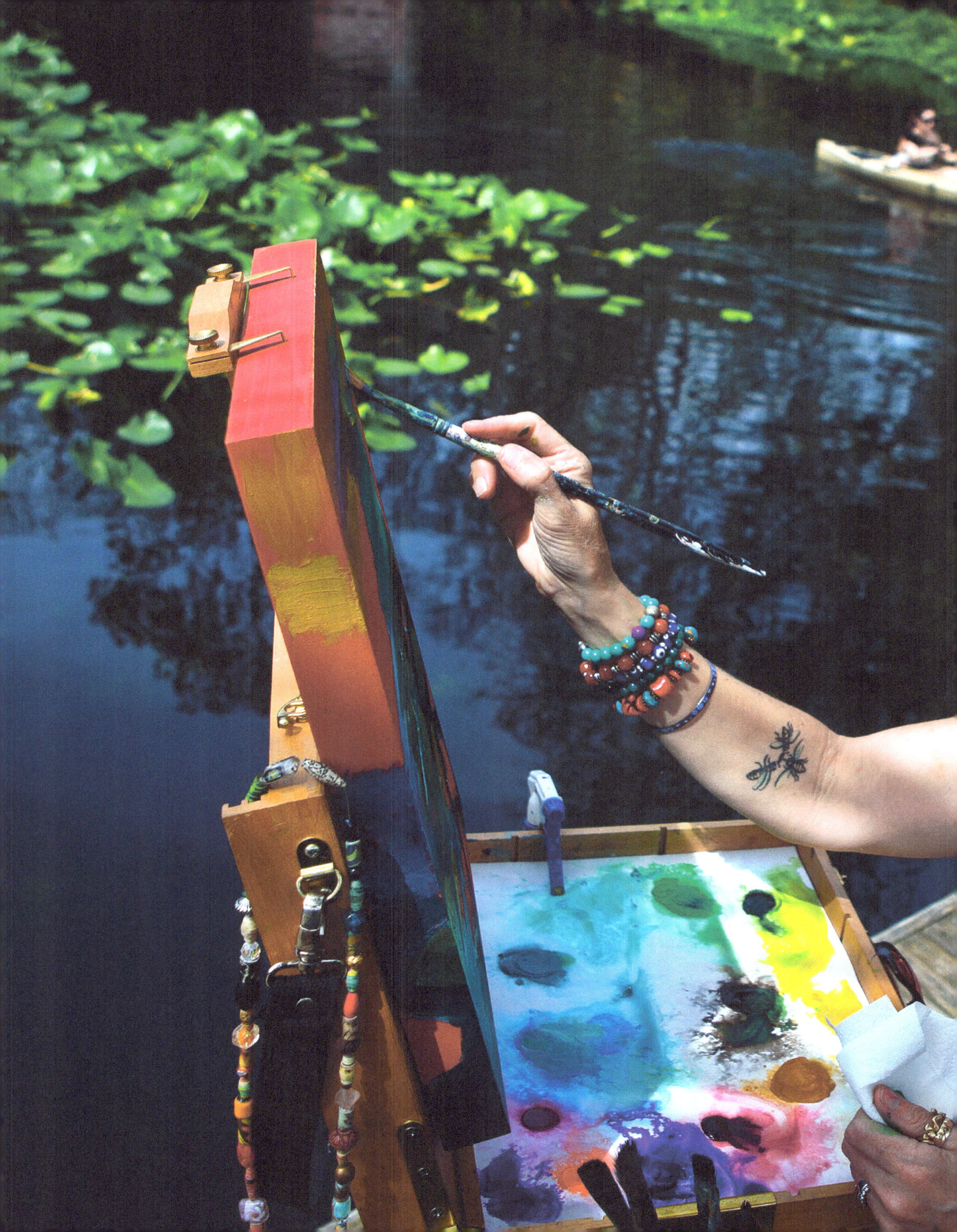

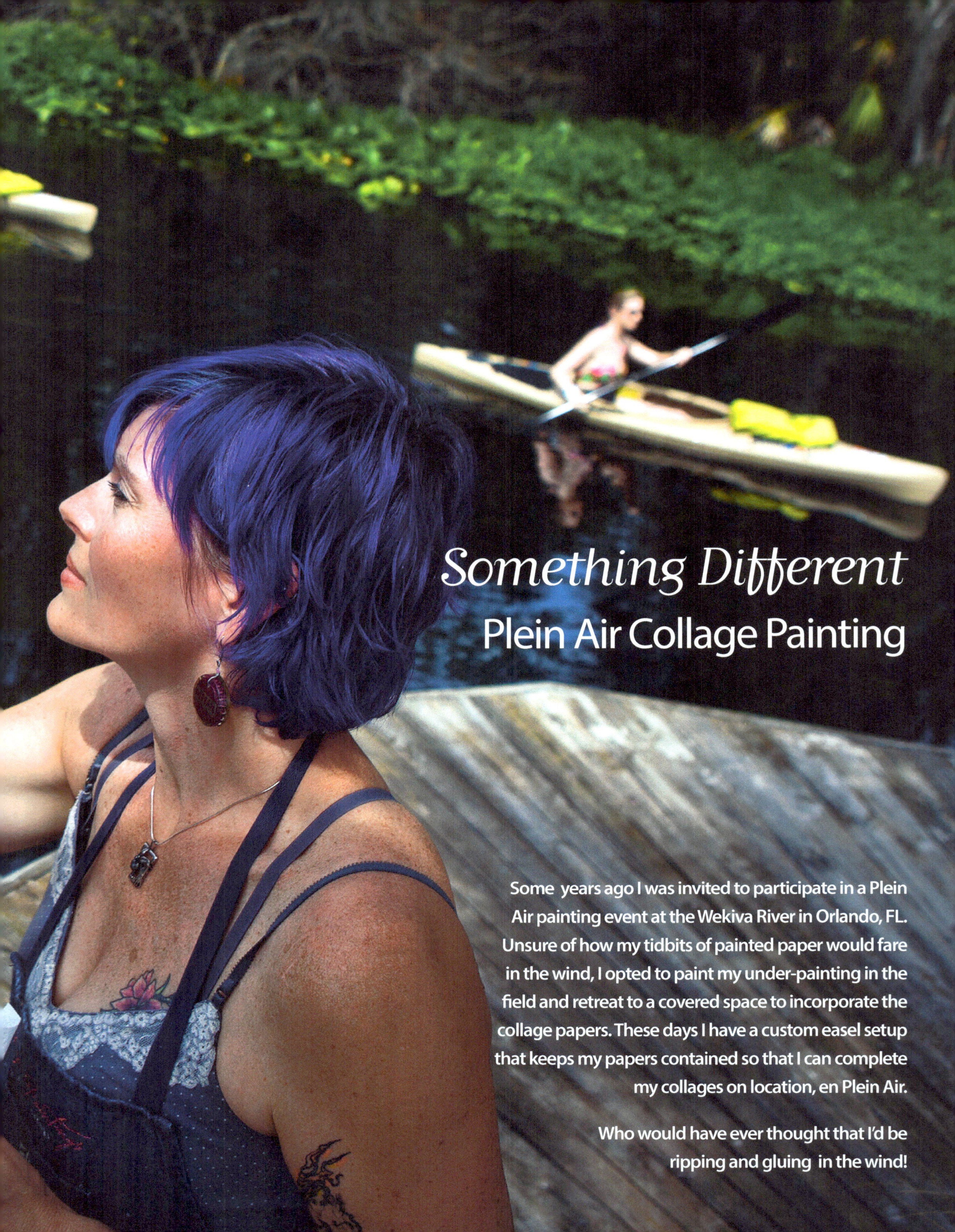

Something Different
Plein Air Collage Painting

Some years ago I was invited to participate in a Plein Air painting event at the Wekiva River in Orlando, FL. Unsure of how my tidbits of painted paper would fare in the wind, I opted to paint my under-painting in the field and retreat to a covered space to incorporate the collage papers. These days I have a custom easel setup that keeps my papers contained so that I can complete my collages on location, en Plein Air.

Who would have ever thought that I'd be ripping and gluing in the wind!

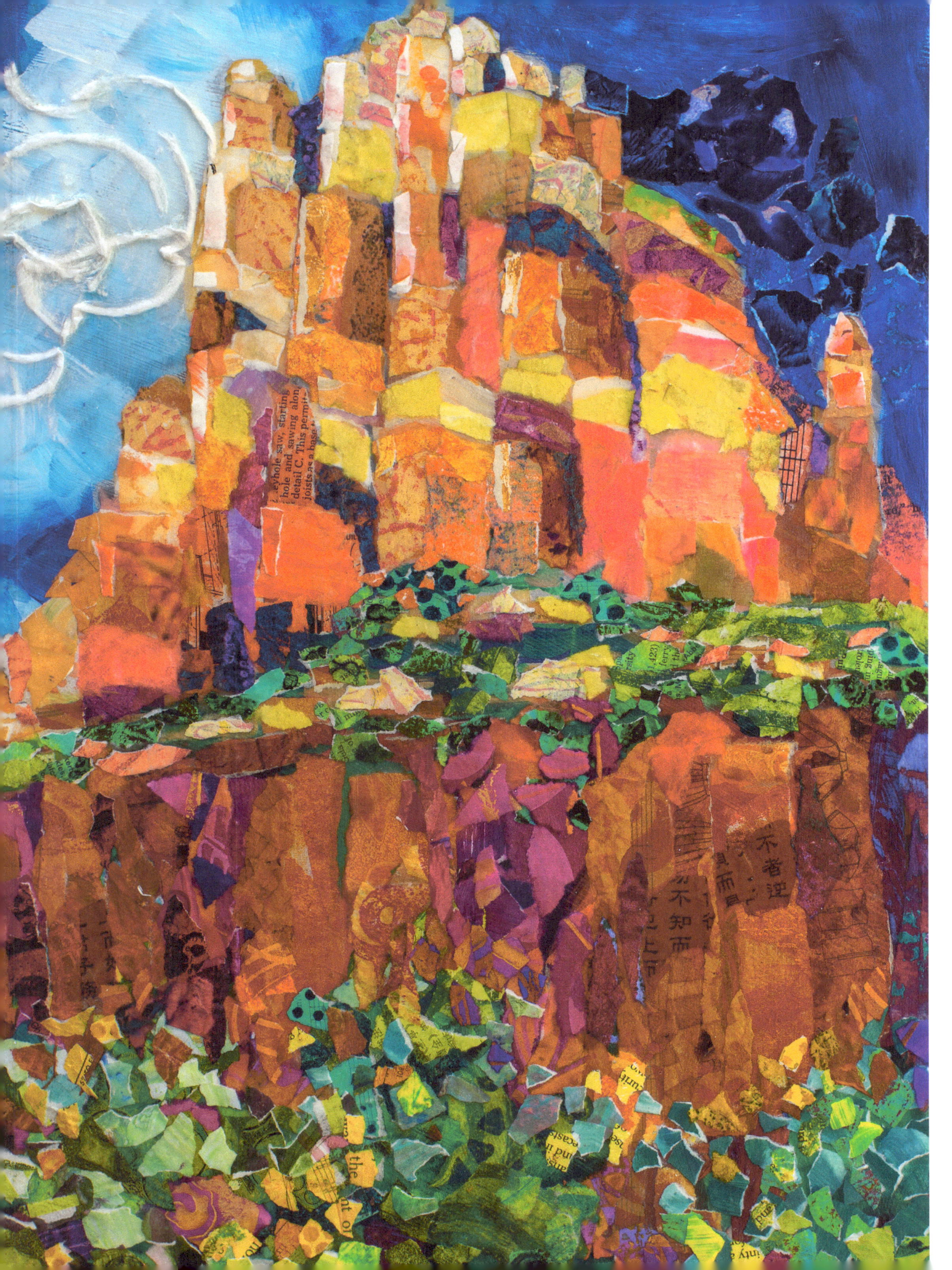

COLLAGE

My technique has evolved and changed as a result of experimentation with hand-painted, hand-made, textured, and patterned papers. Layering and weaving, pushing and pulling the colors, patterns, and values makes the collage process like a dance. Undulating, alternating, and overlapping, until the rhythm creates something I love.

My love of the landscape began about six years ago when I said "yes!" to an invitation from the Wekiva Paint Out to join 30 other landscape painters for a week-long event at the Wekiva River. Prior to this Plein Air event, landscape really hadn't been my subject matter. I was busy painting animals, birds, and florals. Stepping outside of my box (and outside my studio) opened my eyes to the beauty of the natural world around me and the process of drawing and painting from life, in the field. Since then I have participated in a number of other Plein Air painting festivals and events, including the Sedona Plein Air Festival in Arizona. I have learned to embrace landscape as a subject, both en Plein Air and the studio.

In my work I highlight the extraordinary within the ordinary, focusing on intense and vibrant colors combined with a sensibility of design. My collages invite the viewer to look, and having looked, to linger.

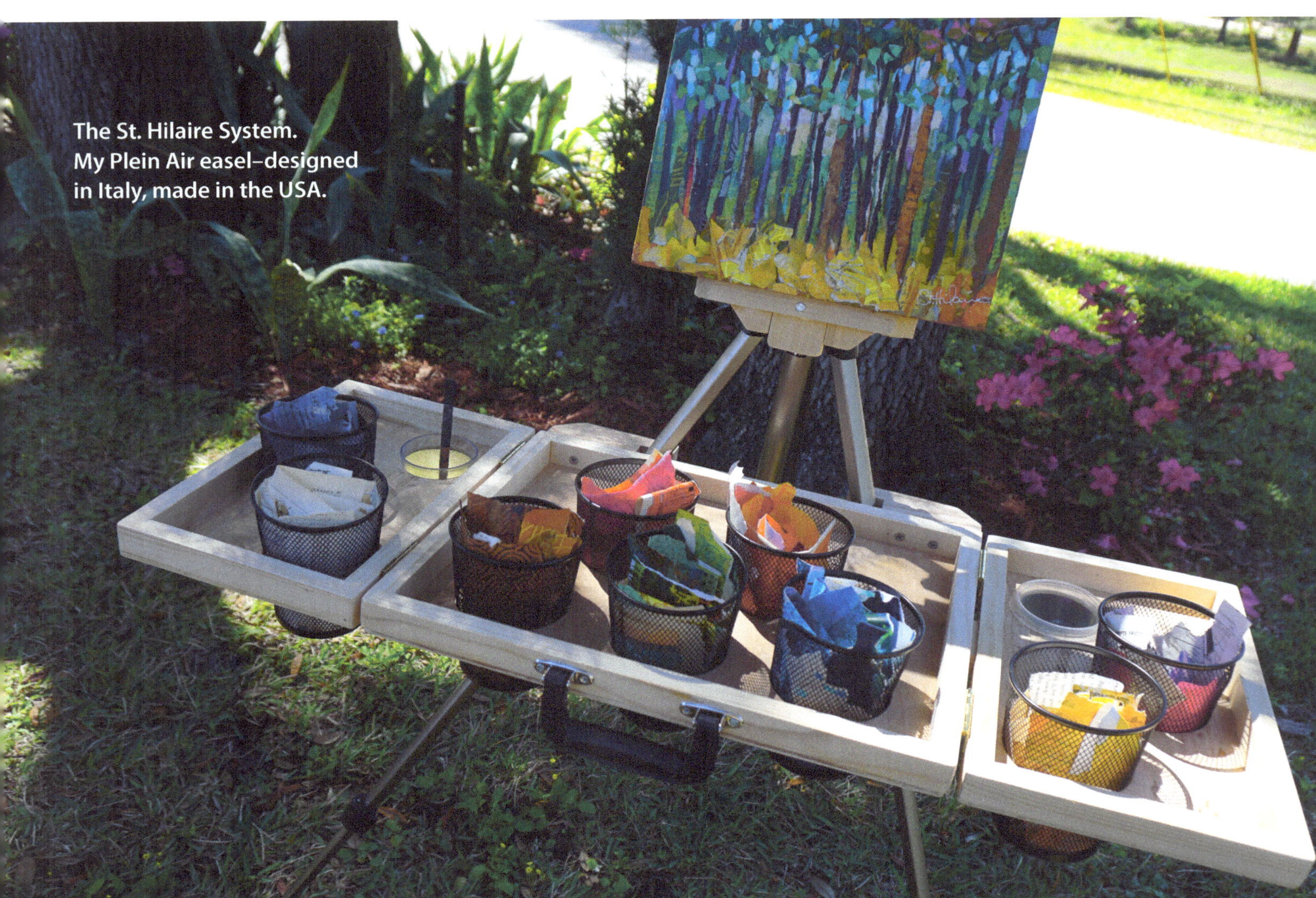

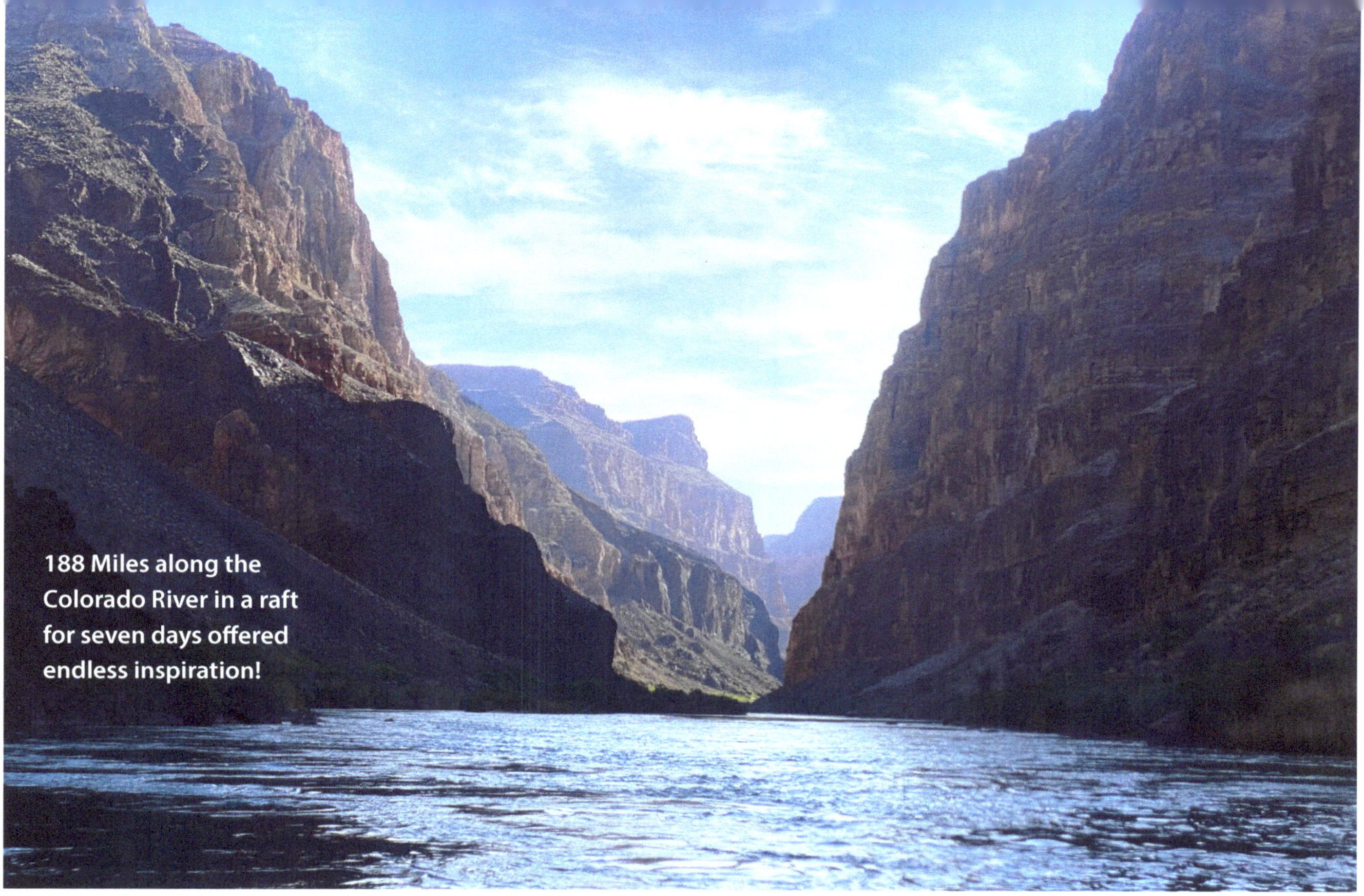

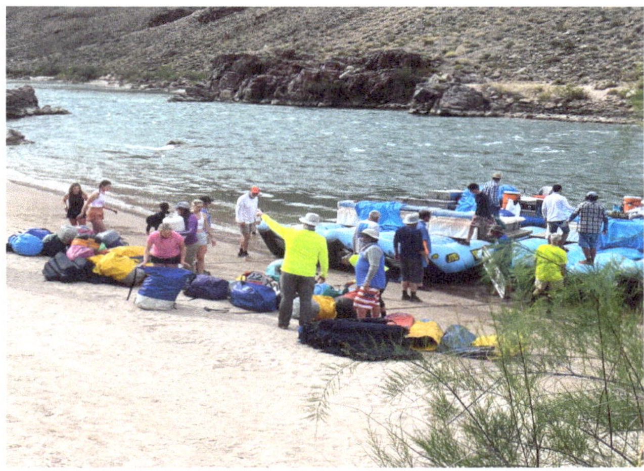

Mother Nature as Muse
INSPIRATION
Grand Canyon National Park

Whether it's the emerald green rapids of the Colorado River as it meanders through the Grand Canyon, the awe-inspiring light of Tuscany, the intense red-rocks of Sedona, or your own back yard; nature offers endless inspiration for landscape painting. Whether you work outdoors from life (en Plein Air) or in your studio from photographs, capturing the colors, light, and textures of nature in collage is both a challenge and a joy.

Remember to always look closely at your subject—draw what you see, not what you think you see. Capturing the essence of a scene requires layers of looking. Translating the landscape into collage requires breaking things down into simple shapes, simplifying the details, and working in an impressionistic manner.

It's about the process, not the product. Enjoy the journey!

A rafting trip inspired a body of Grand Canyon landscapes

Landscape Collage TECHNIQUES

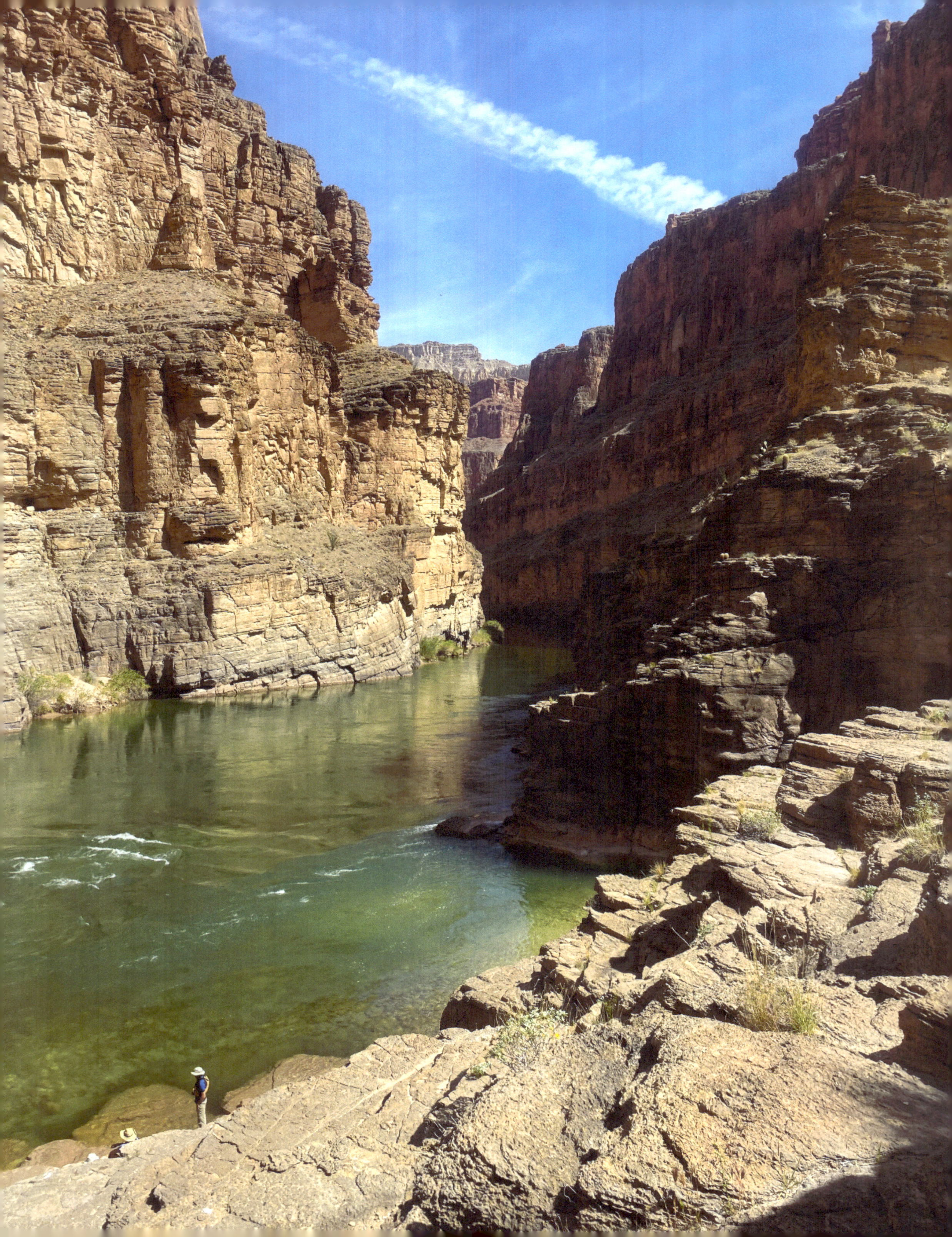

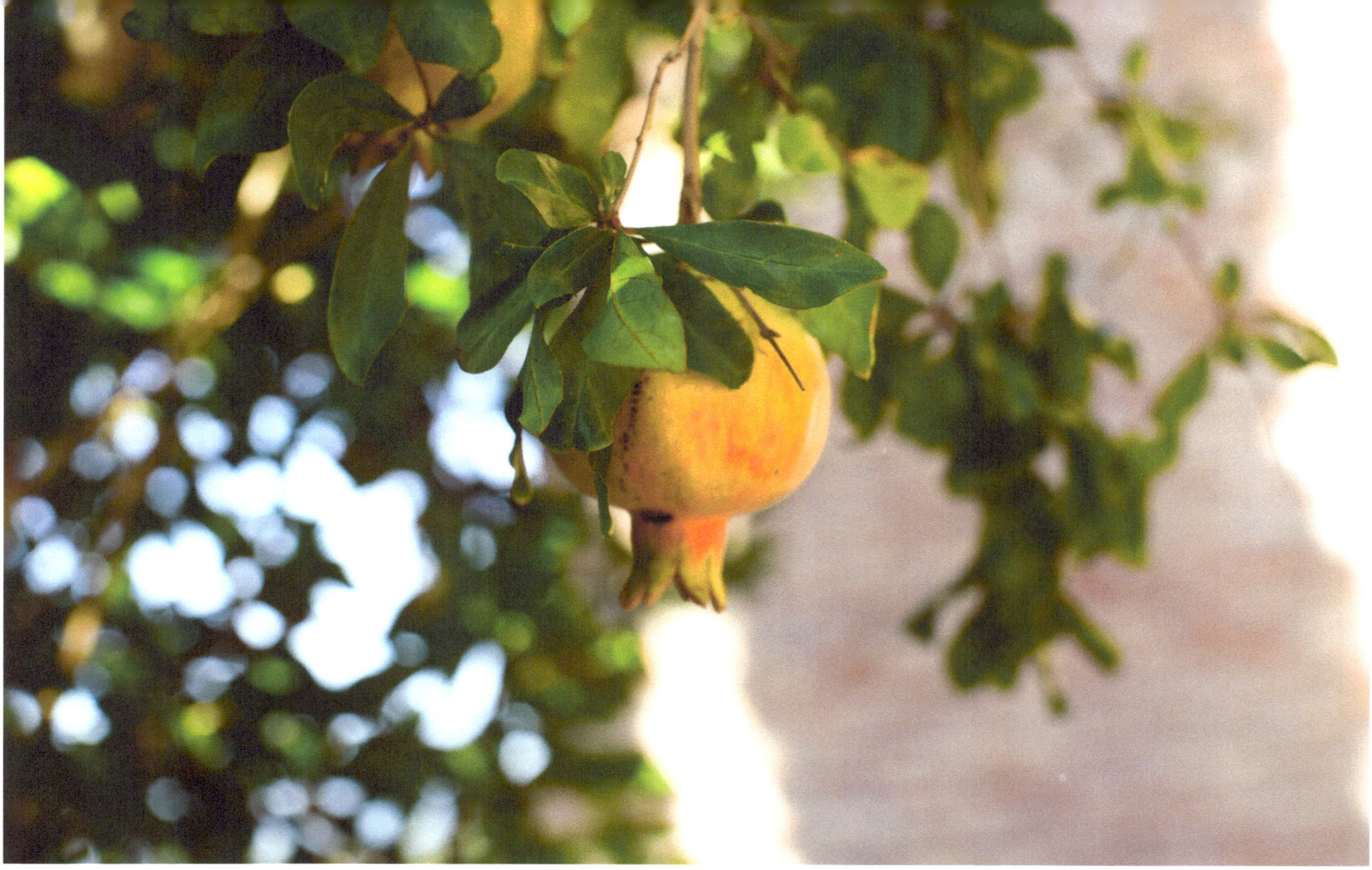

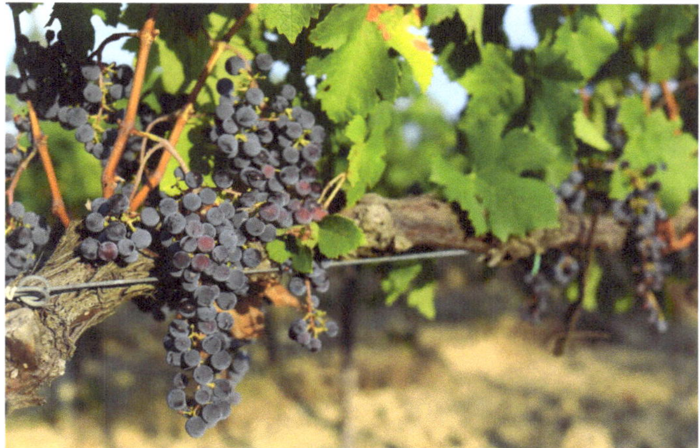
The grape harvest offers rich color and texture

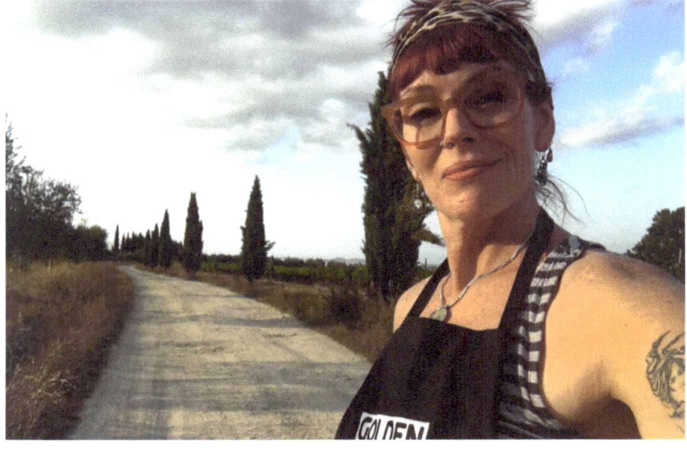
I have painted many a cypress tree-lined dirt road in Tuscany!

Tuscany offers such amazing light, it makes simple details remarkable

Tuscany

My first Paper Paintings Tuscany Retreat was in 2016. I had never visited the countryside of Tuscany and I was immediately taken with the amazing light and incredible skies of the region that was the birthplace of the Renaissance.

Landscape is such a common subject in art that we take it for granted. Yet landscape as a category of European painting emerged only during the Renaissance.

In Renaissance Italy the study of perspective brought forth a careful rendering of scenery. Venetian painters excelled at pastoral vistas that recalled scenes from classical literature. Flemish works enhanced by meticulous landscape detail became popular in Italy hand inspired Italian artists.

One of my favorite places to paint is the dirt road that leads to the private villa that hosts my workshop students. The elongated cast shadows from cypress trees at the end of the day inspire me; I have painted this scene many times both en Plein Air and from photographic reference.

Landscape Collage TECHNIQUES

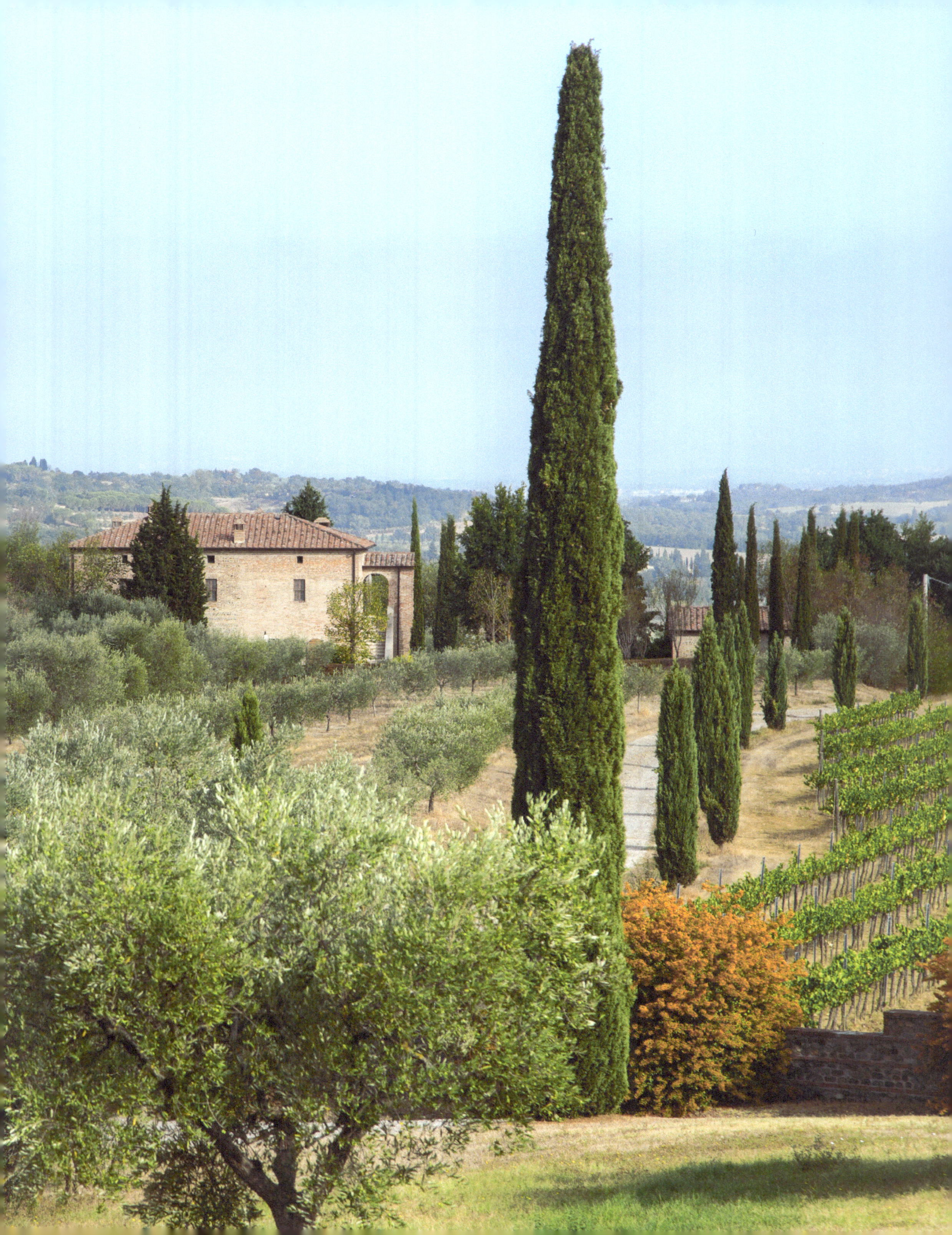

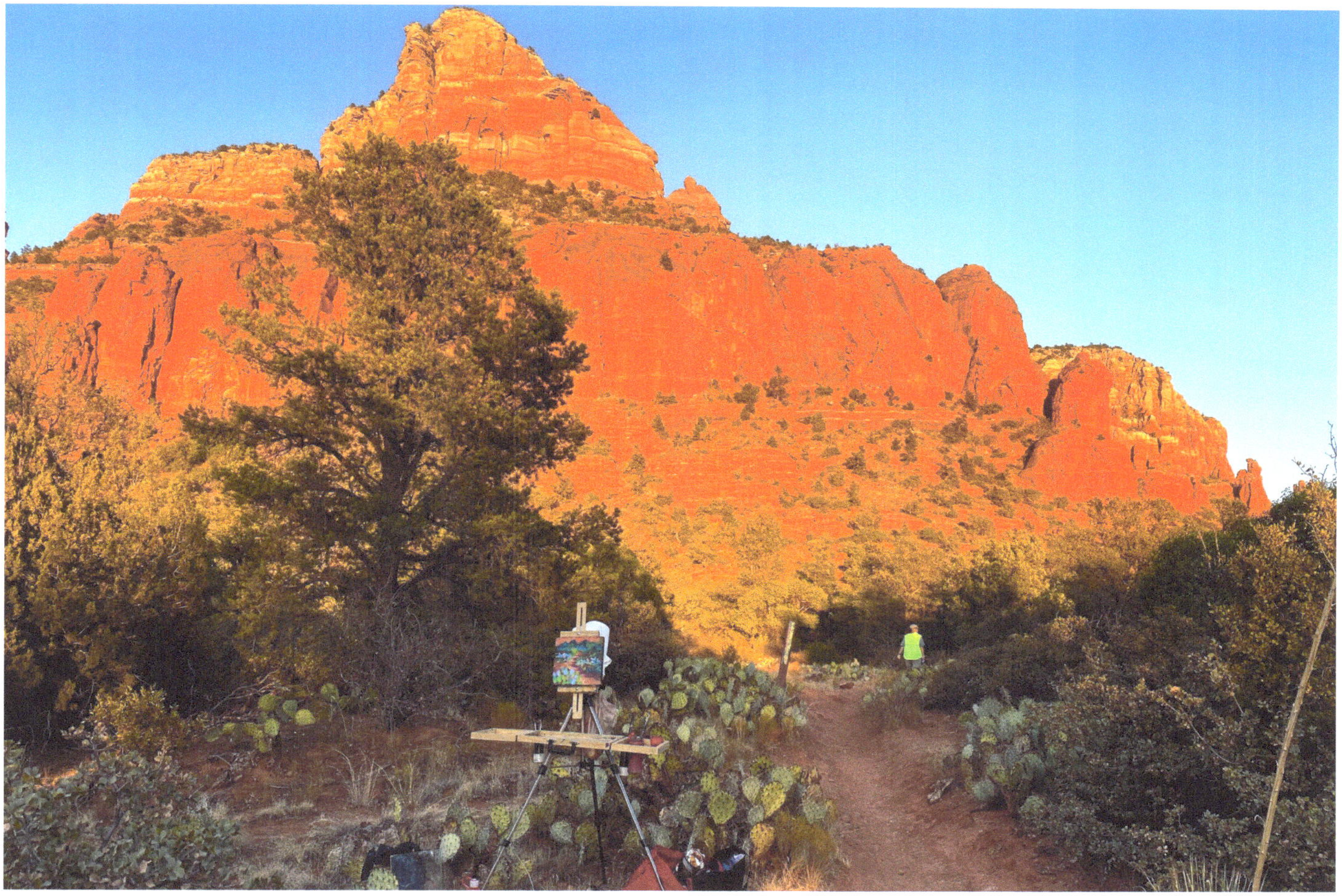

Sedona has beautiful color and remarkable rock formations

Sedona

Sedona has been my Happy Place for many years, I originally visited there with my family and was captivated by the red-rock terrain. Upon returning home, I reached out to several galleries in Uptown Sedona for representation–I was lucky enough to earn a spot with the Lark Art Gallery which represented my work for nearly ten years.

Sedona is a desert town near Flagstaff that's surrounded by red-rock buttes, steep canyon walls and pine forests. It's noted for its mild climate and vibrant arts community. Uptown Sedona is dense with New Age shops, spas and art galleries. On the town's outskirts, numerous trailheads access Red Rock State Park, which offers bird-watching and fabulous hiking.

I also connected with the Sedona Arts Center in Uptown, where I was added to the curriculum

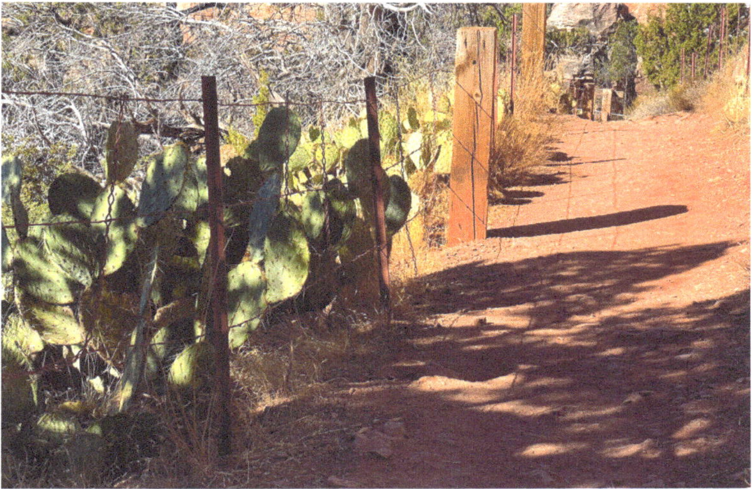

A hiking trail in Sedona, AZ

as a workshop instructor under the category of mixed media. I have been teaching Paper Paintings workshops there for over ten years. In 2019 I was invited to participate in the Sedona Plein Air Festival and that's when I really was able to appreciate painting the desert landscape from life.

Landscape Collage TECHNIQUES

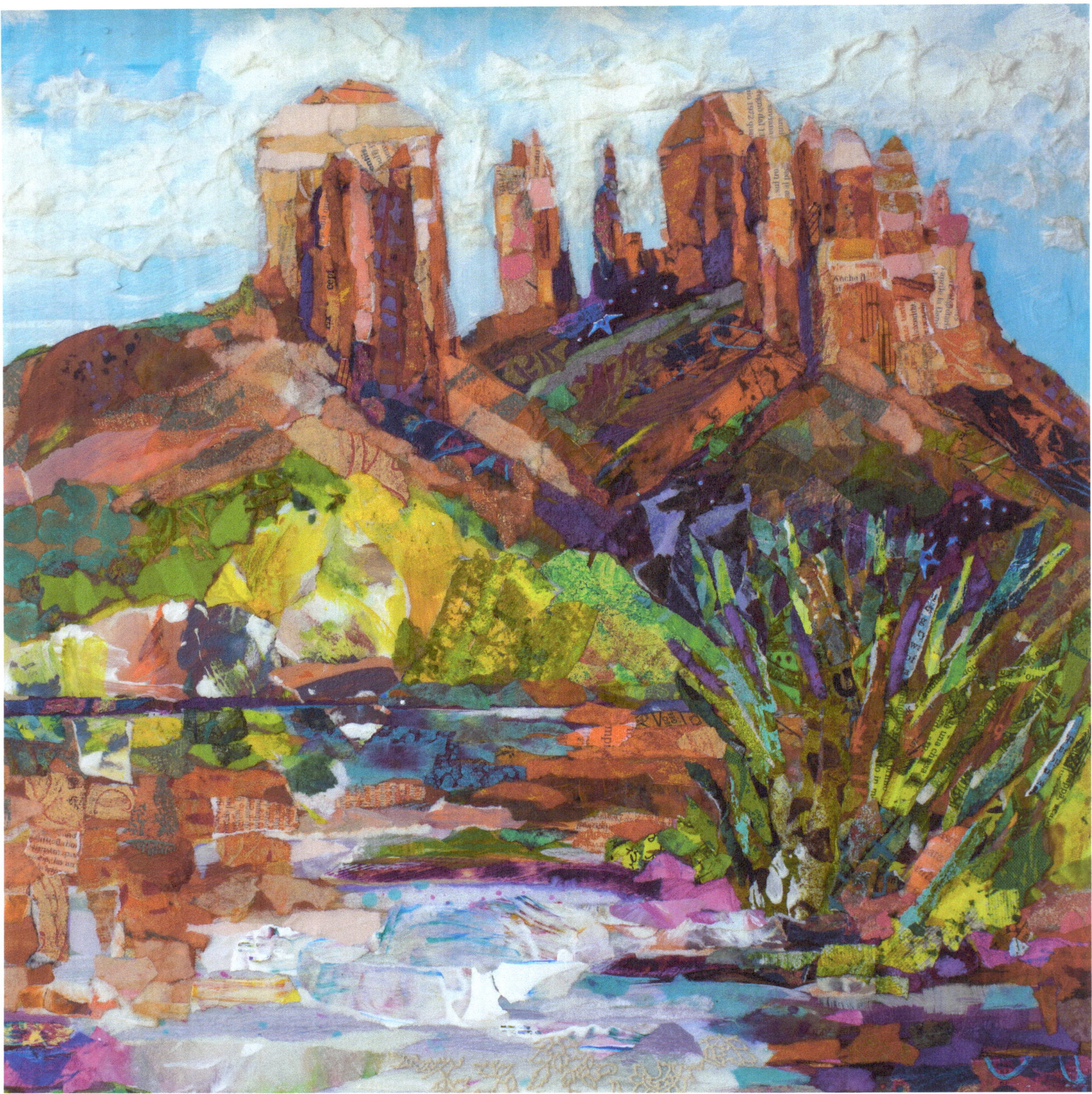

Spring in Sedona / 24x20

nature's color palette

In a perfect artistic world, all colors can be blended from the primary red, yellow, blue, white and black. If you are not skilled at color mixing, you are in luck... You may purchase pre-mixed paint in a seemingly endless variety of colors and shades at your local art supply store or on-line. Painting your own collage paper with professional artist colors is the key to having all the colors, patterns, textures, shades, and values you will need.

looking closely

Capturing the simple shapes of landscape requires close visual examination. You must forget what you think you know and really study the scene in order to reduce (and draw) landscape to its' most simple and effective shapes.

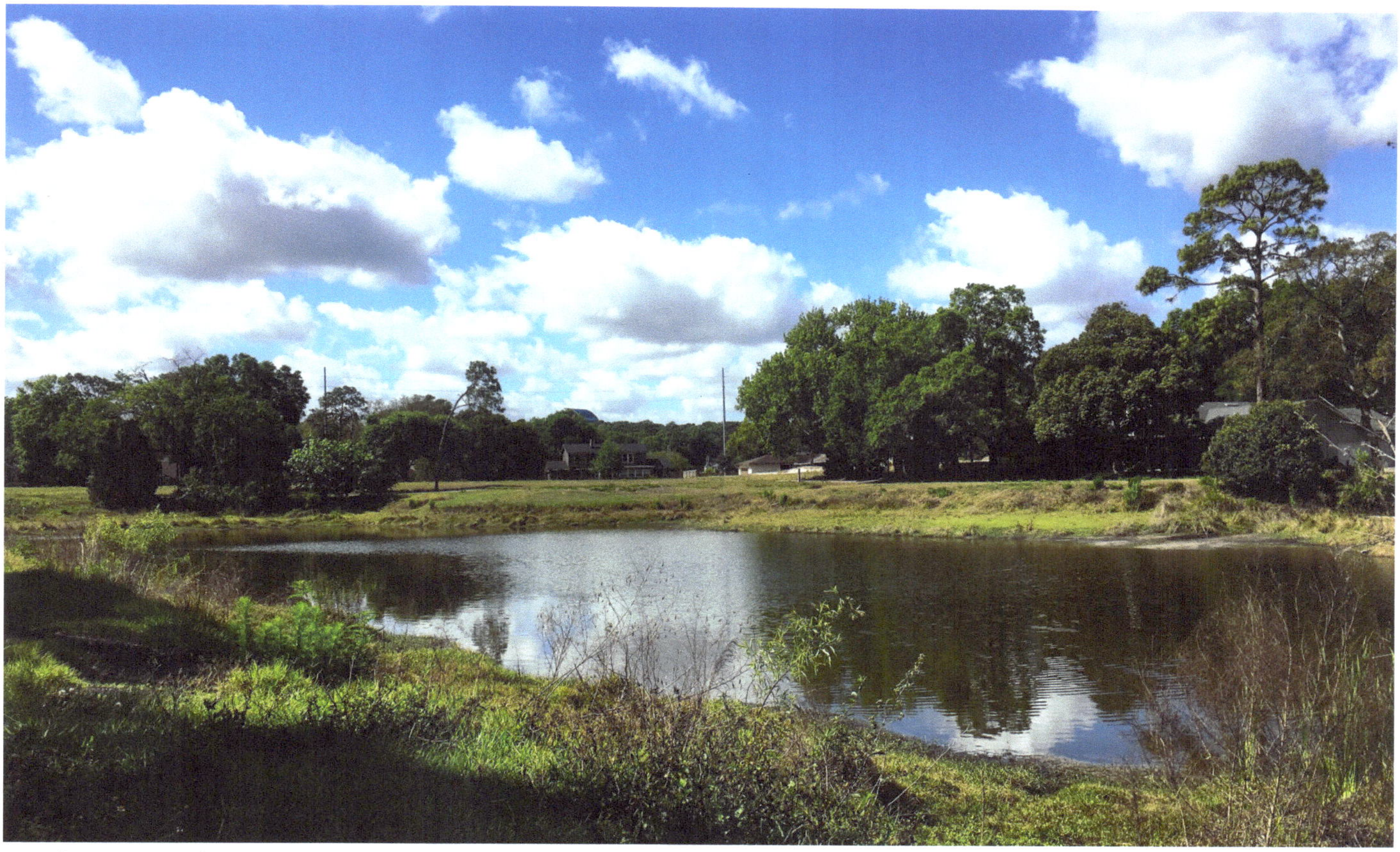

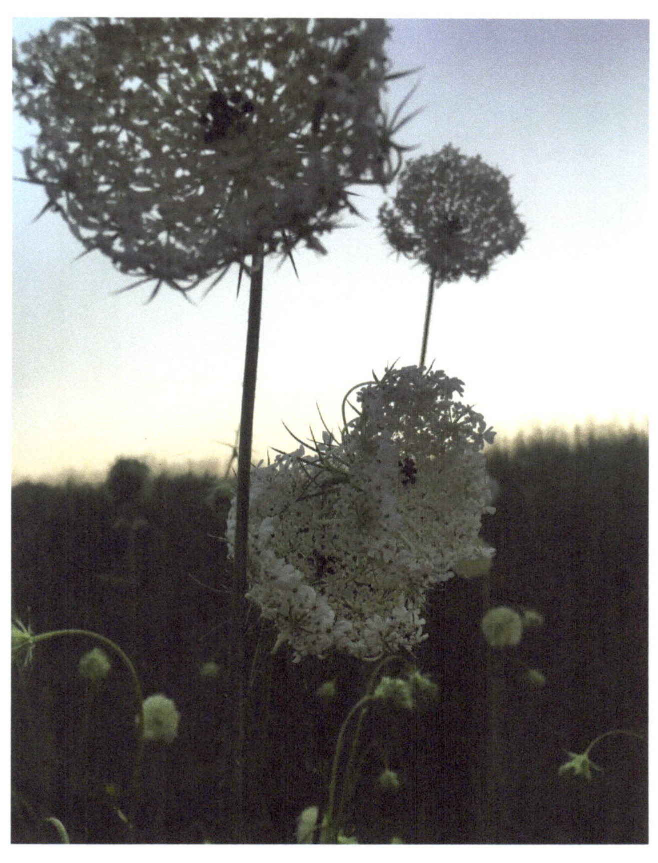

A walk around my former Florida neighborhood offered wonderful natural views of an abandoned golf course

Here at Home

You don't have to travel to exotic places to find great landscape inspiration. You can be inspired by the simplicity your own back yard. I used to walk my dogs through my neighborhood's abandoned golf course. At times it felt as though I lived right in the middle of the country, even though you could hear the traffic from Interstate-4!

I take lots of photos, hoping to create paintings from them. The key is remembering where you filed them when you are looking for them. Try putting all your painting reference images in one folder on your computer so that you can refer back to it when you are in need of inspiration.

Remember that landscape does not always need to be vast or expansive, intimate portraits of a place are just as interesting. Look closely at some elements of the landscape that you might find inspiring.

Queen Anne's Lace (right) was taken at the mailbox of a dear friend in Upstate NY.

Calla Lilies (overleaf) was taken in my front yard after weeding and mulching and feeling pretty good about my landscaping skills.

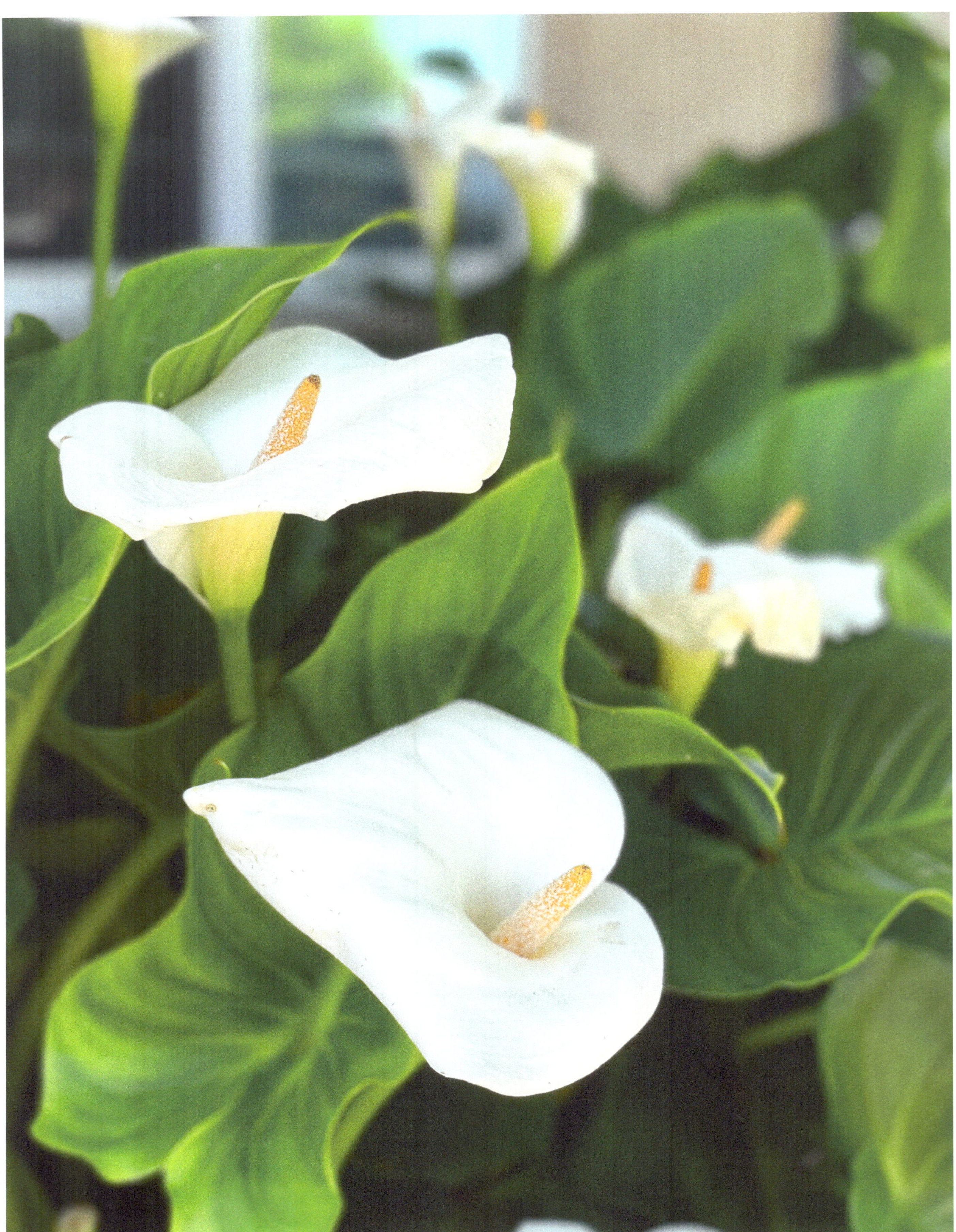

BASIC SUPPLIES

Gathering and collecting art supplies is a source of great joy for every artist. Mixed media collage offers endless possibilities for combinations of supplies. I encourage you to experiment with what you have on hand in addition to what I list below, as you may have already gathered lots of wonderful art tools and goodies that appeal to your personal sense of adventure.

preferred supplies

- **PENCIL AND ERASER** for sketching your image

- **REFERENCE IMAGE** sized to fit your canvas panel, printed out on basic copy paper, non photo paper

- **GRAPHITE TRANSFER PAPER** to transfer your reference image to the substrate if you struggle with drawing.

- **VARIETY OF FOUND PAPERS**, sheet music, maps, wallpaper, hand written notes, old book pages, hand made papers, deli paper, white tissue – variety of thickness and textures. You can do this totally with found papers.

- **DECORATIVE PAPERS**, papers you purchase at your local art supply store with fiber, embossing, metallic patterning, iridescent patterning. Please purchase in white or natural if possible, this allows for the most color options.

- **NO MAGAZINES** no shiny coated printed papers (they wrinkle), no scrapbook papers (too thick)

- **GEL PRESS MONOPRINTING PLATE AND BRAYER** Gel printing 8x10 plate and 6-inch hard rubber brayer

- **GOLDEN FLUID ACRYLIC PAINTS & WHITE GESSO** for under-painting on panel AND hand-painting papers—colors of your choice, keeping in mind the subject matter and your ability to mix color. Small container of gesso for adding white to certain paint colors.

- **CANVAS PANELS** economy surface for support. This is mat board covered with pre-primed canvas, NOT stretched canvas. 12x16, 16x20, your choice on size.

- **CRADLED WOOD PANELS** more expensive option but requires no framing when you finish the 1- or 2-inch edge

- **PAINT BRUSHES** (various sizes and shapes) for painting your image and applying glue. Use what you have on hand. I like Princeton Catalyst short handle #8 filbert specifically for glue application.

- **LIQUITEX GLOSS GEL MEDIUM**, this is the collage glue. Please purchase Liquitex brand in GLOSS

- **PALETTE PAPER** or Masterson Sta-Wet Palette system for mixing and keeping paint

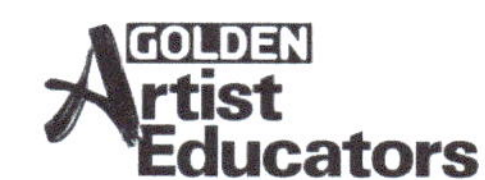

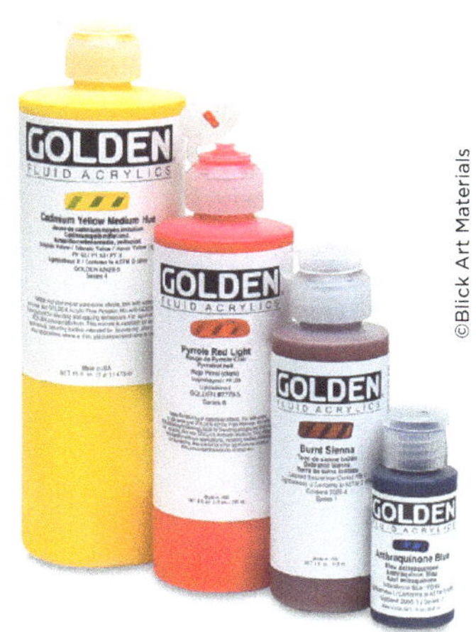

I have been trained by Golden Paints in the use and application of all their products.

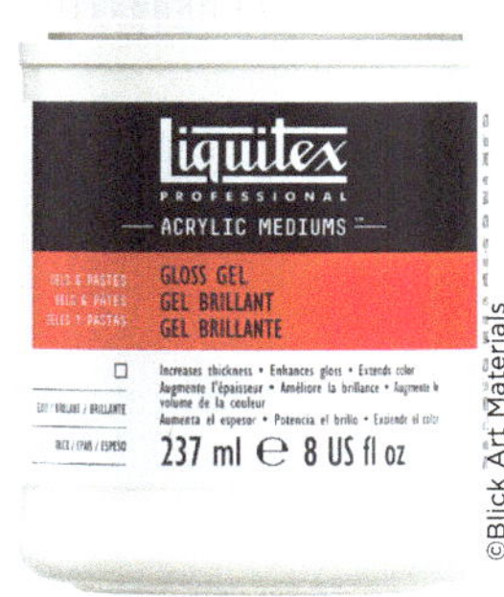

I use Liquitex Gloss Gel Medium as my collage glue, it's thick and stays in place while I work upright at the easel.

Canvas panels are pre-primed and are an economical surface for beginners.

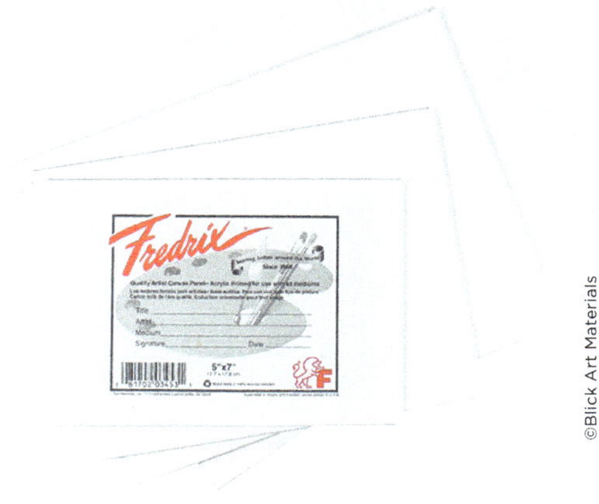

Landscape Collage TECHNIQUES

why I'm wild about painting rice paper

These acid-free papers are strong and highly absorbent. They are made in the centuries-old Japanese tradition. They are white and natural tones which make an excellent base for creating your own brilliantly colored collage papers. All are available on-line and most can be found at your local art supply store in the Chinese brush painting section.

Rice paper takes the color all the way through and lays flat when glued because of its' absorbent properties. I purchase rice papers on a roll versus in a pad, this way I can determine how large of a sheet I want to use. Rice paper comes with and without fibers, both have different applications in collage.

Hosho — Hosho is a traditional kozo (mulberry fiber) paper that doesn't shrink or tear easily, making it ideal for woodblock or line printing. Hosho paper is sized.

Kozo — Kozo rice paper is highly absorbent, making it ideal for calligraphy and watercolor painting. Kozo paper is not sized.

Unryu — Unryu rice paper has been used for centuries in Japan for creating Shoji screens and is extremely strong, thanks to molded-in fibers. It's excellent for calligraphy, sumi-e, watercolors. Unryu paper is not sized.

Ricer Paper Sheets — Hanshi Japanese rice paper for brush writing or calligraphy is mouldmade in the centuries-old Japanese tradition makes excellent base for fluid acrylics, available in sheets if you prefer, versus a roll.

Assorted Japanese Sheets — You may purchase a 10-sheet assortment of fine Japanese papers from DickBlick.com. This assortment includes two full sheets of Chiri (sized), Okawara (sized), Unryu (not sized), Kitakata (sized), and Mulberry (not sized). A nice way to experiment and find which papers work best for you.

Thai Unryu — Long, swirling strands of kozo provide contrast and texture in these traditional style unryu papers. Lightweight and translucent, choose from a range of natural tones, perfect for painting your own colors, textures, and patterns.

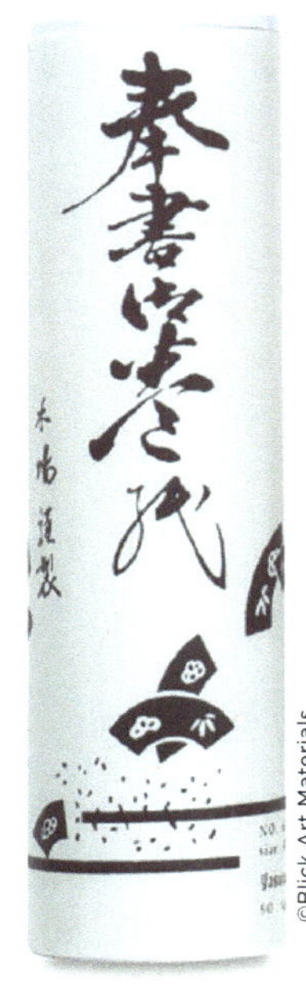

Rice paper comes on a roll in Hosho, Kozo and Unryu

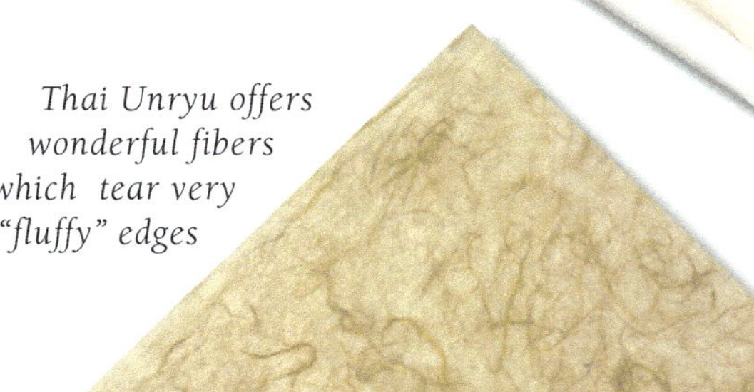

10-sheet assortment of fine Japanese papers

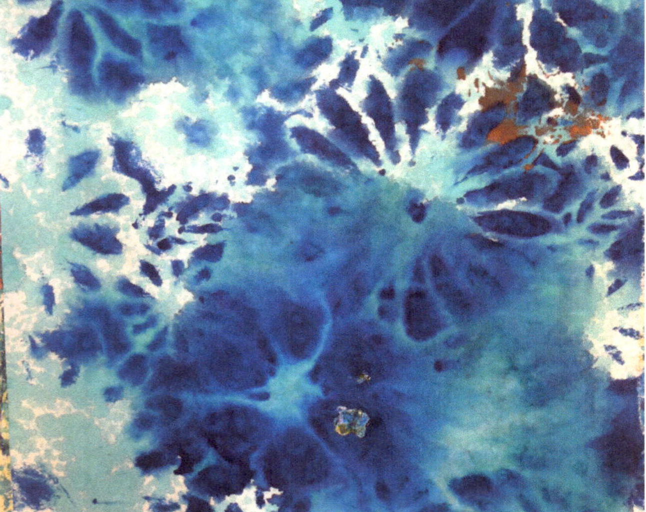

Working wet into wet on rice paper gives a watery, tie-dyed like effect

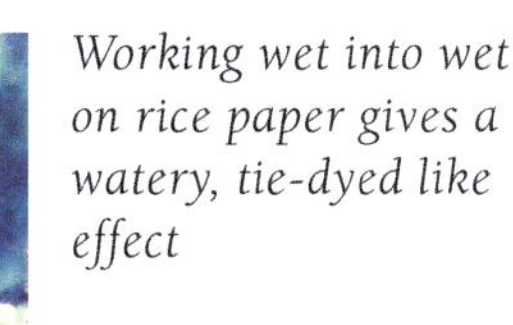

Thai Unryu offers wonderful fibers which tear very "fluffy" edges

painting collage paper

There are so many papers that are great for collage. I paint anything from old maps to printmaking paper to rice paper to my kids' homework.

I am also a fan of found papers, so check out your local used book store or library for some old books that you can take the pages out of. This paper is often great quality (less recycled content), the text adds another layer of creativity in the hand painted paper process, and the books are typically inexpensive.

I have learned through experimentation that glossy coated paper stock is not good for collage. This type of paper tends to cockle and that means the viewer's eye knows it's paper, even from afar. Since I want my artwork to appear as a painting, all papers must lay completely flat.

I also enjoy purchasing decorative papers from my local art supply store with fibers, metallic patterning, and textures. I grab these papers in white or natural tones so that I can paint them any color from yellow to black. In painting paper, experimentation is key, and practice makes perfect.

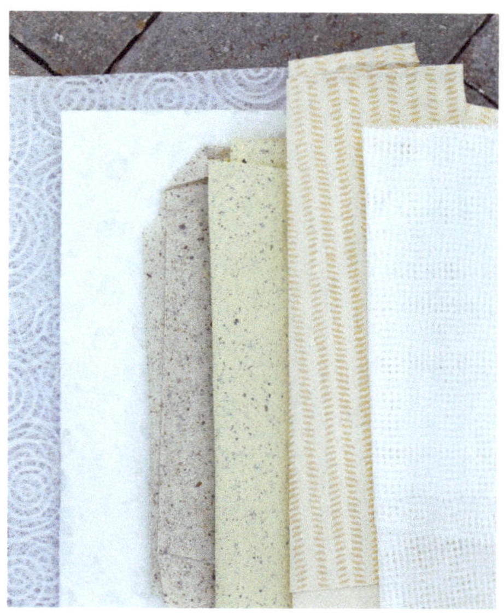

Some samples of my natural toned art store purchased decorative papers. I like the fibers, textures, inclusions, and lace cut patterns.

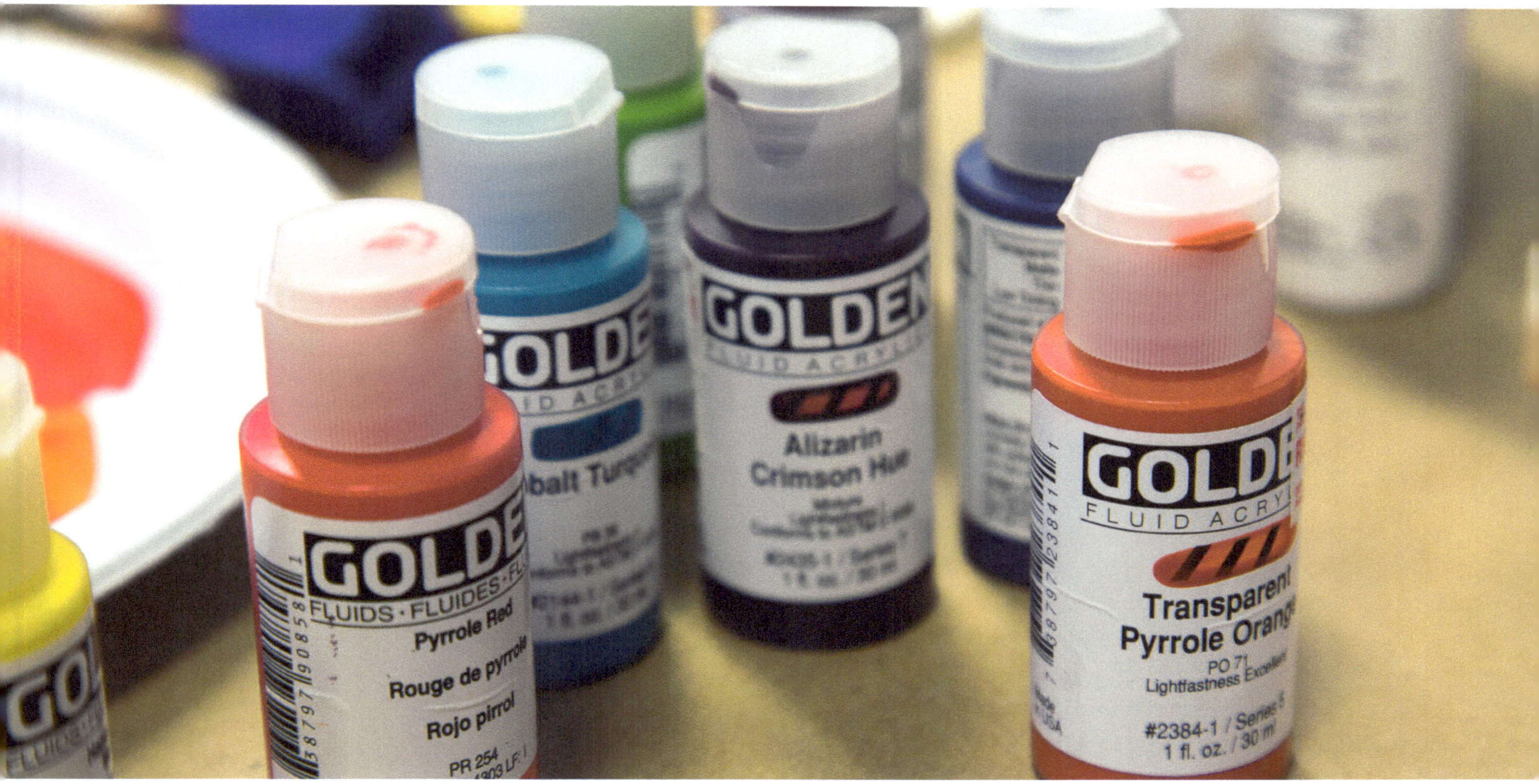

I prefer Golden Fluid Acrylic colors for painting my collage papers and my under-painting. These paints are light-fast, durable, and flexible. They are wonderfully versatile, professional quality acrylic colors with the consistency of heavy cream. Visit them on-line and request a color swatch chart for accurate color representation at *GoldenPaints.com*

Fluid Acrylics are highly pigmented and translucent, this is important. Every layer of paint allows the previous layer to shine through. This is the effect of translucent paints, they multiply and blend as you lay one technique of painting paper over another.

Landscape Collage TECHNIQUES

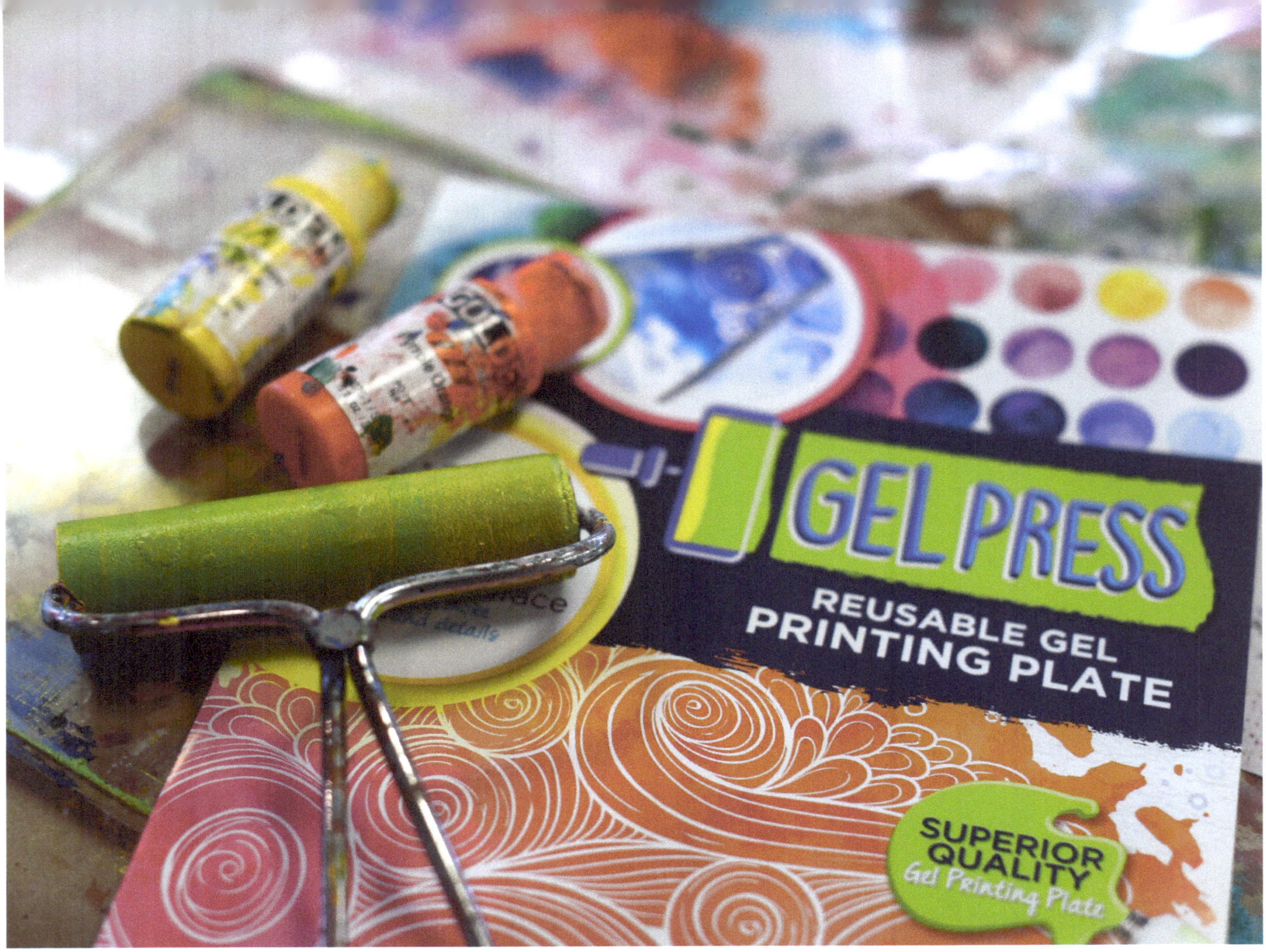

I use the Gel Press plate to create about 98% of my collage papers

why paint your own paper?

In the beginning, I used pre-colored papers in my collage work. I found the most richly colored, textured, patterned papers in the art store and I collected and coveted them on every trip I took. On a trip to New York City I must have spent over $100 on sheets of luxuriously colored papers at the store Kate's Paper.

What happened next was sad, but true. Most pre-colored papers fade! These papers are possibly colored with dye and not pure pigment (the color that is the base of all fine art paints and pastels). Dye fades over time, depending on its exposure to sunlight. It will break your heart to see a collage fading right in front of you, little by little, as the years go by. At first you might not even notice it, until you look at a photo of the artwork on your computer, and all of a sudden you realize that your original just does not look as vibrant as it used to.

To combat this dilemma, I started painting my own collage papers. I use Golden Artist Colors Fluid Acrylic paints, these are professional grade paints. Painting my own papers offered me a whole new world of possibilities of color, texture, pattern, shading...A perfect *paper palette!*

Fluid Acrylic paints are an excellent choice for painting your own collage papers. You can water them down extensively and they keep the same level of vibrancy, making them excellent for dripping and splattering.

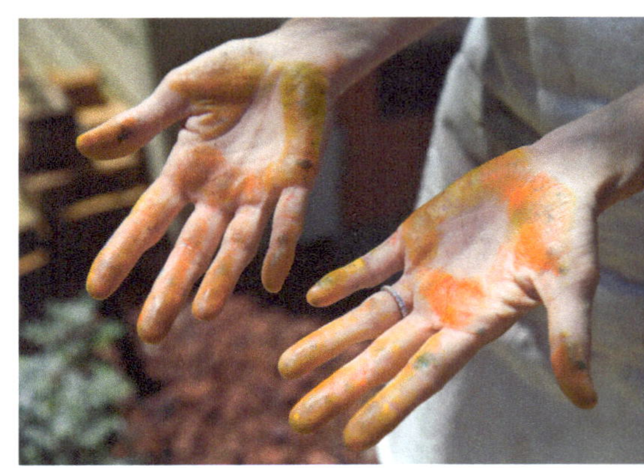

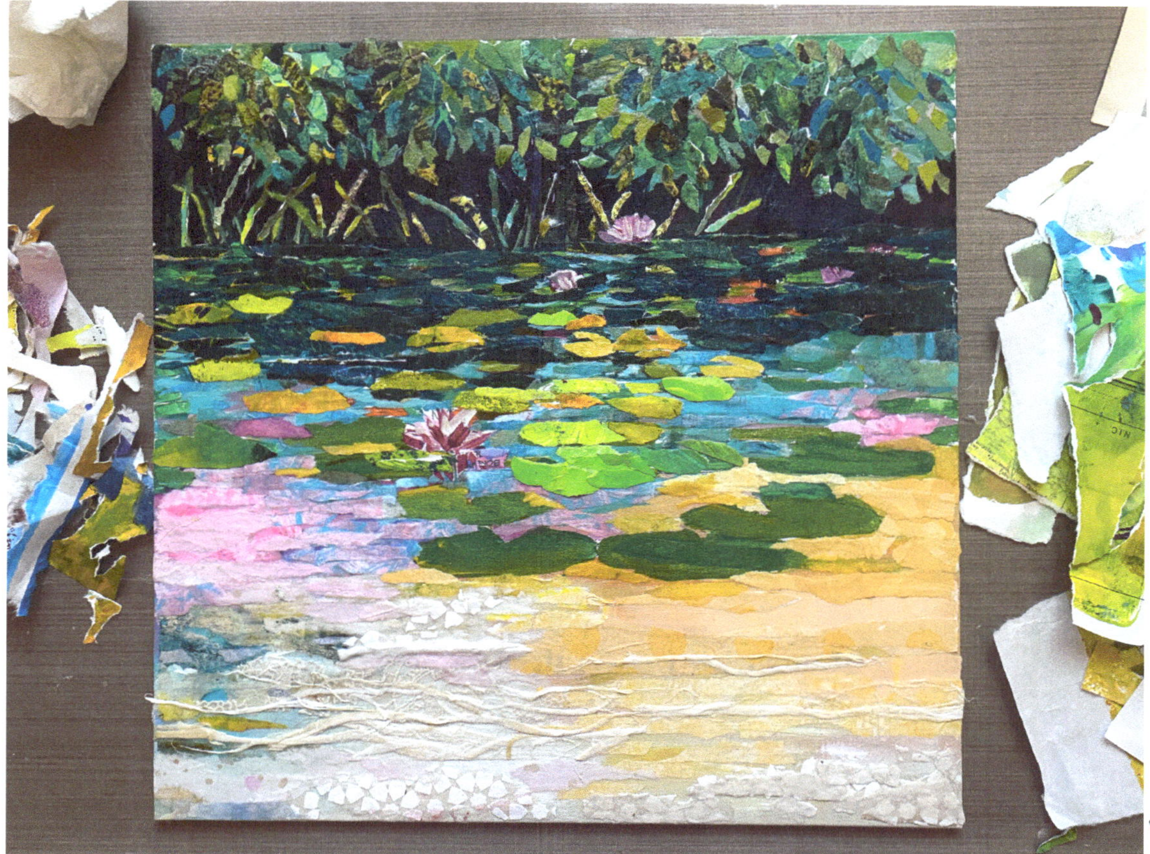

A full range of values in every color is imperative for accurate shading

PAINTING
with paper

variety is key

Keep in mind that you'll be painting papers in a full range of values, from the deepest darkest shadow color to the very lightest highlight color and *every* value in between. The landscape above makes use of the range of green papers to the right, every one of those swatches employs a different pattern and layering of techniques.

You can never have enough paper, because each paper brush mark and petal must be different from the one that is glued down next to it. Why is this so? Because if you glue the same paper next to itself, visually the two pieces become one. In order to create a collage that looks like a painting, we must maintain individual paper brush marks—this means within every value of every color there must be many *different* papers.

Landscape Collage TECHNIQUES

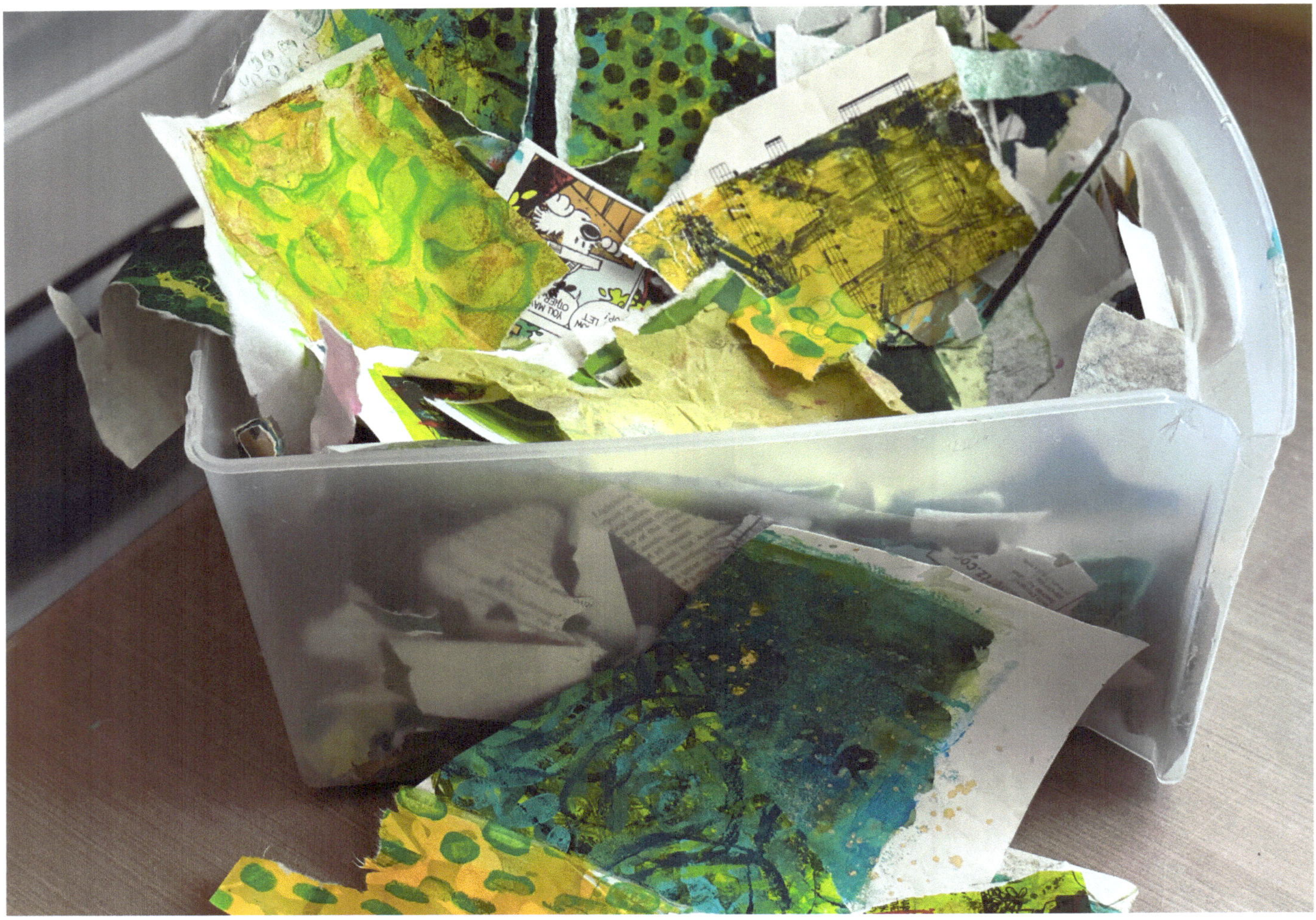

The green drawer from my organization system pulls out and sits on my taboret

color organization

In my studio I divide my papers into nine plastic drawers, the same organization I use for my Plein Air easel. If a paper incorporates two different colors, I tear it in half and put it in both drawers.

When you are ready to collage, it's much easier to find the perfect value of green when you have organized your colors so that all of your green is in one place. I use three sets of clear, stacked drawers by Sterilite. They pull out of their framework and I set them on my taboret to dig through the color I am looking for.

Storage solutions are personal. Although nine plastic drawers work for me, you may need more or less depending on your own organizational process.

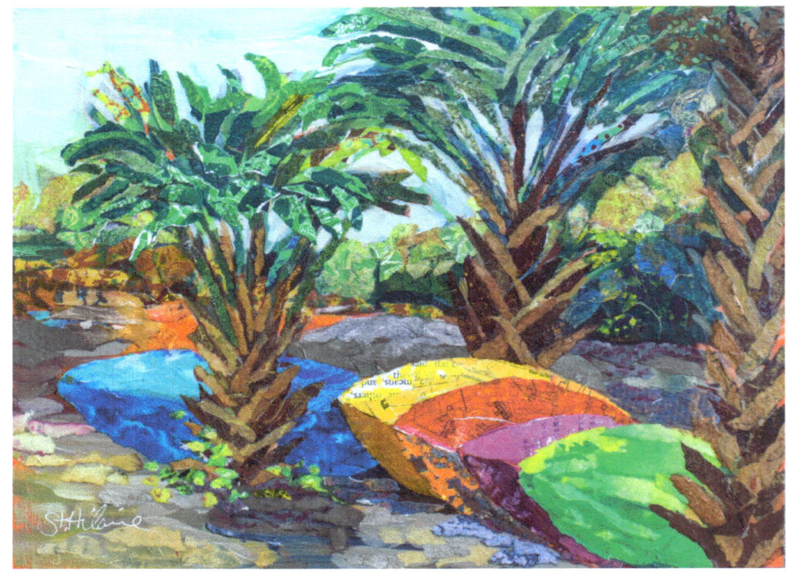

Shades of green are imperative for this painting of palms and kayaks

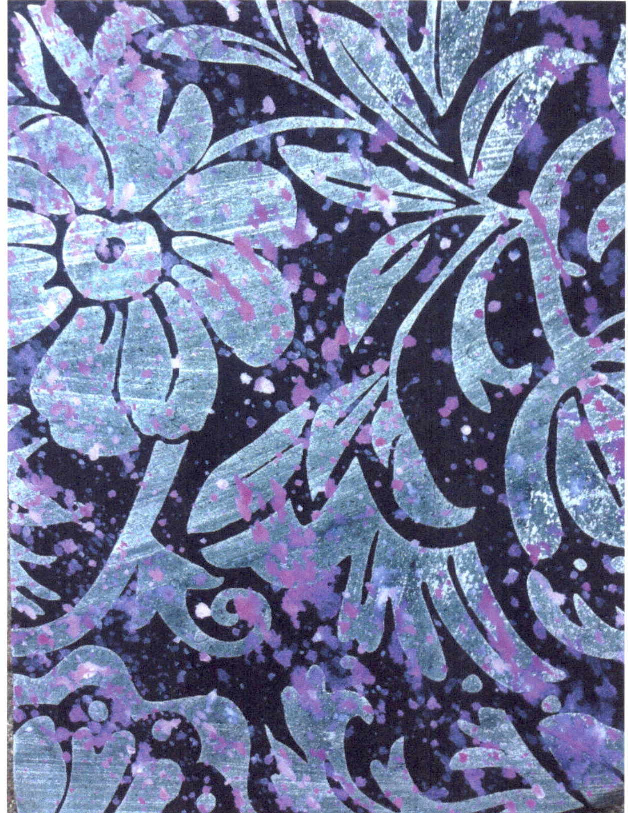

Every couple of weeks I pull out the paints, the tools, the Gel Plate, the brayer, the brushes, and I make myself a batch of custom colored collage papers.

Beyond just tinting papers with fluid acrylics, I have developed some interesting techniques over the years. To achieve texture and variety of colors, I layer these techniques over and under one another until I achieve highly textured, rich, colorful collage papers in a variety of colors and a full range of values within those colors.

making the most of decorative papers

I gave up using pre-colored decorative papers from the art supply store due to fading. Now I only buy white or natural decorative papers and paint them with Golden Fluid Acrylics.

I do like to utilize the printed patterns of decorative papers. The papers shown with gold printing below were purchased on a trip to Binder's Art Supply in Atlanta. What's fun about painting these types of papers is that the metallic pattern resists the Fluid Acrylic paint, leaving it to show through multiple layers of techniques.

The paper (below) started out brown. I painted some of the oversized sheet dark brown, some red, some blue and some purple. I stayed with dark colors because the translucency of the paint does not allow for lightening the base value.

Decorative paper that is white or natural the most successful starting point for any color I want–from the lightest yellow all the way down to deepest black and any color in between.

Top: White paper with silver swirls included in it serves as a great base for creating custom colored versions.

Hint: Take your oversized art store sheet and divide it into four, or even eight pieces, paint each one a different color. Collage utilizes a variety of bits and pieces of paper, one sheet goes a long way.

Below: Art store decorative papers come with some wonderful printed patterns that you can take advantage of by painting over with diluted fluid acrylics which will allow the patterning to show through. Be sure to paint dark colors over dark papers.

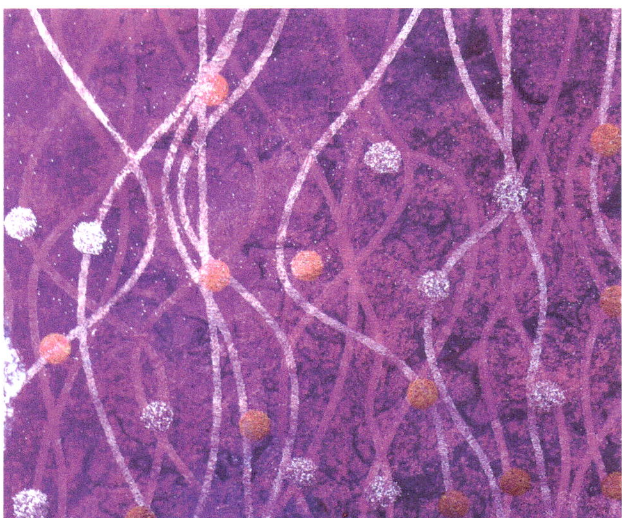

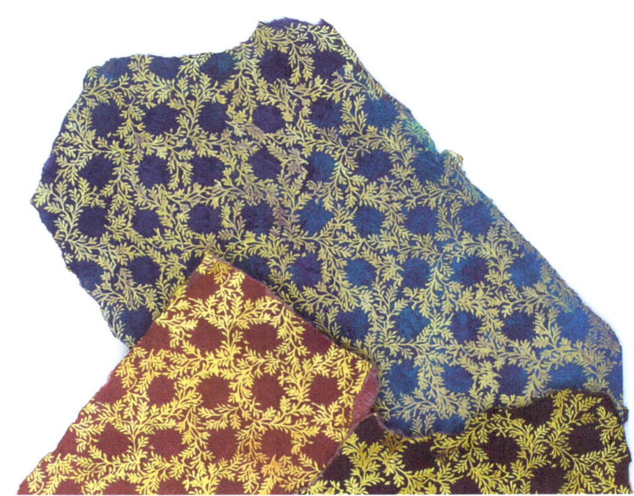

Landscape Collage TECHNIQUES

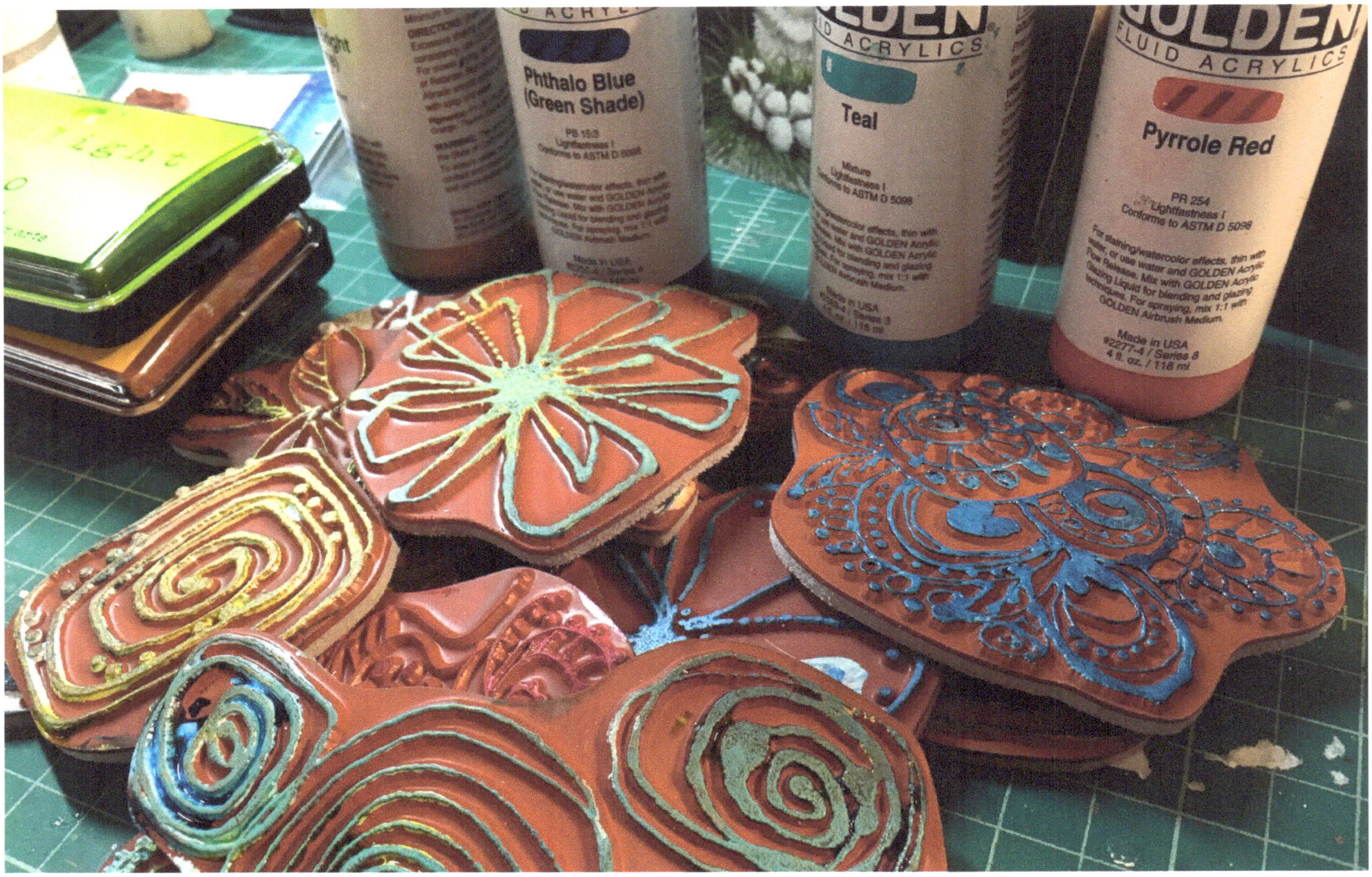

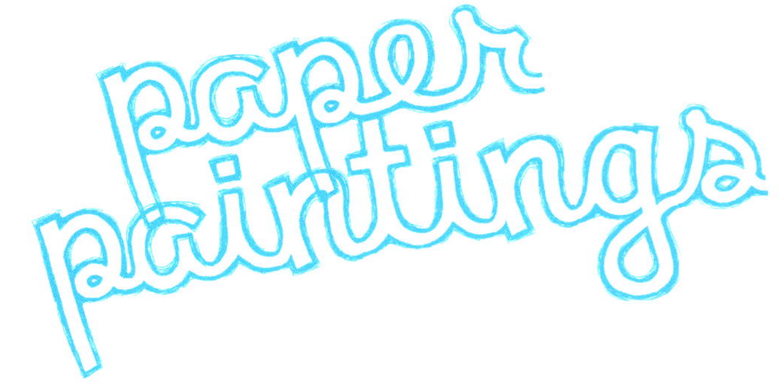

my rubber stamp designs

Purchasing stamps at your local craft store can offer immediate gratification in terms of adding patterns, textures, and marks to your hand painted collage paper.

I have designed a line of art stamps with RubberMoon, an American company based in Missouri. RubberMoon has a full line of Elizabeth St. Hilaire stamps (in foam and rubber) which they sell in sets as well as individuals.

my foam stamp designs

Commercially produced foam stamps are lightweight, easy to store, economical, and FUN! I have designed foam stamps for both RubberMoon and Joggles over the last year. Visit RubberMoon.com and Joggles.com for a full selection of my foam stamp designs, an ever expanding collection!

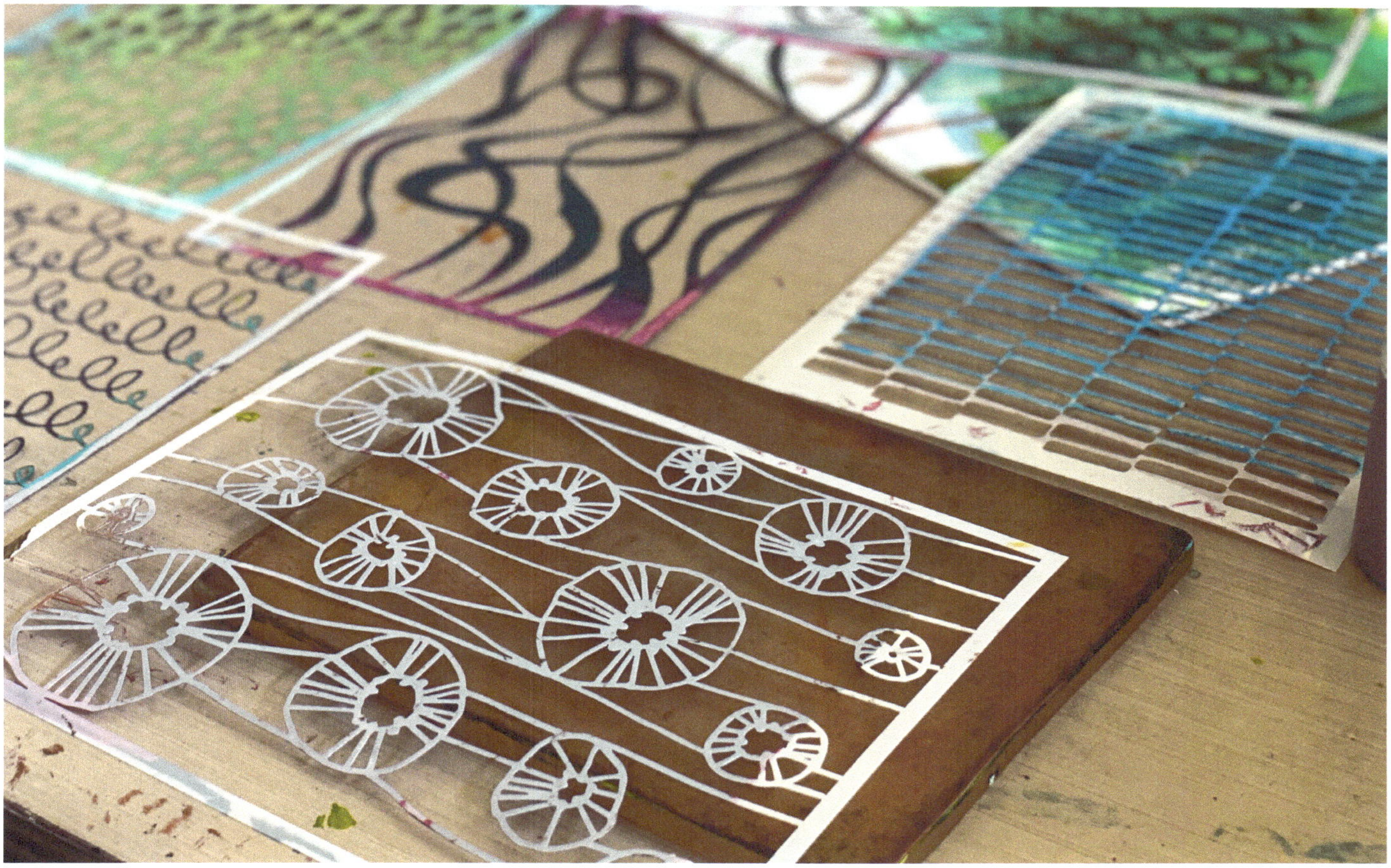

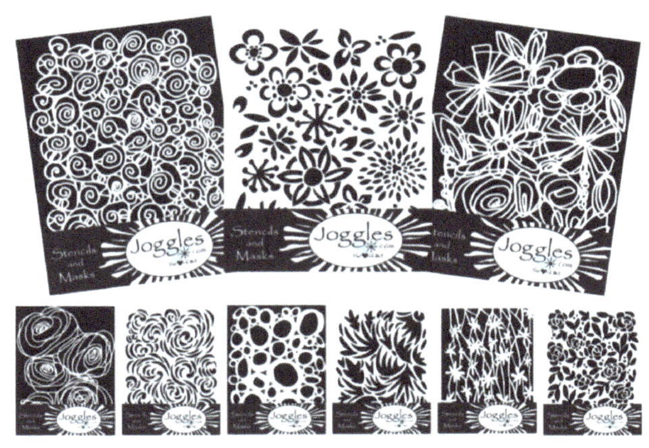

The Peacock Collection Set of 9

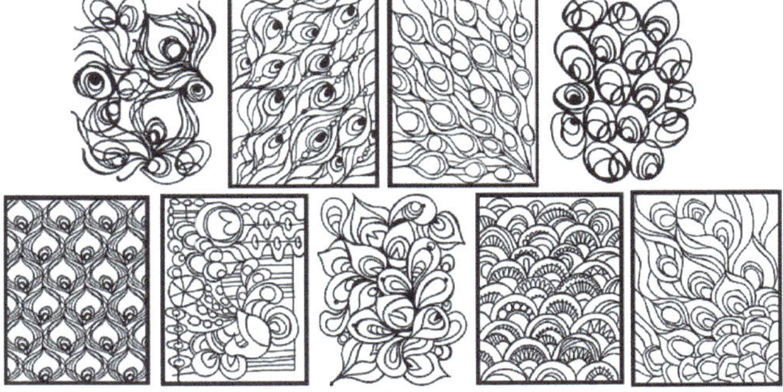

my stencil designs

I create about 98% of my hand painted paper through the monoprinting process using a reusable gel printing plate by Gel Press and my own stencil designs with Joggles.com. I am super excited about my line of stencil designs which debuted in 2019, I have released new designs each year since. I have designed my stencils for the purpose of hand painted collage paper. What does this mean? I am focused on line quality, shape, thickness, and design versus specific and recognizable imagery.

Many of you will already have stencils in your stash. If you are looking to add more or you are new to stencils, you might like to try some of my 9x12 designs which are perfectly sized for the 8x10 Gel Press Gel Plate.

Visit Joggles.com 9x12 Stencils and Masks to view my collection.

Landscape Collage TECHNIQUES

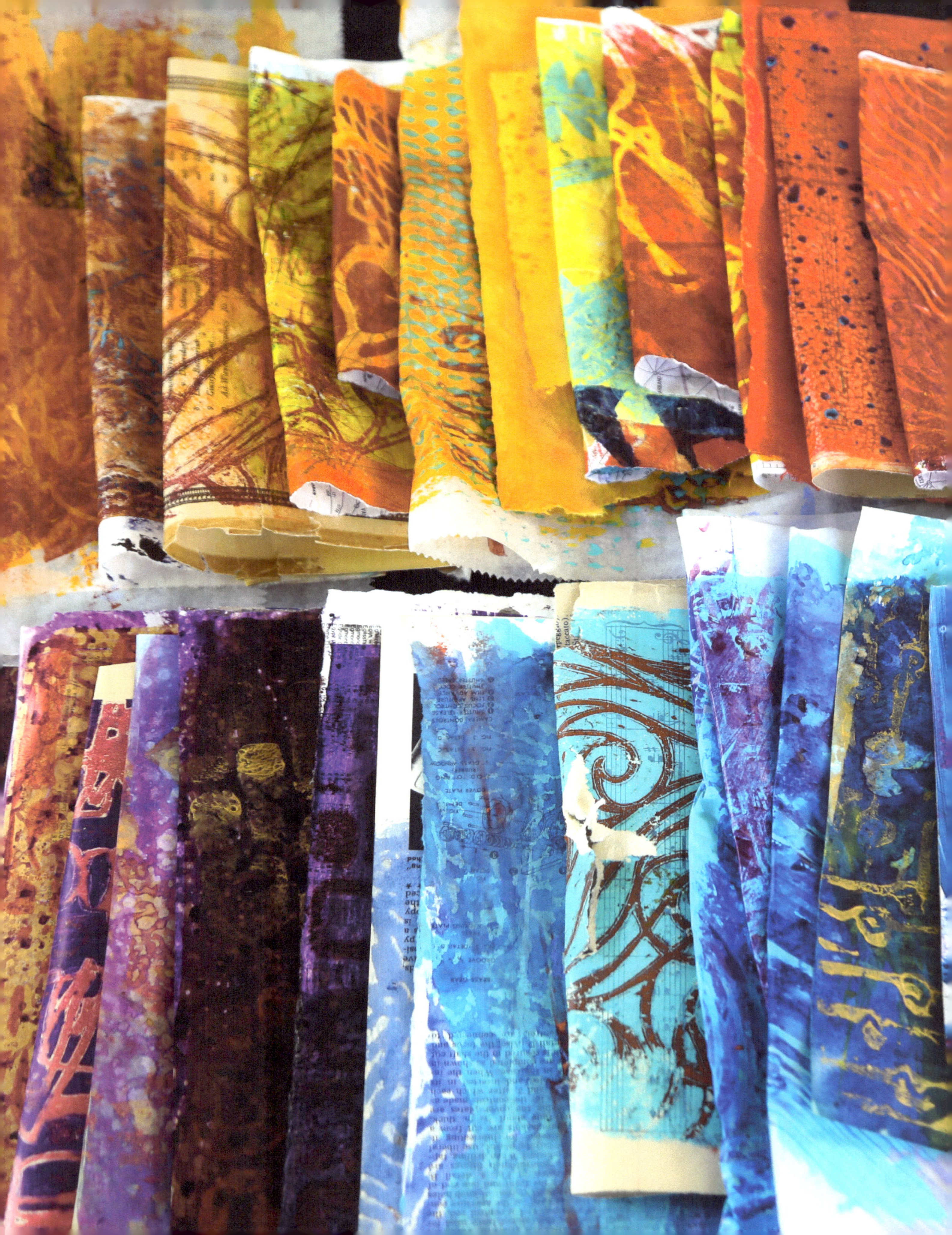

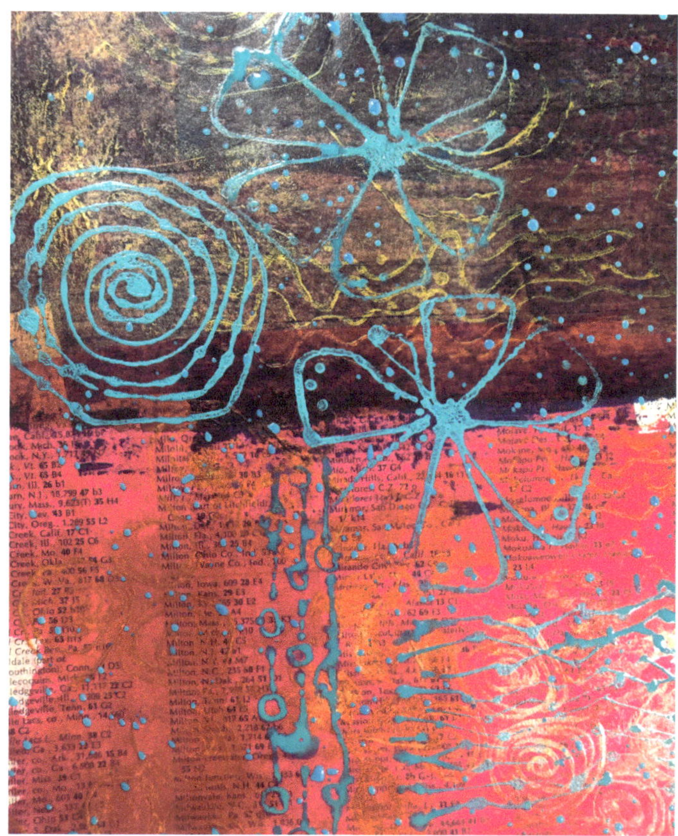

COMBINATIONS: RubberMoon stamps with splatter over an old atlas page

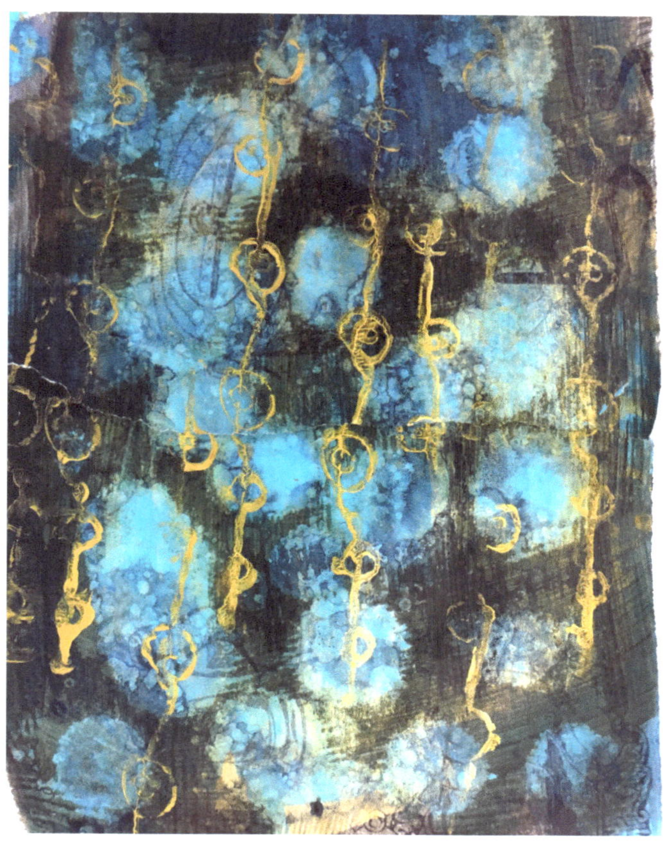

COMBINATIONS: RubberMoon stamps with metallic gold over blotted alcohol resist on an old book page

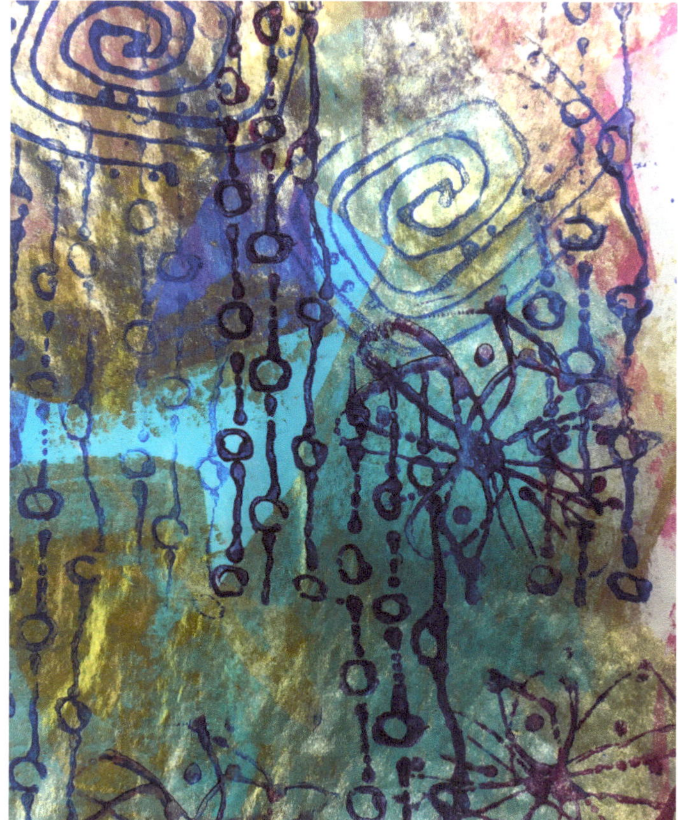

COMBINATIONS: RubberMoon stamps overlapping with metallic paint over credit card scraping on deli paper

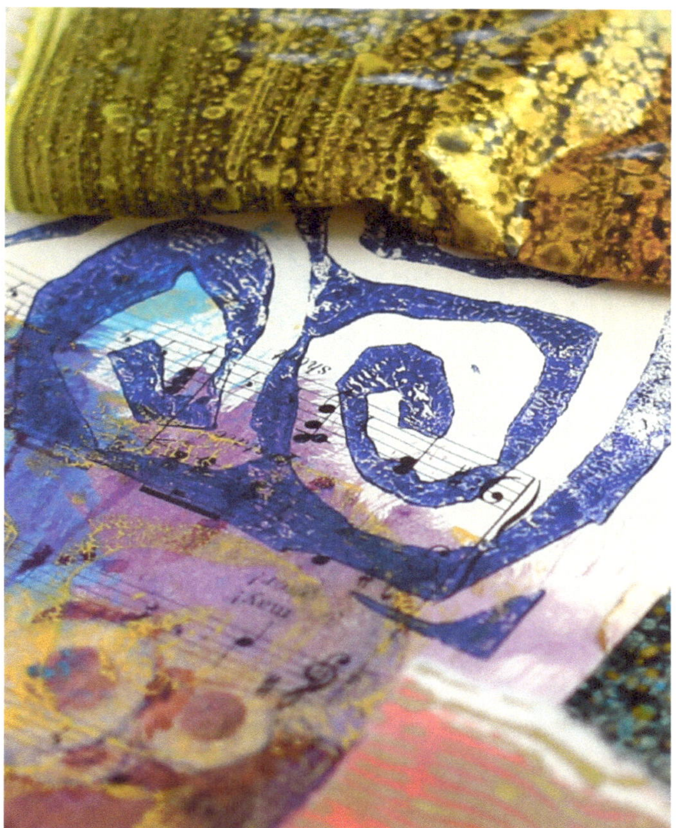

COMBINATIONS: RubberMoon stamps overlapping with alcohol resist and plastic card scraping on sheet music paper

Landscape Collage TECHNIQUES

painting paper

Stamping

Materials:

- Art stamps from RubberMoon.com
- Paint Brush and/or brayer
- Fluid Acrylic Paint or permanent, archival ink pad

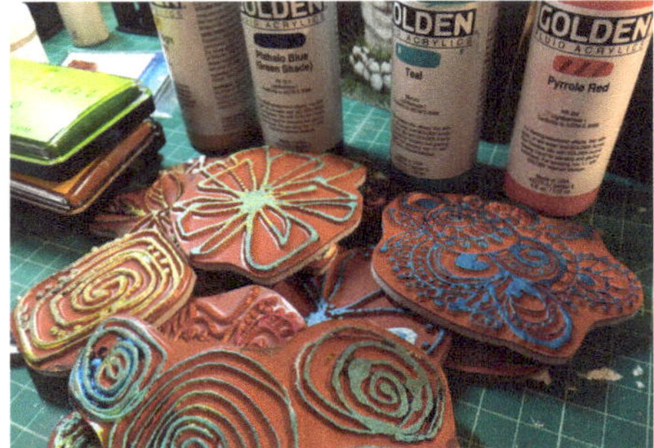

My designed stamps with RubberMoon

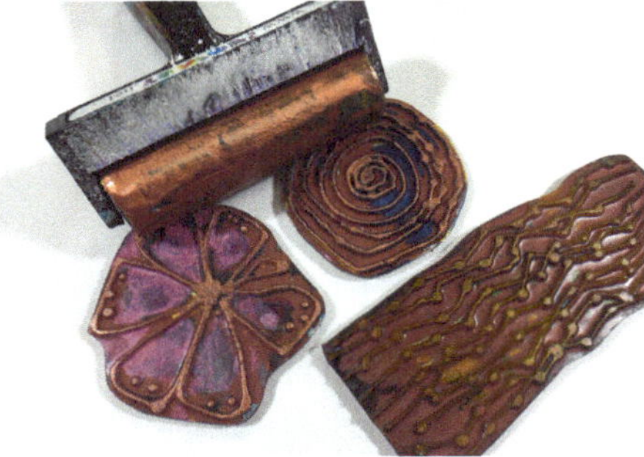

Add paint to stamps

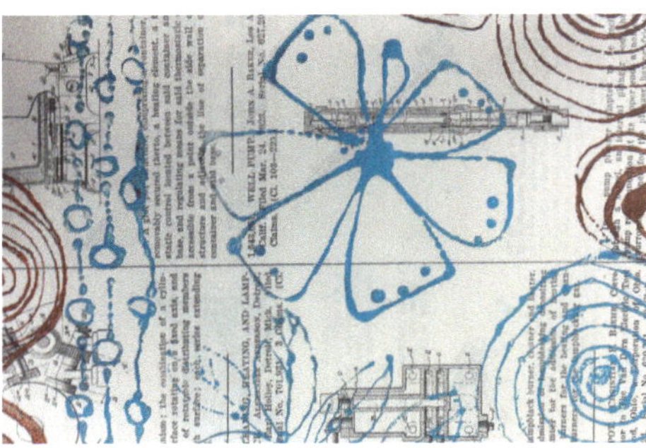

Press stamps onto paper

I typically use my brayer to spread Golden Fluid Acrylic paints directly onto art stamps of my own design with RubberMoon. I use the brayer so that the paint stays on the patterned area of the stamp and does not fill into the negative spaces. You can clean your stamps with baby wipes immediately after spreading paint on them, you can also use a toothbrush with The Masters Brush Cleaner to get dried paint off them. It is not recommended that you soak them in water. I typically print my stamp multiple times in order to remove as much paint as possible before wiping them down.

Companies such as Ranger offer stamp pads that are permanent and fade proof. You can use these for your paper painting or you can use acrylic paint, the effects are different and the choice is yours.

Stamping is just one of the techniques you will use in creating hand-painted papers. The idea is to take one sheet of paper through multiple techniques, adding layer upon layer of texture and pattern. This multi pass process is what makes your papers rich and painterly.

Using your archival ink pad or painting your stamp with acrylic paint, make impressions in multiple colors, overlapping the images over the surface of a white sheet of rice paper or a paper that you have already layered with other techniques. Once the stamped impressions dry, try adding a wash of color over them to tone down any white areas of the base paper. Colors next to each other (analogous) on the color wheel offer harmonious effects, and colors more close to opposite on the wheel offer more intense and color vibrating effects, both are effective in different applications.

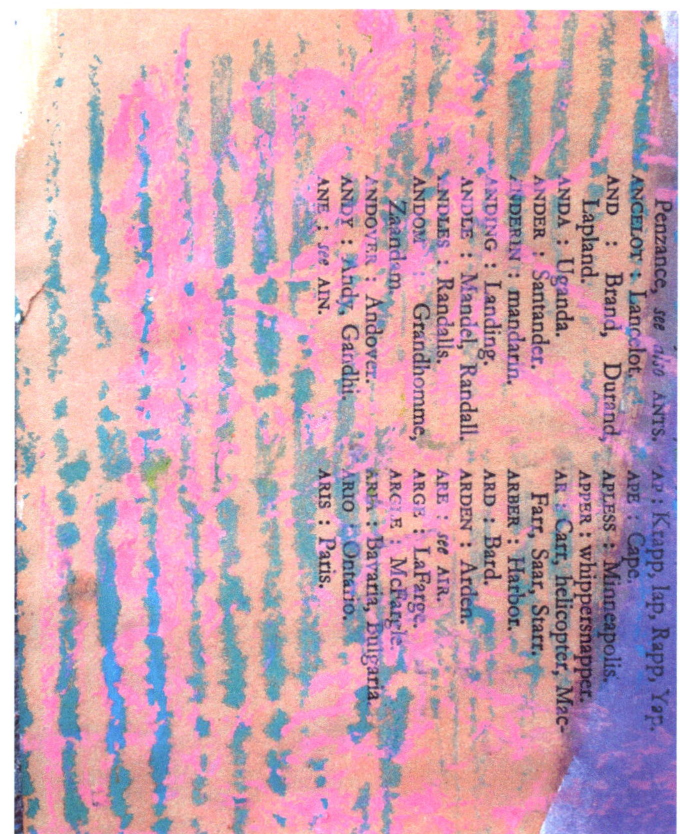

COMBINATIONS: Corrugated cardboard stamping combined with crayon resist & washes of color over an old book page

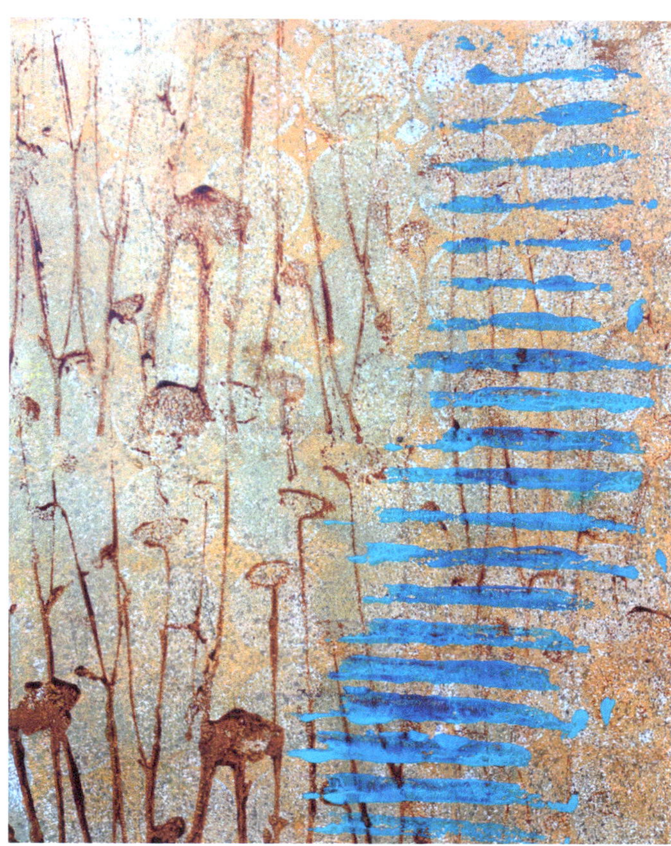

COMBINATIONS: Corrugated cardboard stamping over subtle sink liner stamping with commercial rubber stamping

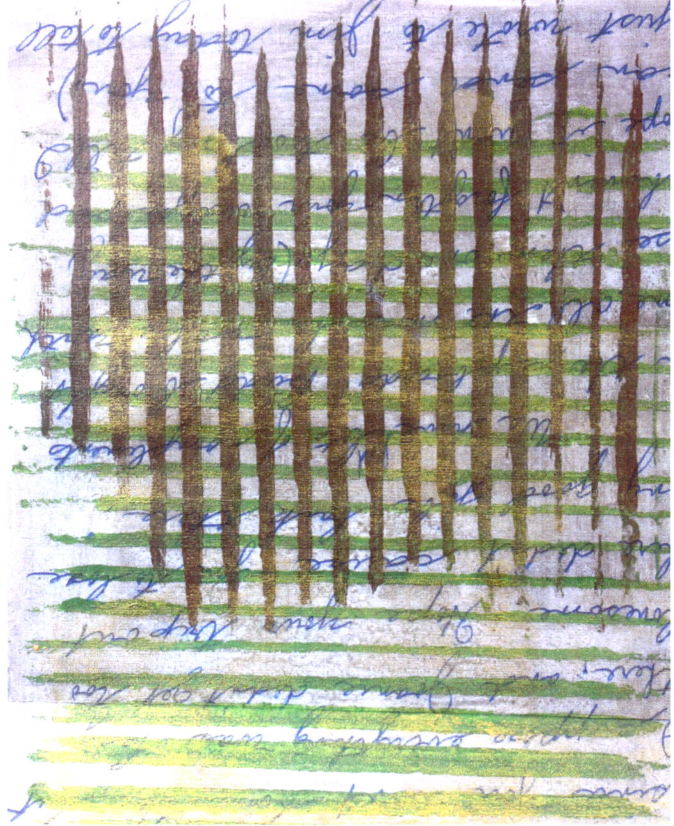

COMBINATIONS: Corrugated cardboard stamping with metallic paints over old hand written letter and pale wash

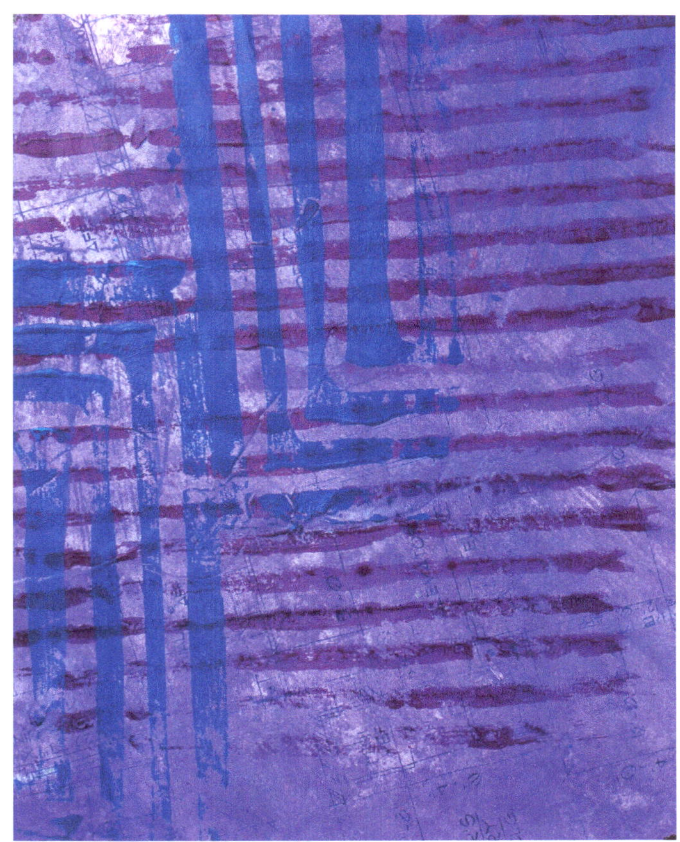

COMBINATIONS: Corrugated cardboard stamping with hand-carved stamp in opposite direction

painting paper

Corrugated Cardboard
Materials:

- Corrugated cardboard box material
- Gesso
- Acrylic paint
- Paint brush

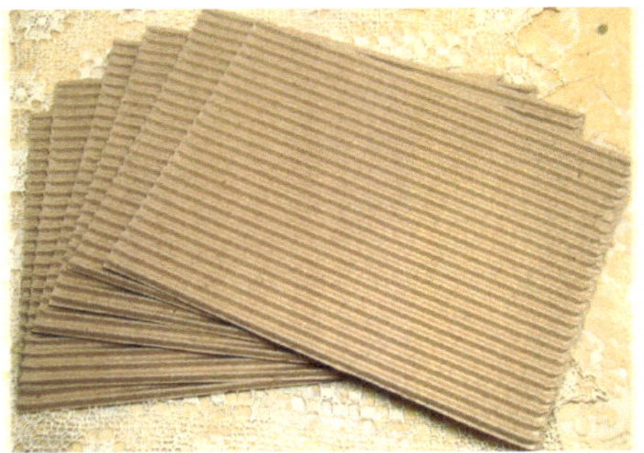

Corrugated cardboard box material

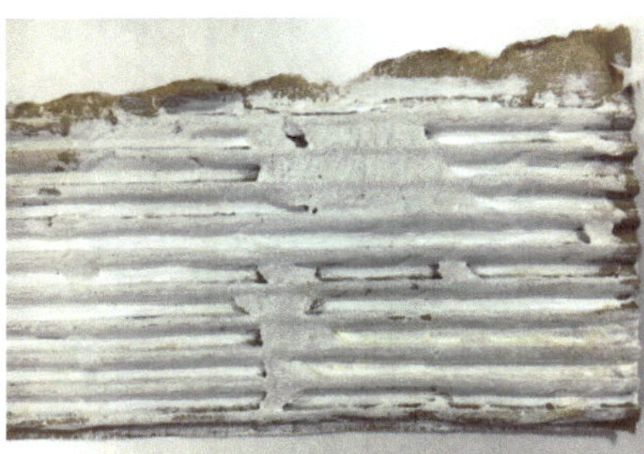

Gesso over corrugated cardboard pieces

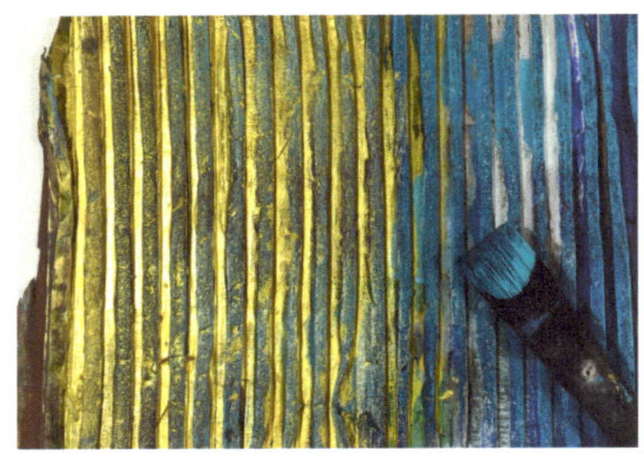

Apply a layer of paint over the cardboard

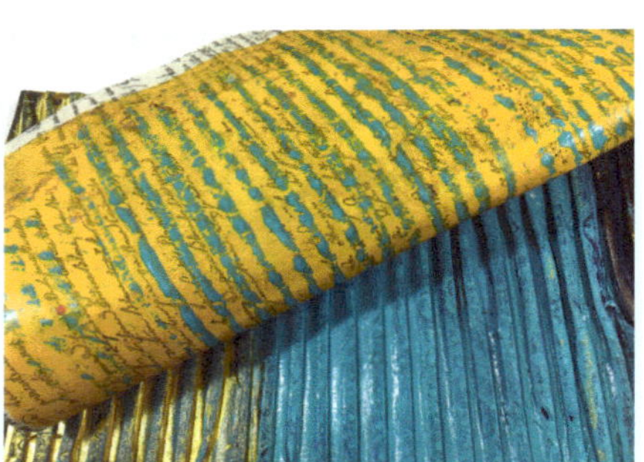

Press the paper onto the cardboard

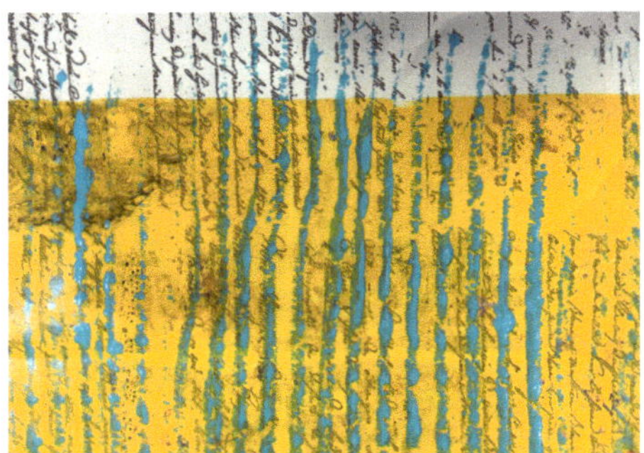

Corrugated lines over a yellow letter

Corrugated cardboard is something that arrives at your door on a regular basis if you are an *Amazon Prime* shopper like I am. If not, you can find free cardboard boxes from your local grocery store or COSTCO. This technique makes a wonderful second or third pass for your already embellished papers. The corrugated lines are much more organic and non-uniform once the cardboard has been pressed several times, it gets better with age!

Separate the cardboard to reveal the

corrugation in the middle. Coat the corrugated surface with a layer of gesso on both sides and allow it to dry. This prevents absorption of moisture from the paint, which will deteriorate the cardboard before it gains character.

Apply undiluted paint onto the corrugated surface with a brush. Press the cardboard in either the same or overlapping directions onto any paper surface, experimenting with different types of paper and colors.

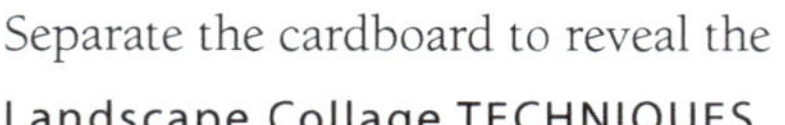

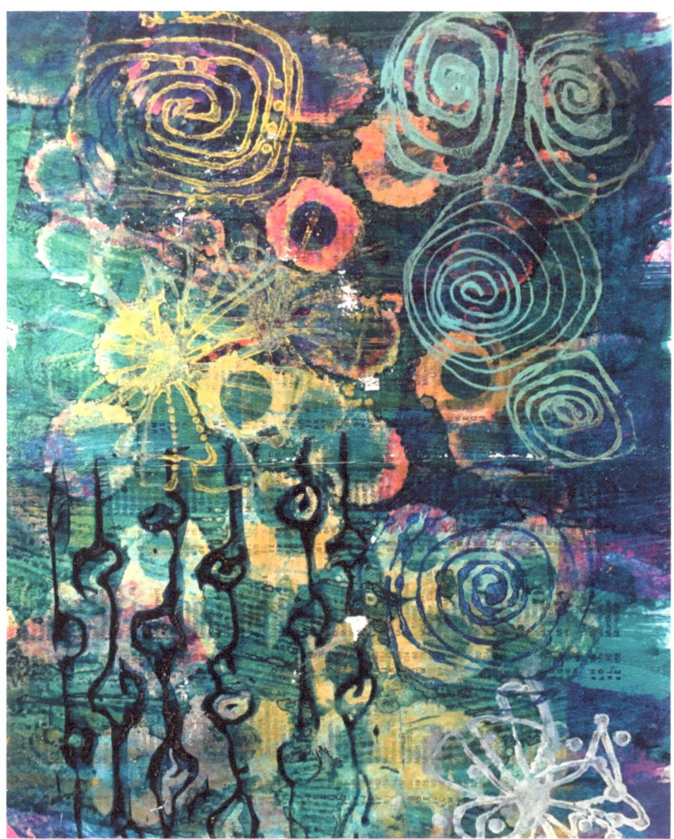

COMBINATIONS: Alcohol resist with rubber stamping

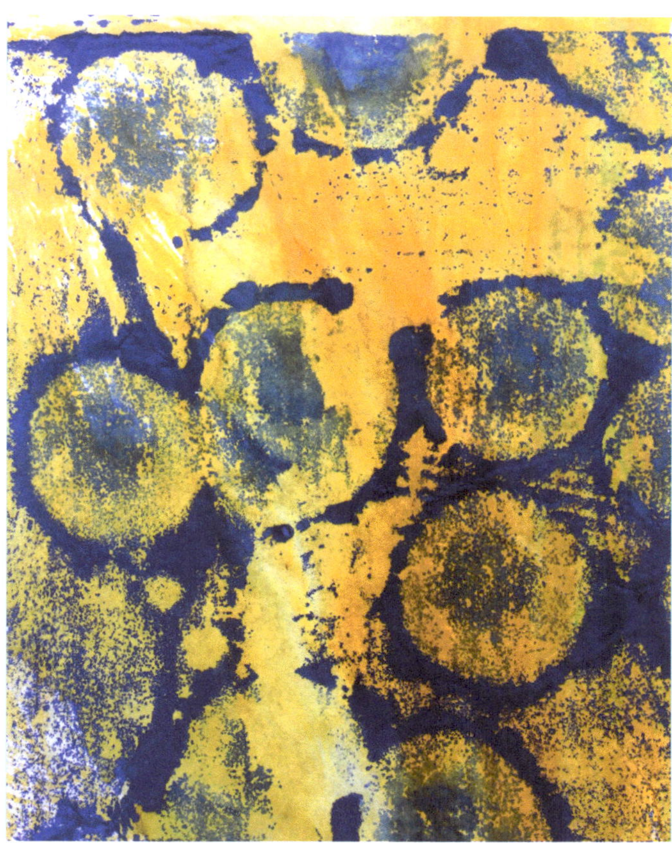

COMBINATIONS: A blotter paper type lift from the alcohol technique onto an absorbent rice paper

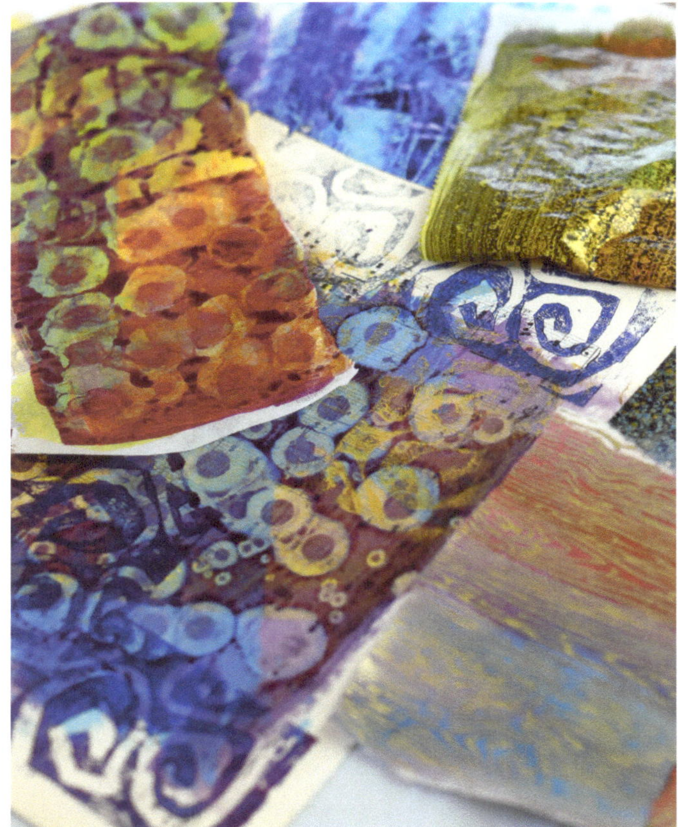

COMBINATIONS: Alcohol resist in various color combos

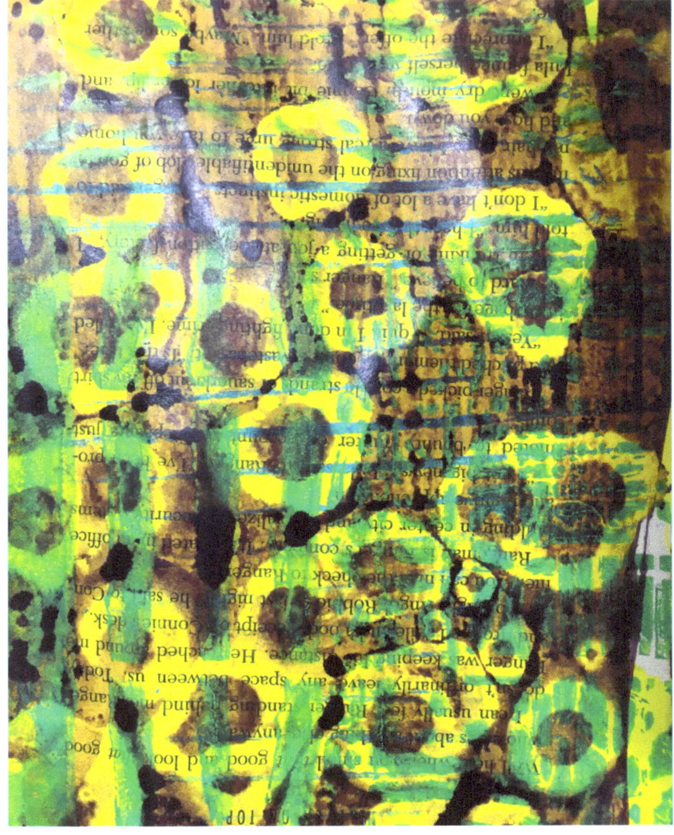

COMBINATIONS: Alcohol resist with cardboard stamping over an old book page

Landscape Collage TECHNIQUES

painting paper

Alcohol Resist

Materials:

- Household rubbing alcohol
- Eye dropper
- Acrylic paint
- Nonabsorbent paper that does not soak up the paint

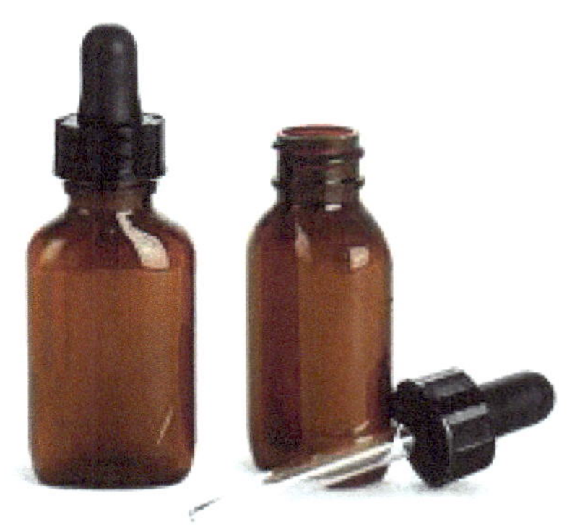

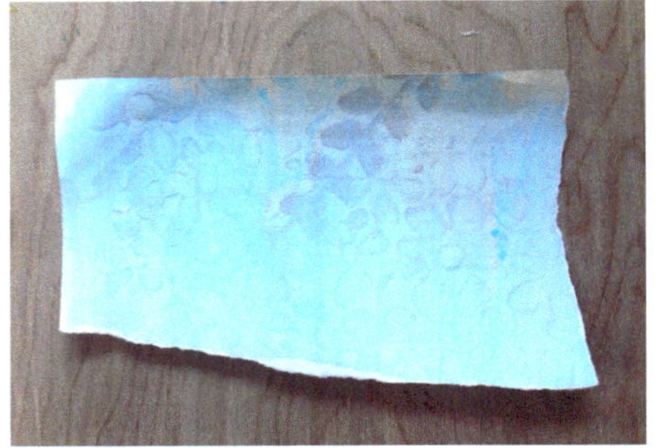

Wallpaper painted a light color and allowed to dry completely

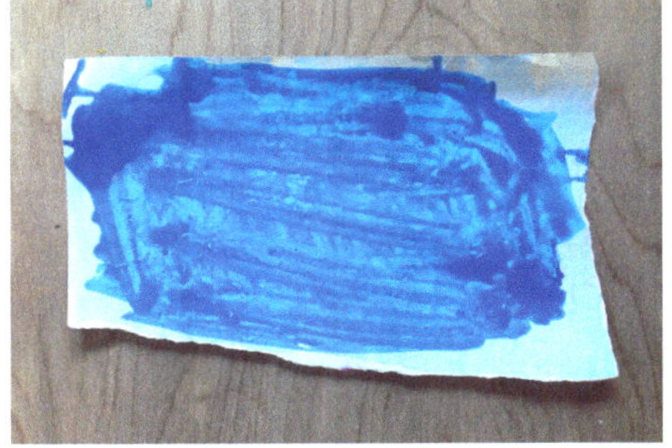

Overlay with a darker color, slightly watered down fluid acrylic paint

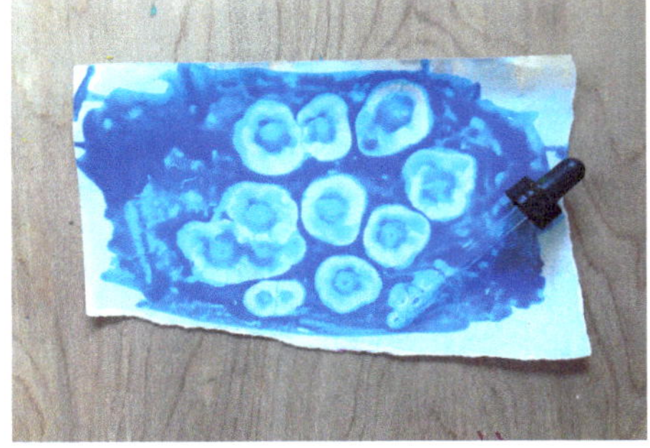

Working quickly, drop alcohol into wet paint with the eye dropper

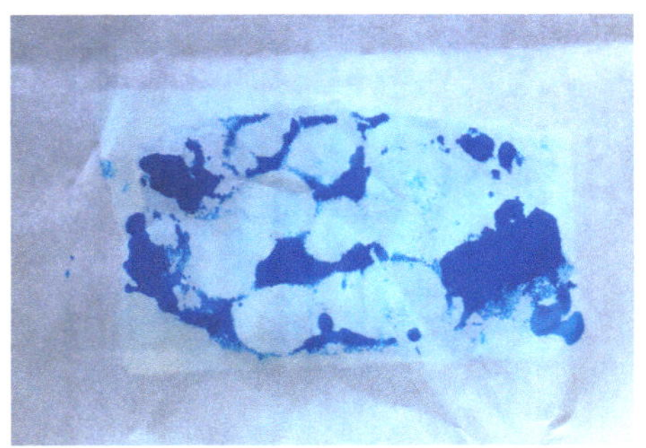

Option: blot off the paint with an absorbent rice paper and a light touch

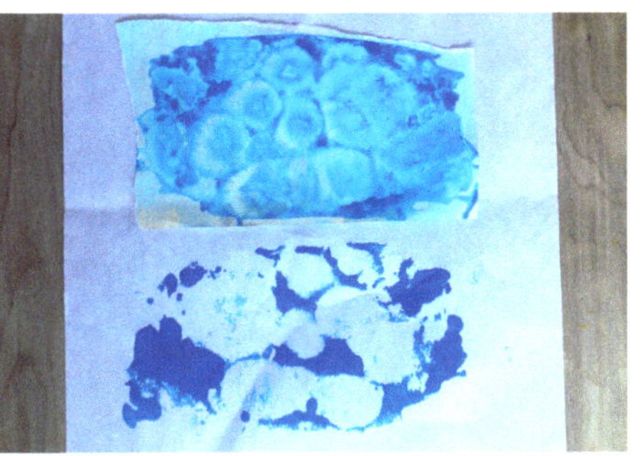

The alcohol pattern is transferred to the rice paper and can obscure the original effect

Rubbing alcohol from the first aid aisle (non-diluted isopropyl) pushes the pigment of acrylic paint away and can offer some wonderful resist techniques.

So many variables come into play with this technique: the type of paper and its' absorbency, the amount of water in the top layer of paint, and how dry the paint is when you drop the alcohol. It's best to experiment with this technique many times to get the best results.

Paint the paper with a light color paint and allow to dry completely. Consider using some of the additive techniques from previous pages.

Overlay a darker watered down fluid acrylic paint on the prepared paper and allow to dry slightly.

Drop alcohol from an eye dropper from varying heights and with varying force to form large and small droplets onto the paper.

Watch the alcohol resist push your top (wet) layer of paint away, revealing the lighter layer underneath. Too wet of paint on top will roll back into the resist space, too dry paint will not move. This technique requires patience and experimentation. If at first you don't succeed, try try again.

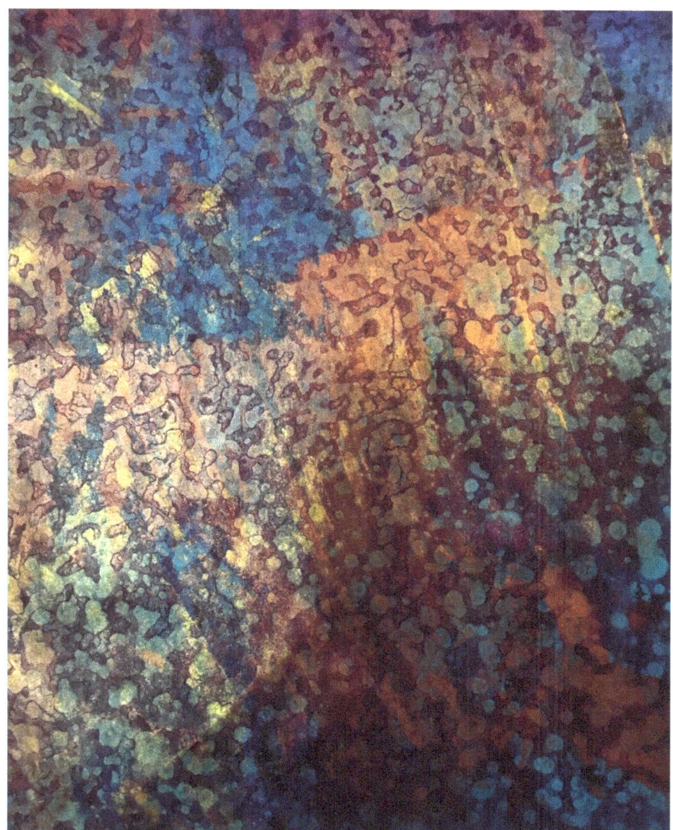

COMBINATIONS: Soap bubble resist over metallic plastic card scraping on deli paper

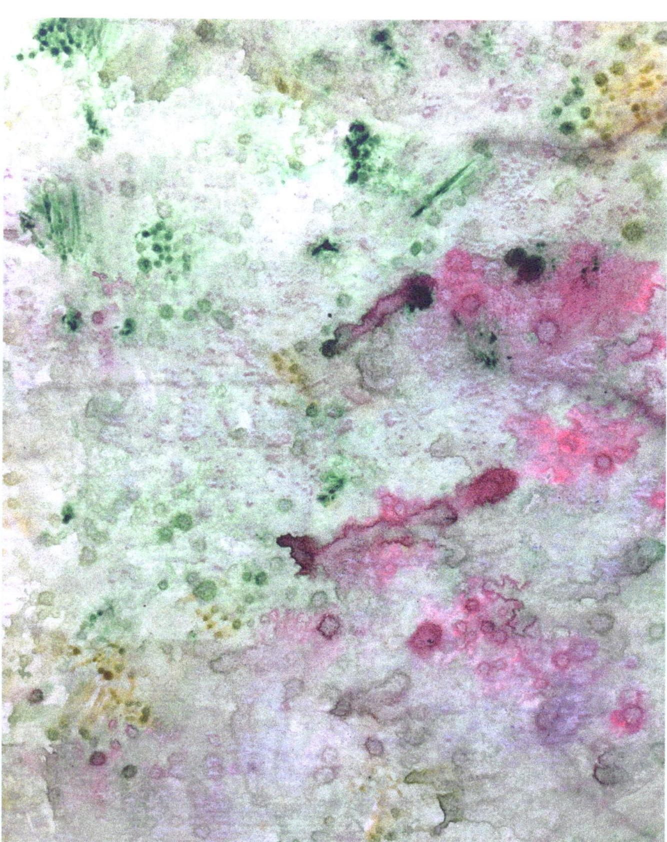

COMBINATIONS: Multiple colors of soap bubble resist on wallpaper, allowed to bleed together

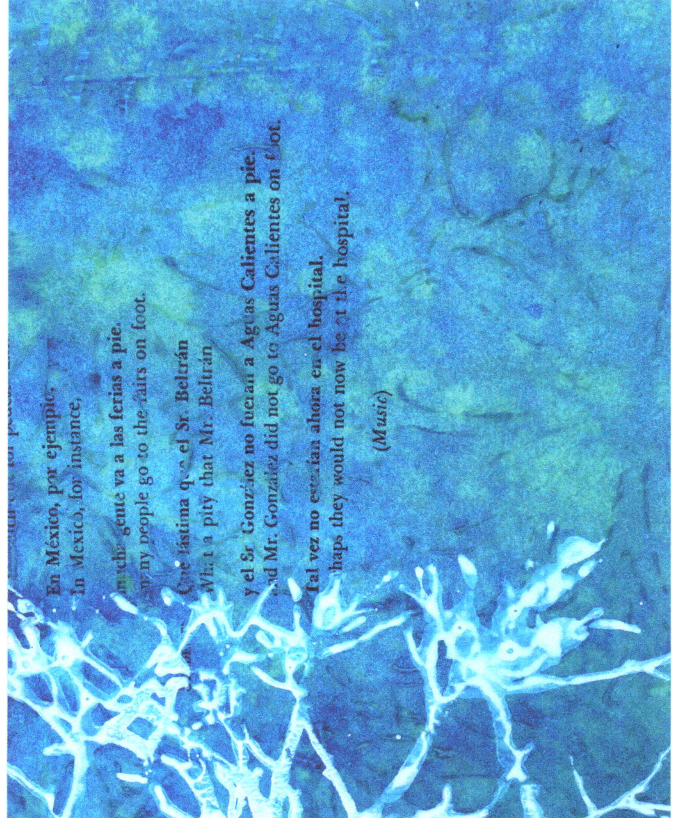

COMBINATIONS: Soap bubble resist over old book page with stenciled pattern in white gesso

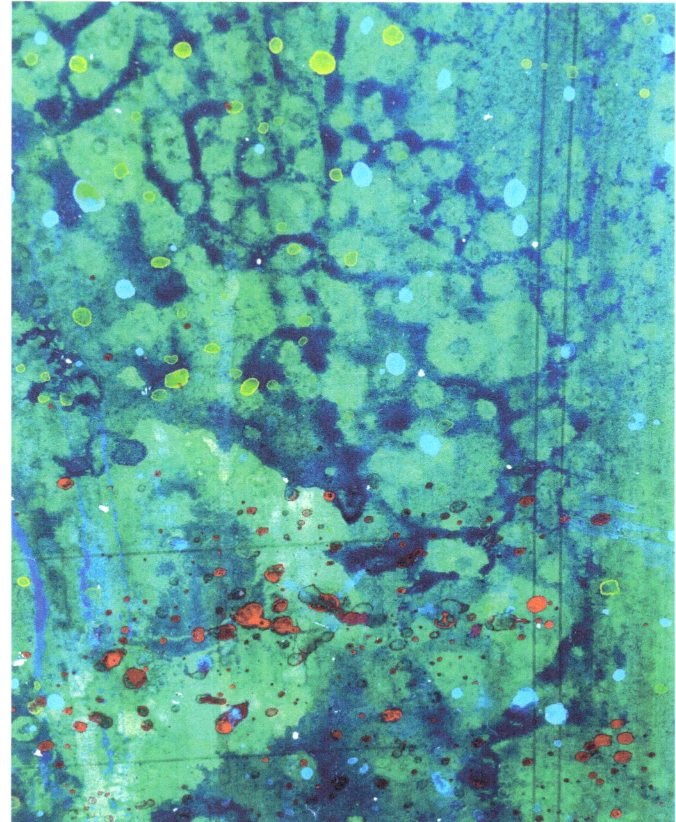

COMBINATIONS: Soap bubble resist over old ledger paper with splattering

painting paper

Soap Bubble Resist

materials:

- Travel size spray bottle with a few pumps of dish liquid–Dawn works best
- Non porous found paper
- Acrylic paint
- Paint brush

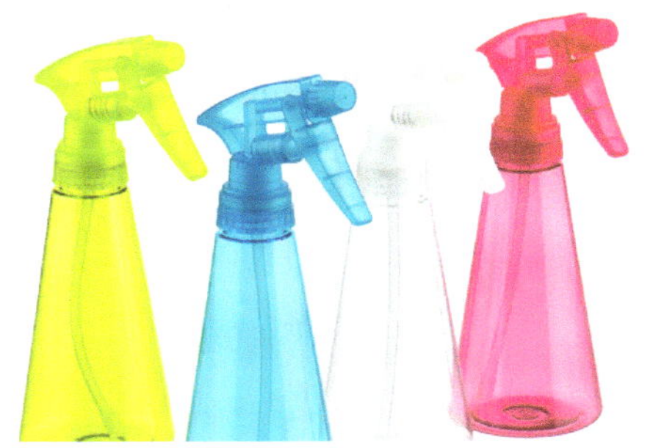

A few tablespoons of dish soap added to a spray bottle and shake

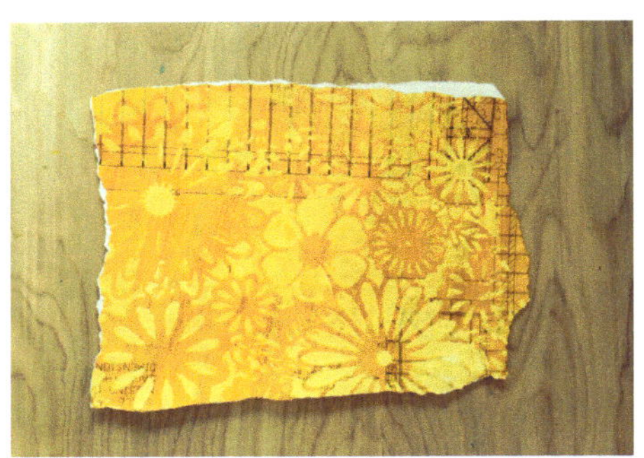

Paper embellished with a stencil pattern in light colors and allowed to dry completely

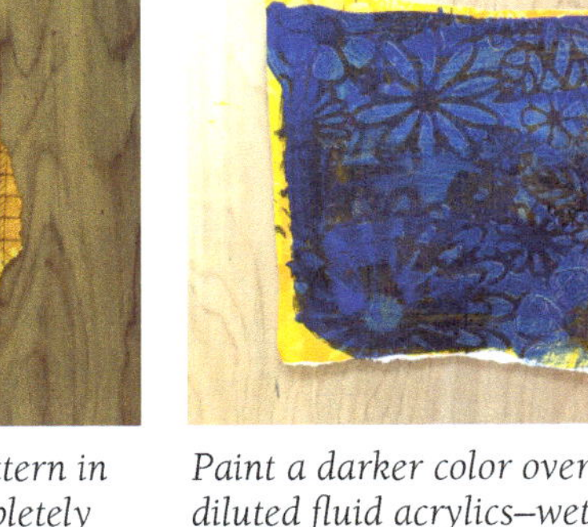

Paint a darker color over the top with diluted fluid acrylics—wet and watery

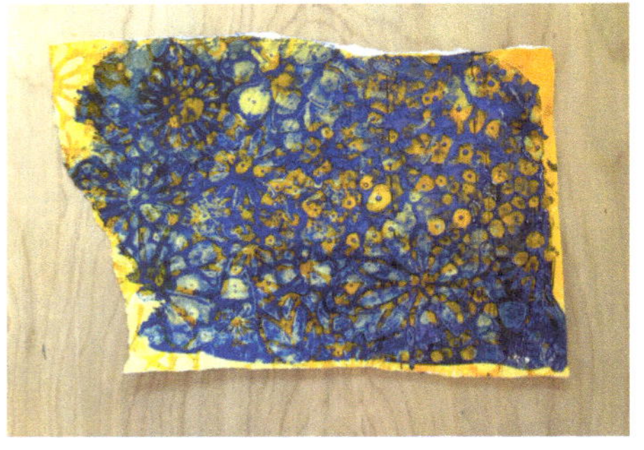

Working quickly, spritz the soap into the wet paint. A pattern will emerge as it resists

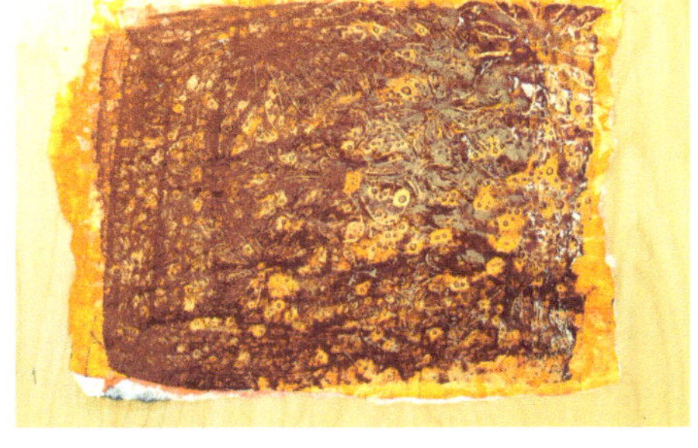

Use a piece of paper that will not allow the paint to soak all the way through. Coat paper with a light colored acrylic paint. Allow to dry completely.

Brush over the top of your painted sheet with a darker color of diluted fluid acrylic paint. (Much like the alcohol technique on the previous page).

While the top layer is still wet, gently spray the soap bubble mixture and allow the droplets to fall onto the paper. Try to spray the soap mixture up in air and let it fall straight down onto the paper in small droplets.

Watch the soap bubbles repel the top layer of paint in a small pattern of spots that sometimes continue to grow bigger and bigger.

There are many variables that come into play with this resist technique, so experimentation is paramount. The amount of water in the diluted top coat plays a role, the amount of drying time before spraying the soap bubbles plays a role, the color of the paint can even play a role. Experimentation is key.

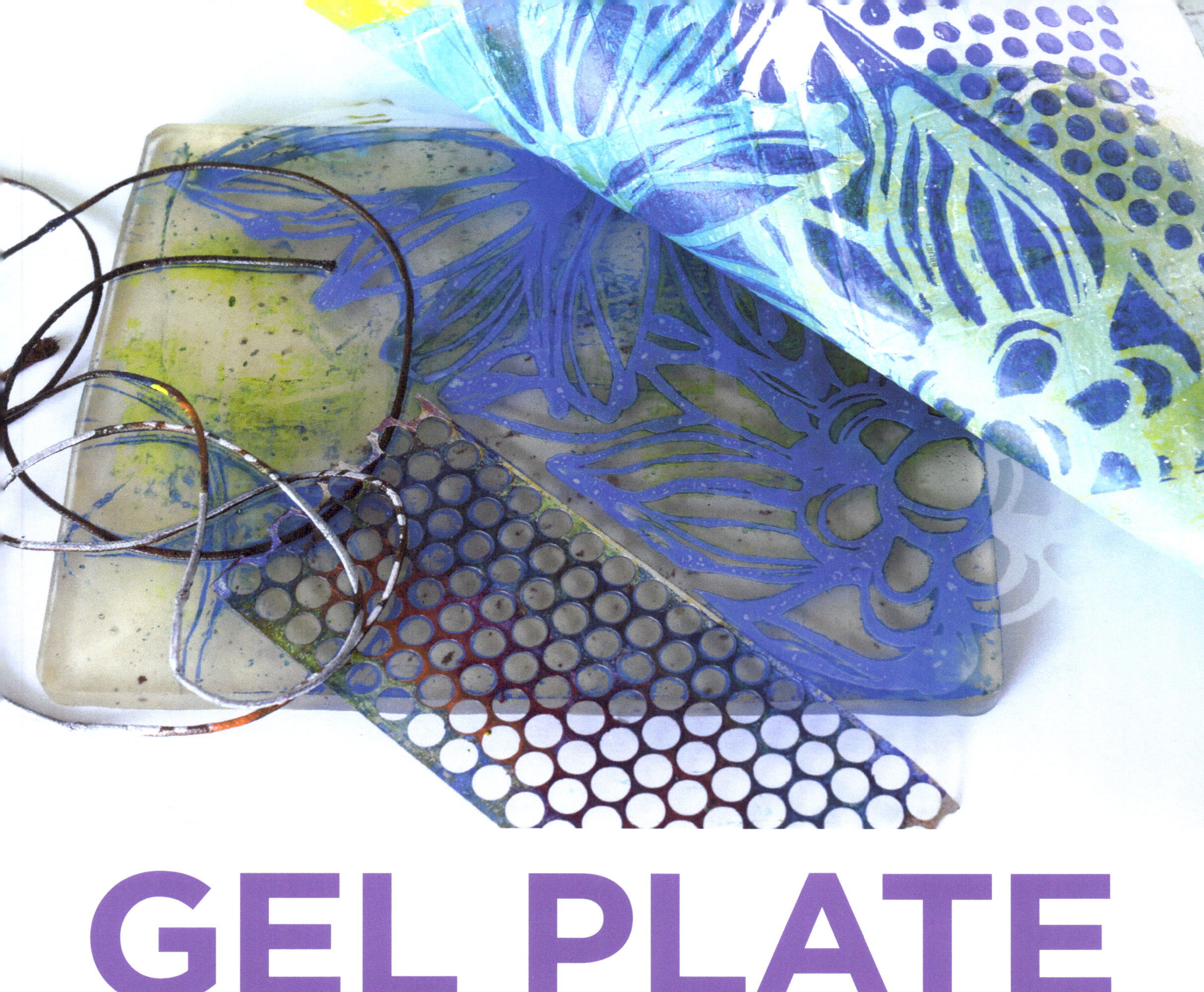

GEL PLATE
monoprinting madness!

The Gel Press printing plate has become all the rage with mixed media artists, and yet I find at least two or three people in my Paper Paintings Collage Workshop who have yet to experiment with it. You are in for a treat.

This Gel Press printing plate looks and feels like gelatin, but is durable, reusable, and stores at room temperature. It doesn't take up room in your fridge like a home-made one, it's easy to clean and always ready for printing. Monoprinting on a Gel Press printing plate is simple and fun. The gratification is immediate, and the prints have endless creative uses.

It is my hope that you will experiment with all of the techniques in this book before you pick your favorites. The effects I get with some of my classroom demonstration papers make the students ooh and ahhh, but they don't necessarily always find them to be the techniques they choose for themselves. Why not invite some friends to join you? Clear a table top and have fun Gel printing papers together, then swap and trade and expand your inventory with the styles and color palettes of fellow paper painters . I've gotten some of the best papers in trade that I would have never made on my own.

color
combinations

painting paper

Starting with light colors and working your way down to darker colors is the way to go with fluid acrylics, which are the paints I prefer in my process. Because fluid acrylics are translucent, a light color will not show up very well over a darker color. For this reason, I start light and every subsequent layer is a little darker. I also like to use colors that are next to each other on the color wheel for harmony, or colors that are across from each other for discord. I suggest experimenting with both to see what appeals to you.

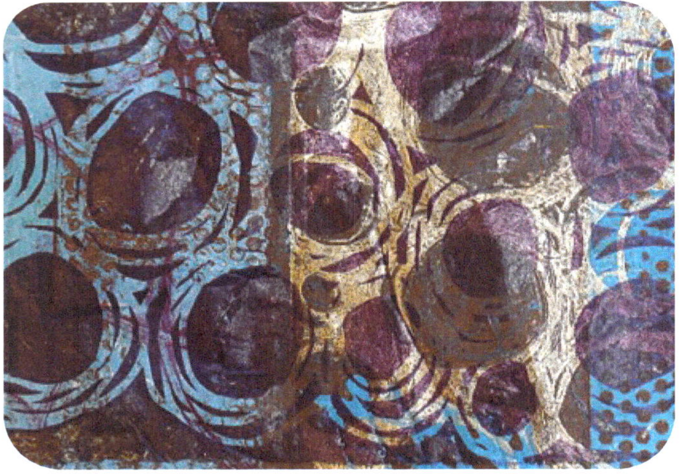

Harmonious colors start with light blue, to dark purple, to opaque gold on top.

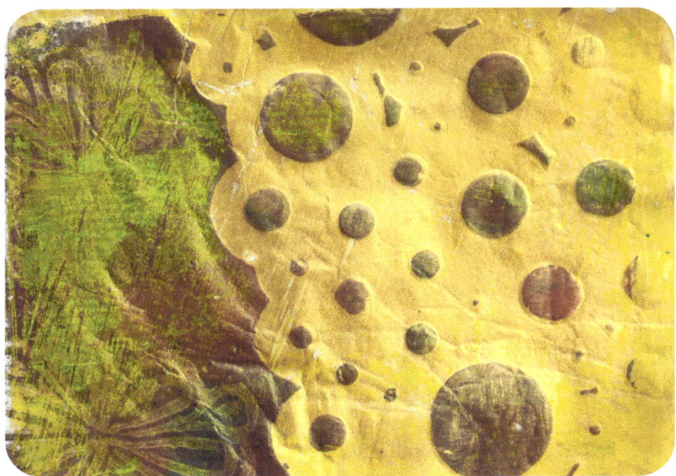

Creating an overall glow by utilizing metallic paint for the base and translucent, darker colors on top.

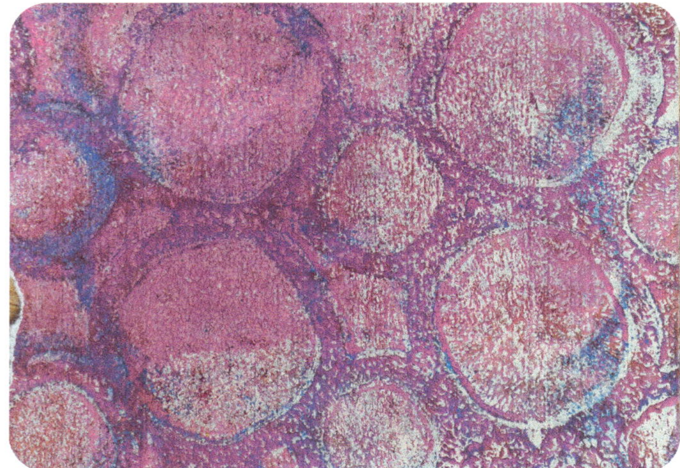

Creating harmony by staying with colors that are next to each other on the color wheel. Staring with magenta, adding darker purple.

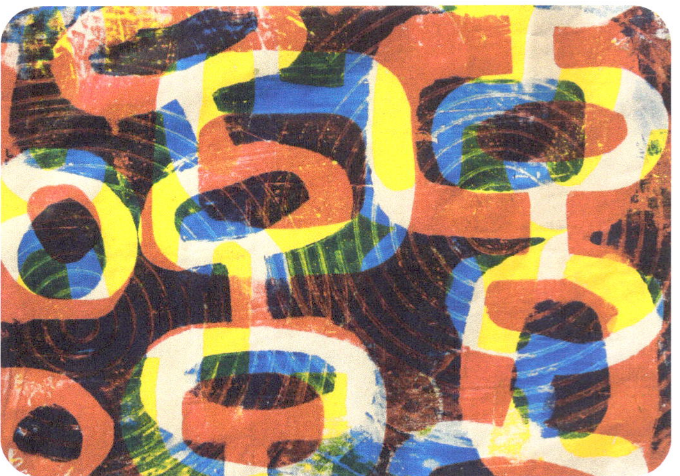

Creating discord with opposite colors. Starting with yellow, adding red, and lastly blue. Working light to dark, starting from white.

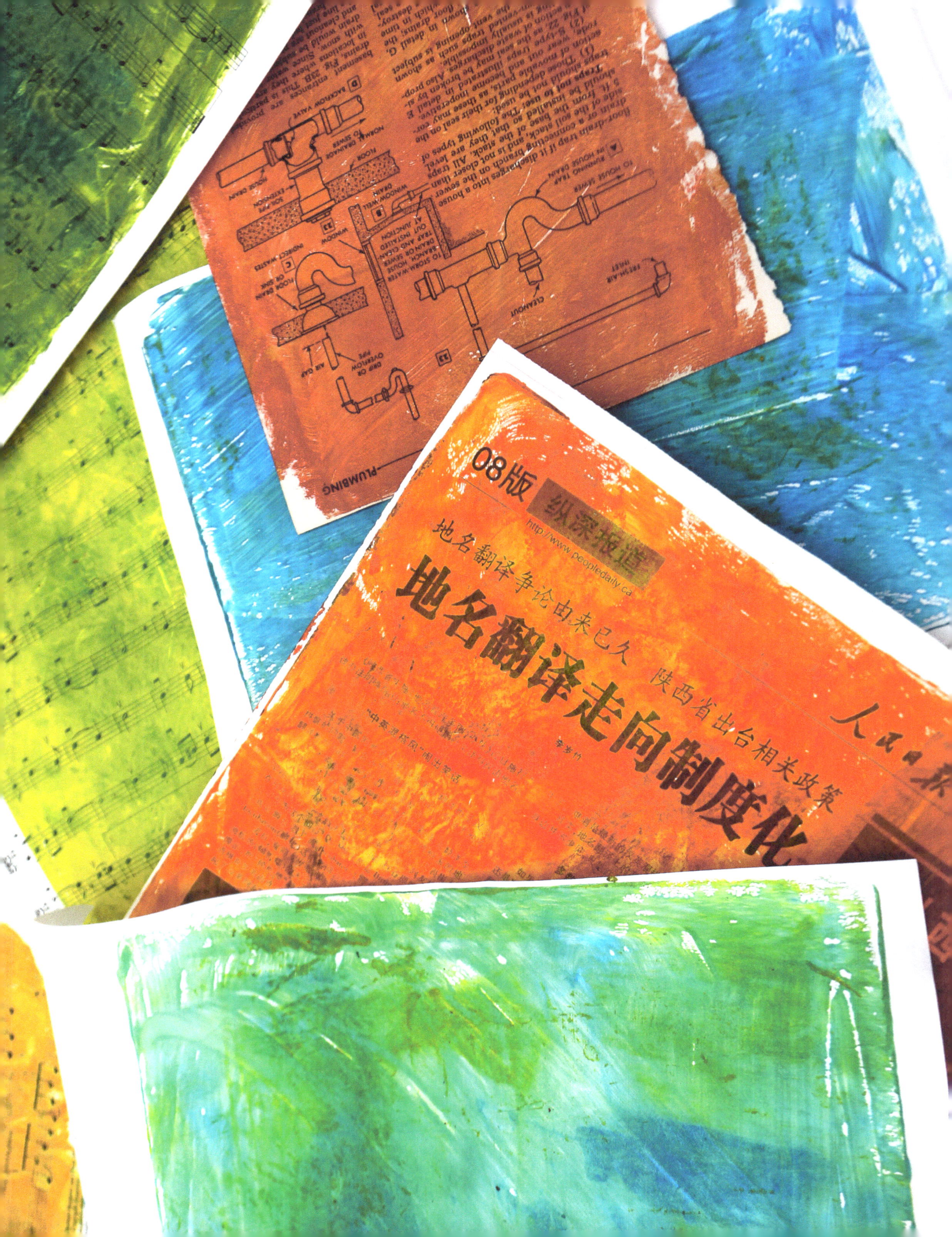
08版 纵深报道
http://www.peopledaily.ca
地名翻译争论由来已久　陕西省出台相关政策
地名翻译走向制度化
人民

starting with light colored solids

I find, in fine art Gel printing, that starting with a light colored solid base is the way to go. I prefer not to have any high contrast white areas in my final prints, as I am hoping to achieve a painterly, fine art feeling. In order to eliminate the whites, without having to wash over the print post production, I always start with a solid base layer. I do not clean my plate between base layers, this process makes use of any residual paint on the plate from layer to layer. I call the leftover dried paint the crust. Your subsequent layers pick up the crust along with the newly applied paint—creating unexpected and beautiful results.

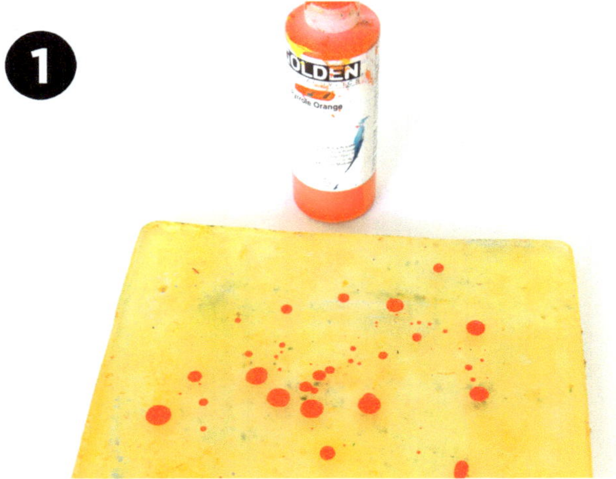

The brayer gives thin, even coverage for a few drops of paint applied directly to the plate.

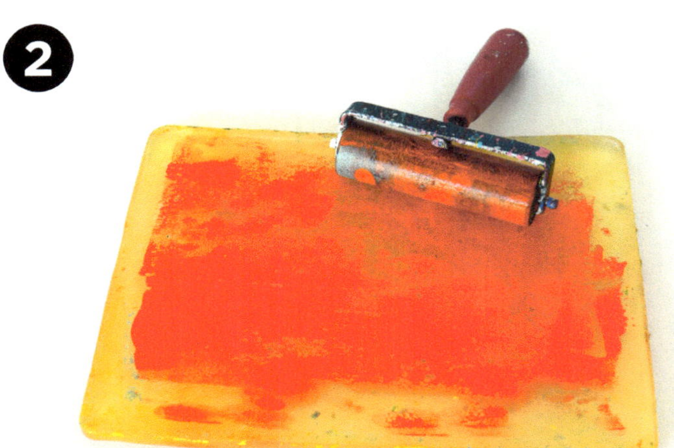

Roll the paint out to evenly cover the surface of the plate with the brayer.

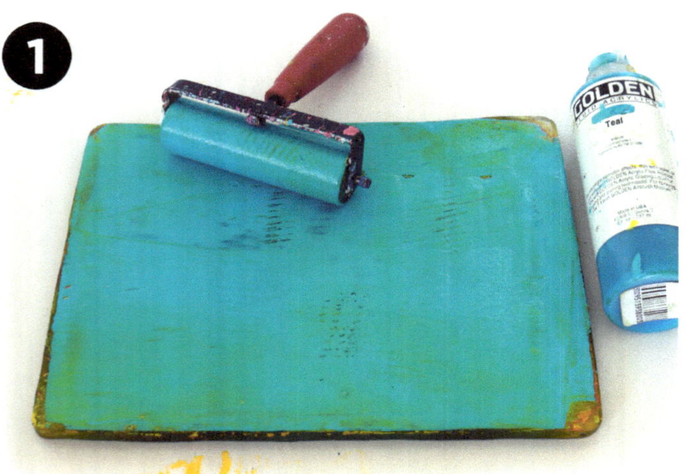

Start your printing process with a light colored solid.

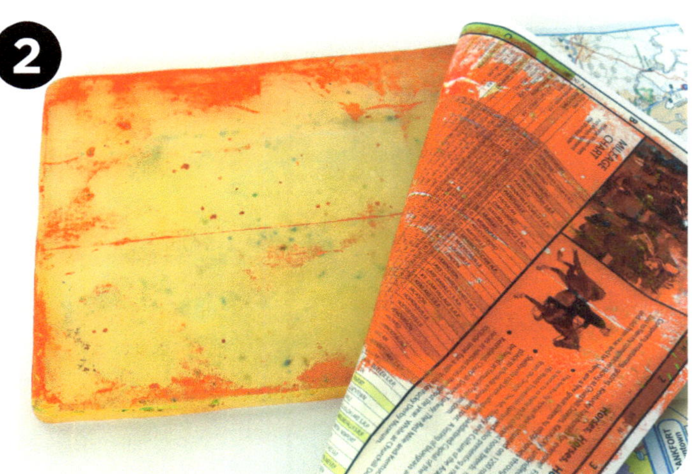

This will act as a base for subsequent, more complex layers

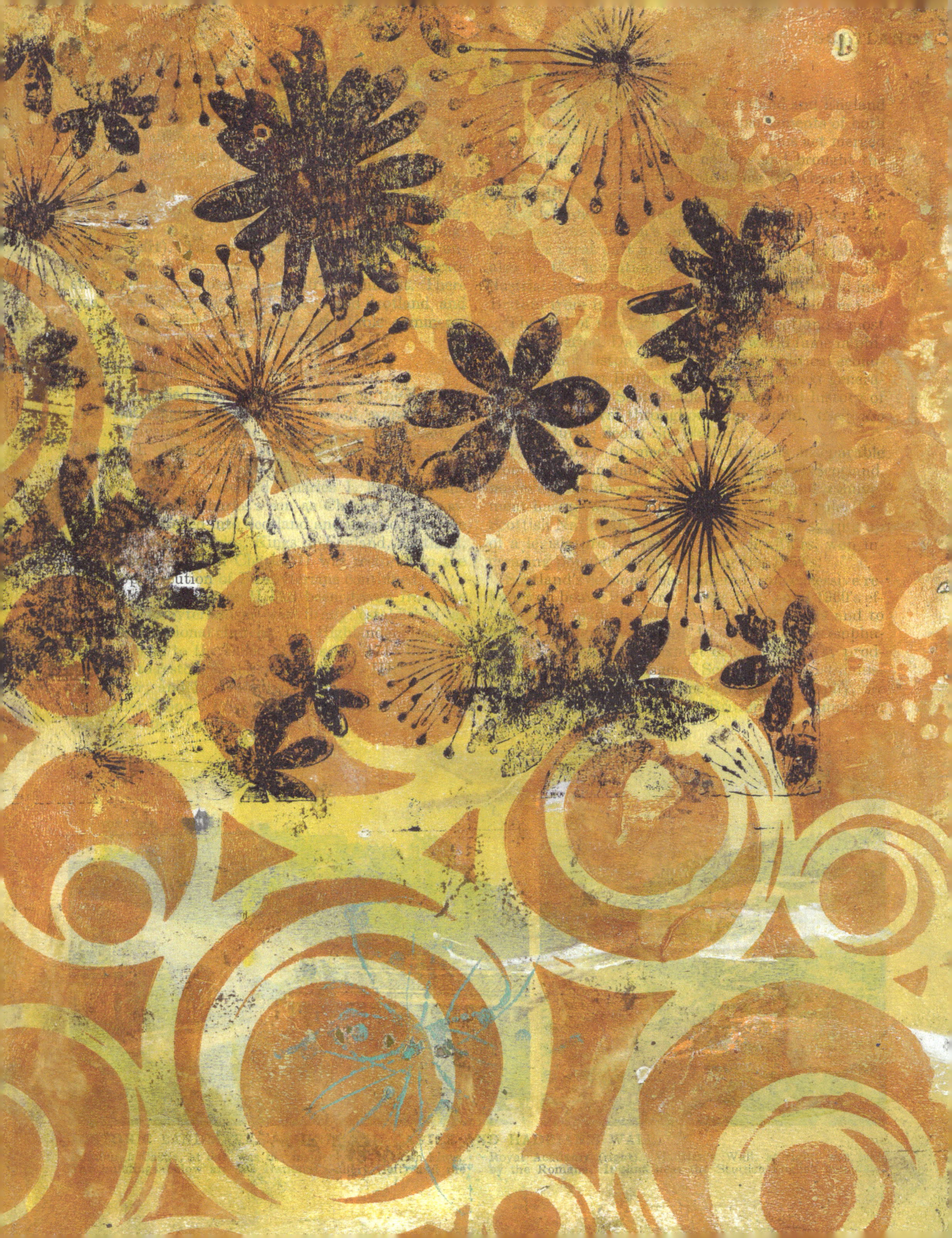

building layers

through translucency

Once you have your light colored base layer(s) printed on several small sheets of paper or an oversized sheet of paper, your goal is to start multiplying prints over and over with the techniques to follow in this book. Because Fluid Acrylics are translucent, every Gel printed layer you apply from here on out is going to show through and multiply with its predecessor. My typical rule of thumb is to combine a minimum of three layers in my Gel Prints, this creates rich papers for collage with lots and lots of depth. Varying the techniques of your layers creates even more visual interest. That being said, stencils tend to be the favorite technique of the Gel Press printing plate for my workshop students. My advice? Be bold, branch out, try different things!

The idea behind starting with a light colored base layer is that your prints don't include the white of the paper, which offers high contrast and can appear busy. High contrast can be distracting in collage papers, apple red should be layers of rich reds, intense oranges, deep yellows; adding white to this palette would be distracting.

I often multiply a print made using scraping tools over a print made with stencils, and then layer that print over one made with hand cut masks. This is the multi layered Gel print process I use for creating collage papers.

Keeping in mind my palette, I'll implement three or more colors (working from light to dark) that are analogous (next to one another) on the color wheel. I love the combination of blues and greens (cool colors) layered over each other through different techniques.

Every rule is meant to be broken! Experiment with combining opposites across the wheel as well.

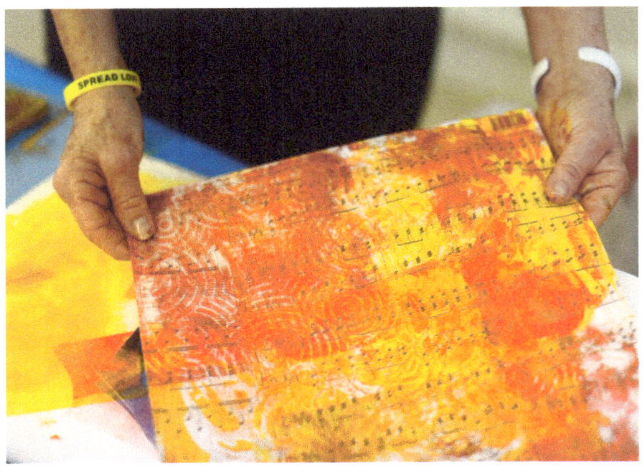

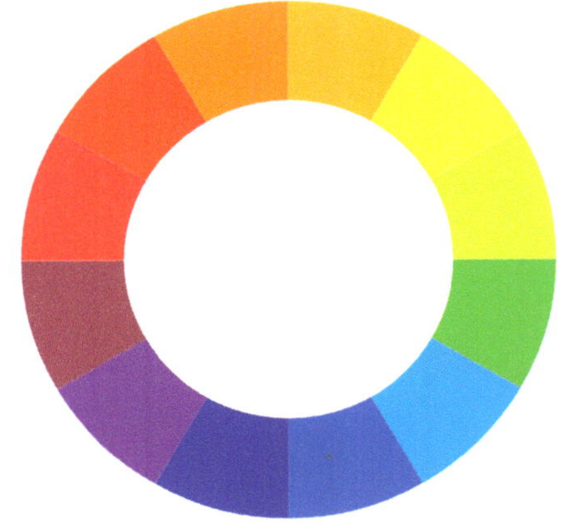

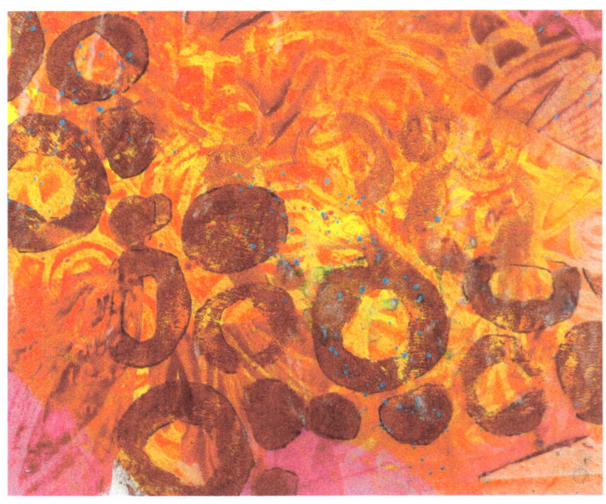

Making use of analogous colors

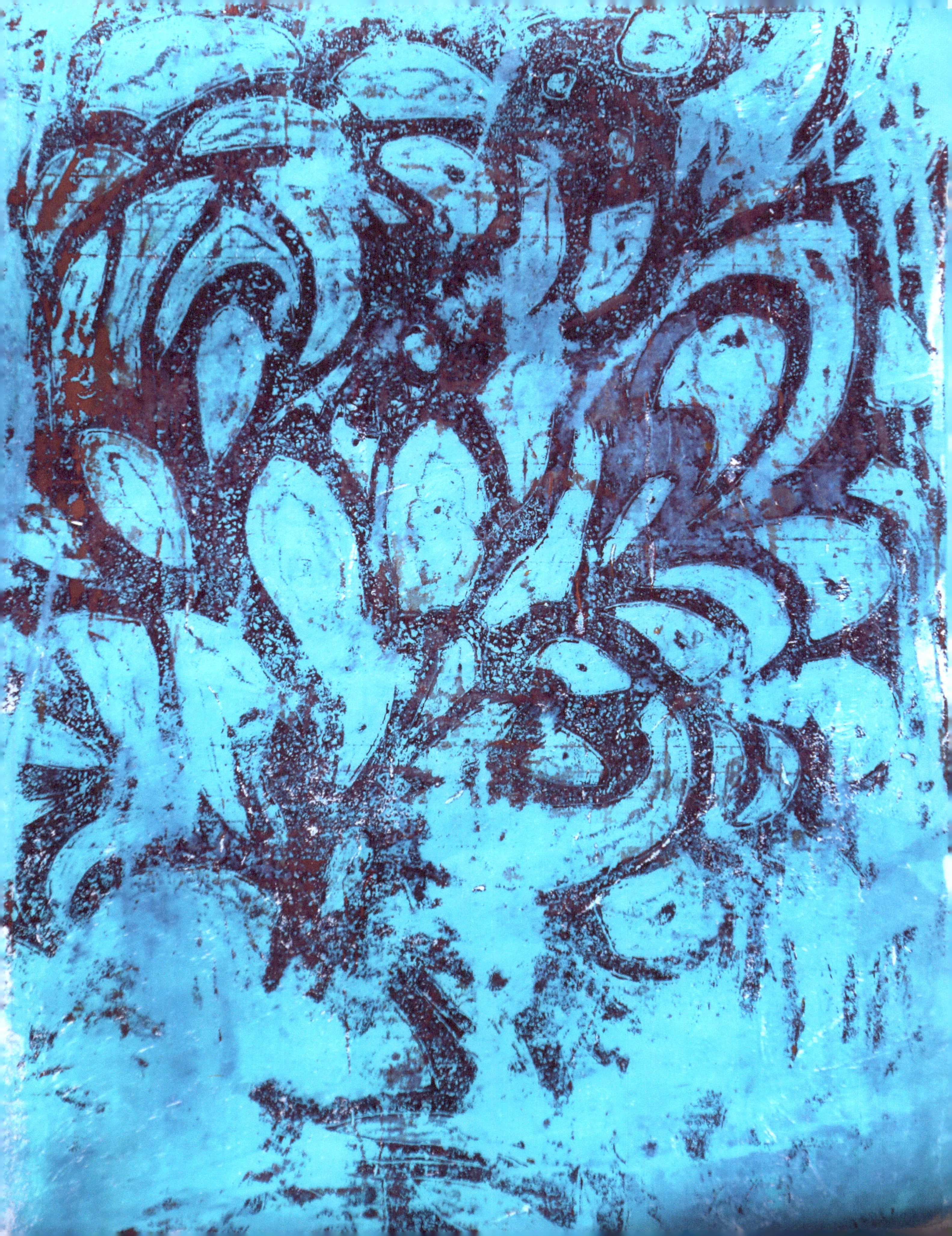

stencils

with ghost prints

Layering ghost prints one over the next (working light to dark) offers rich, painterly printed paper. The more layering the better, when you are trying to achieve painterly, fine art prints. Ghost prints can either be pulled immediately onto a pre-prepared light colored solid, or they can be pulled together with a second layer of paint.

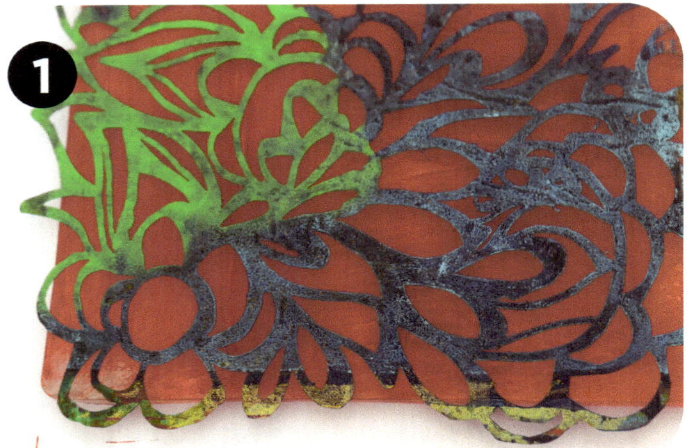

Lay the stencil over a thin layer of paint on the plate.

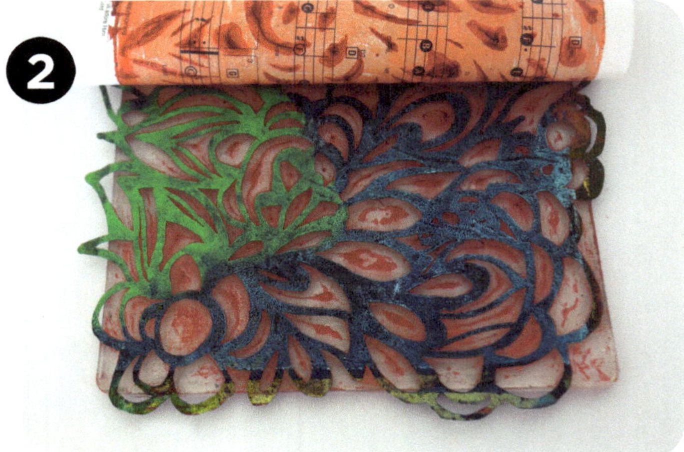

Press and pull a print from the plate

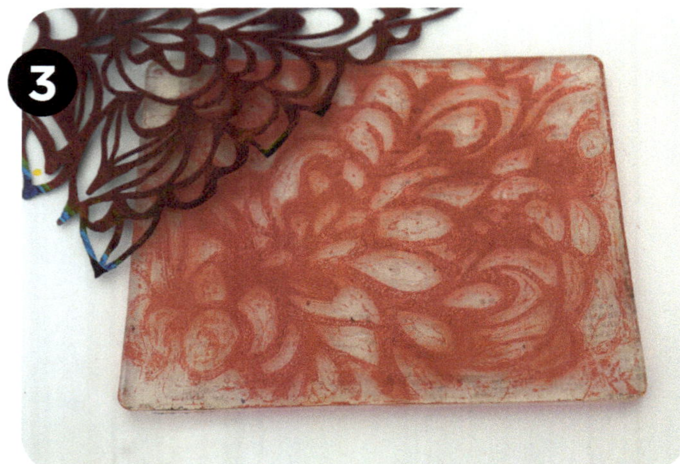

Paint left behind becomes the ghost print, or second print, after removing a stencil.

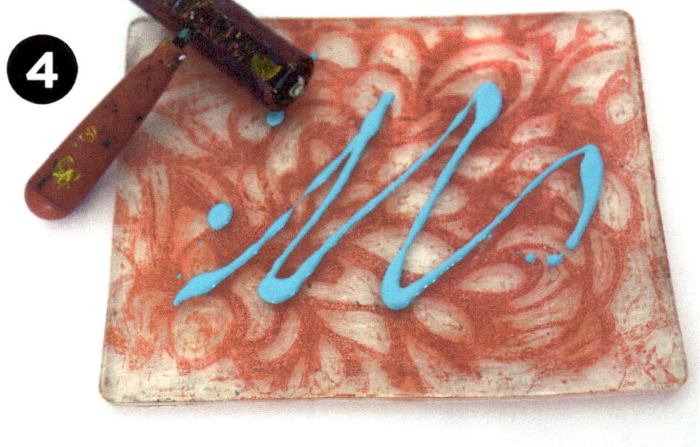

Add a thin layer of a lighter color paint over top of the dried ghost layer, pull the print of both layers together (left).

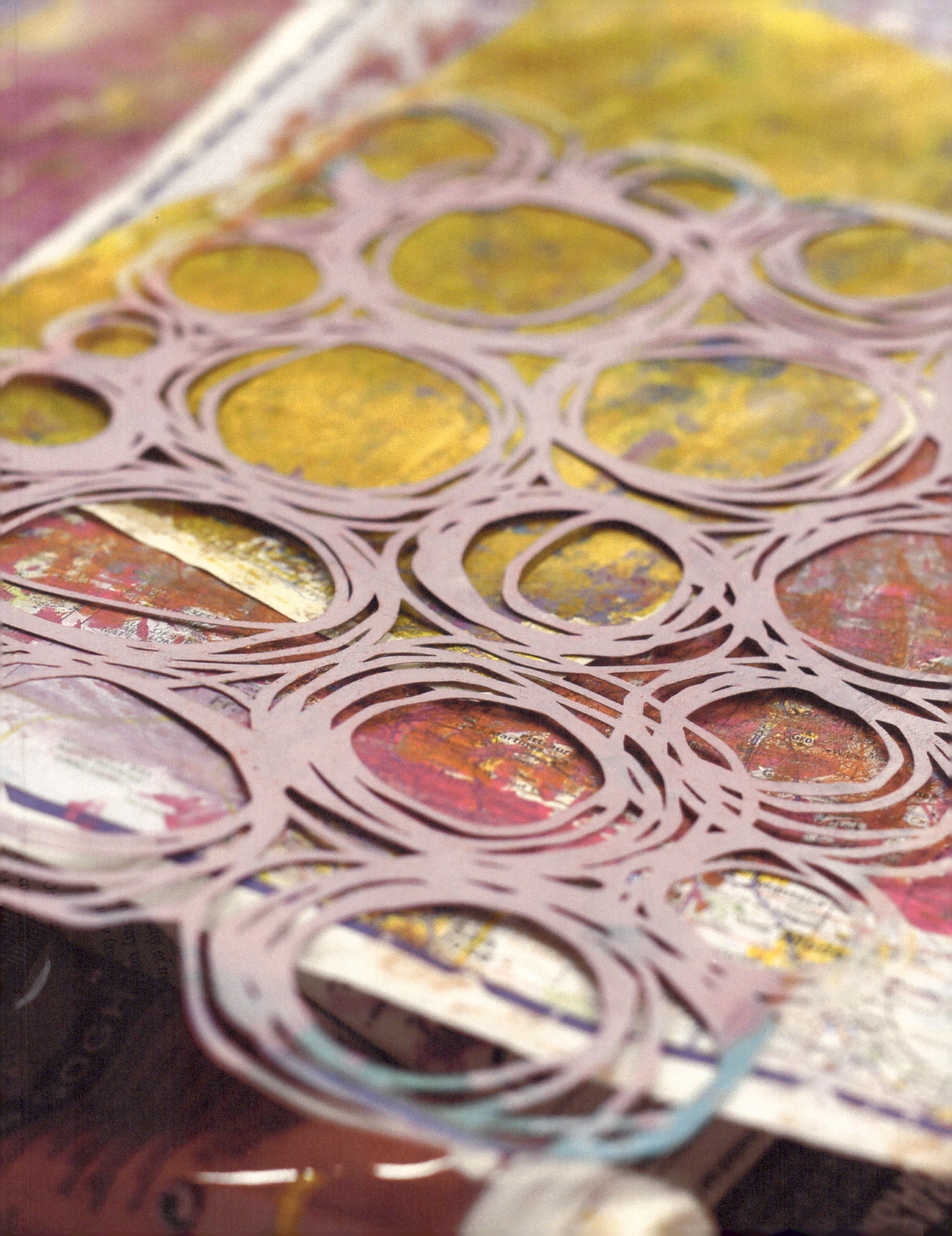

stencils

combining and layering

Layering stencil mask prints one over the next (working light to dark) offers rich, painterly printed paper. Combine stencils with elements such as leaves, string, and place mats for more diversity of patterning.

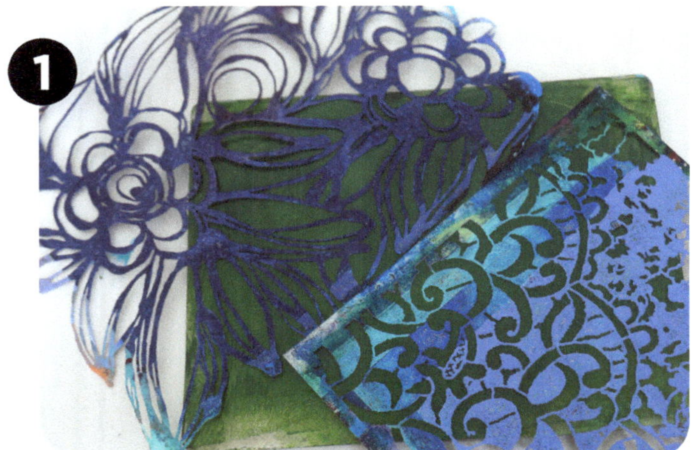

Combining two stencils on dark green paint.

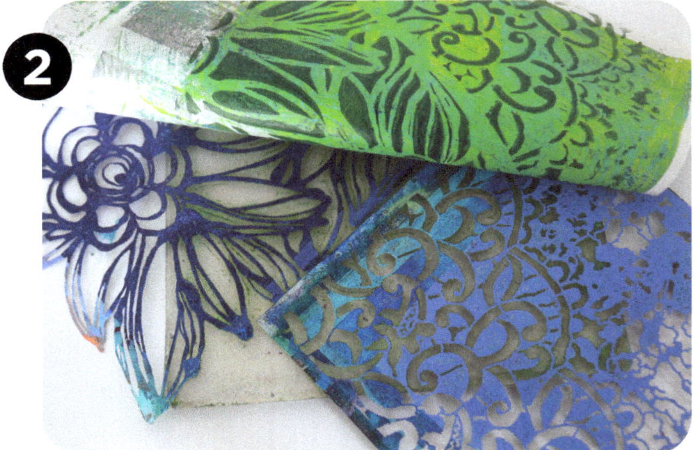

Pulling the multi stencil print on a light green solid.

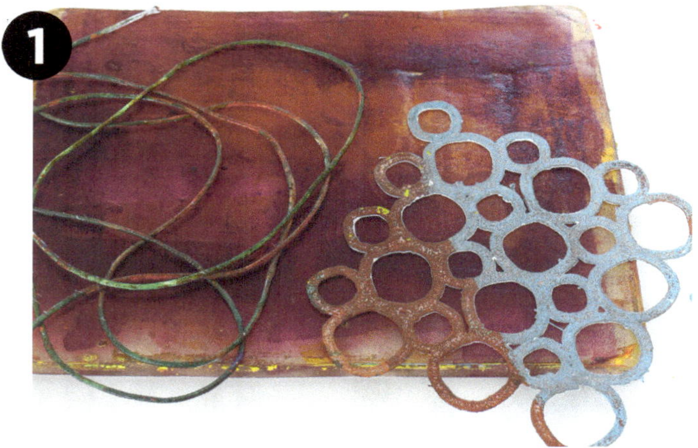

Combining a stencil with string (or other found masking material) on one print.

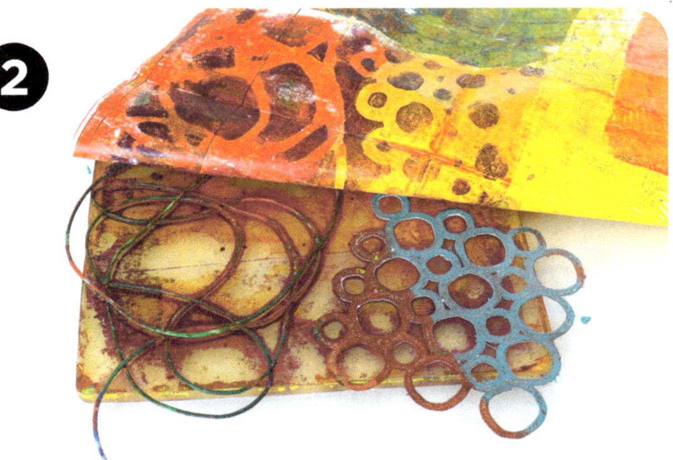

Pulling the print over a mixed solid base layer.

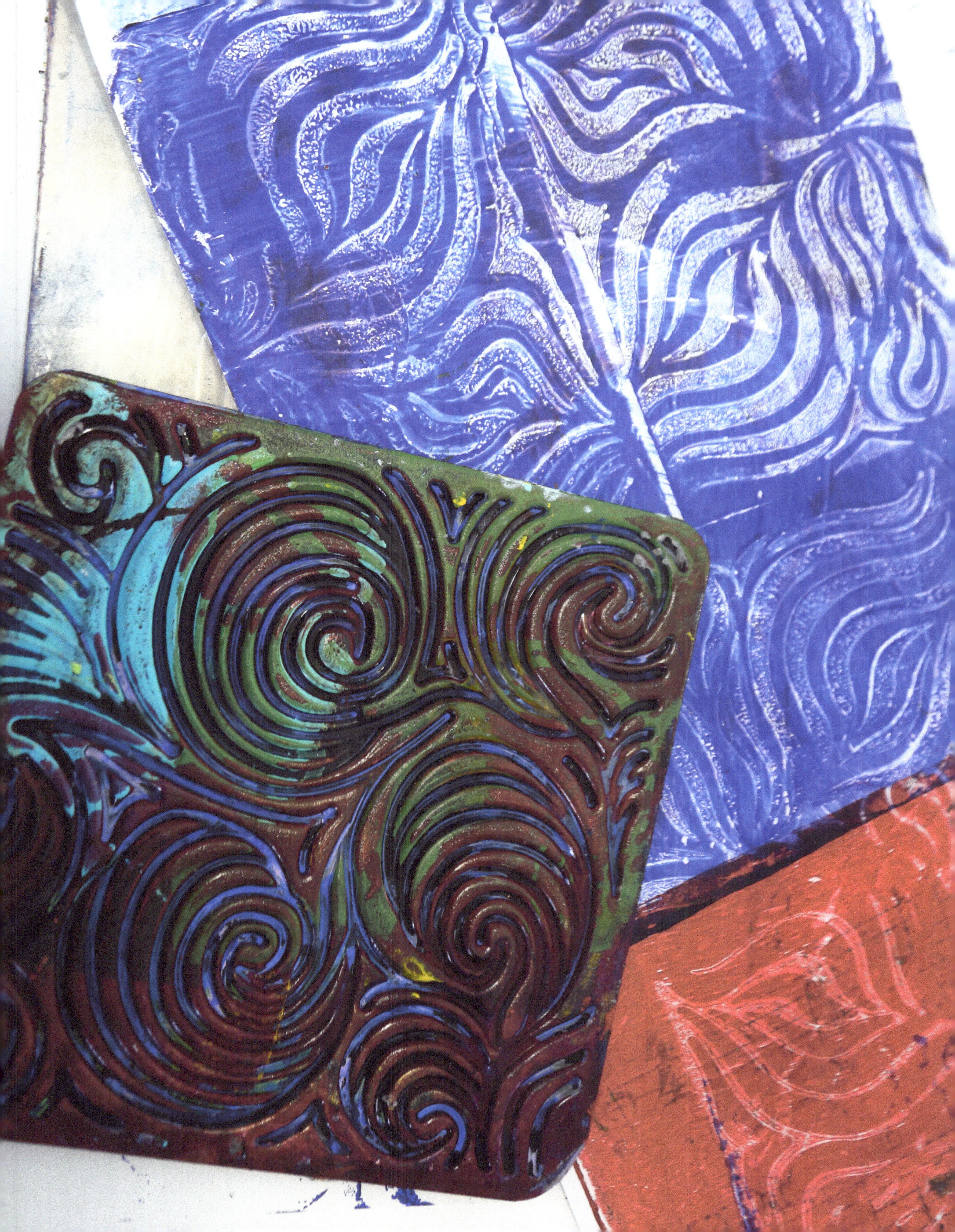

texture

plastic rubbing plates

There are many ways to apply texture to Gel Prints, commercially produced texture plates being just the beginning. Other elements that can be used include, the bottoms of shoes, the circle end of a paper towel roll, potato mashing tools, yoga mats, needle point mesh... The possibilities are endless. Look around you and start thinking about the everyday items in your life and how they would work when pressed into paint on the Gel Press printing plate. It's a whole new world.

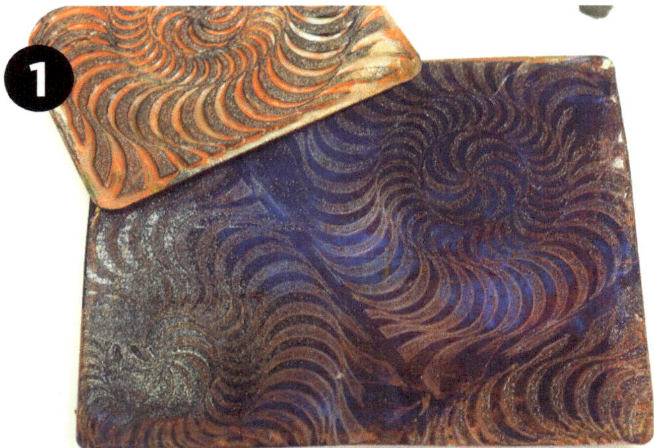

Press a clean, dry rubbing plate into a wet layer of paint to create a pattern by removing paint.

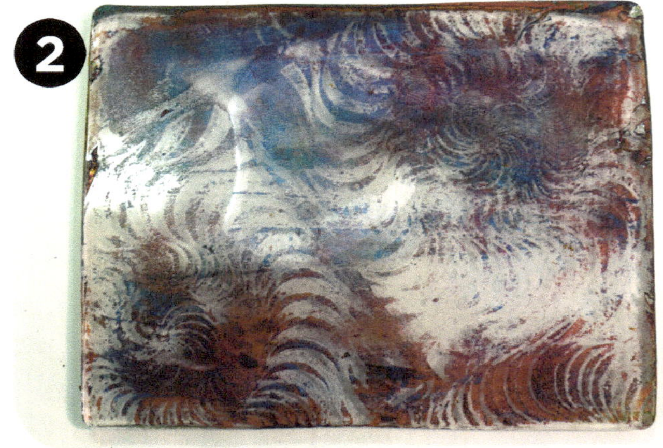

After the first print of the rubbing plate, let the residual paint dry on the plate.

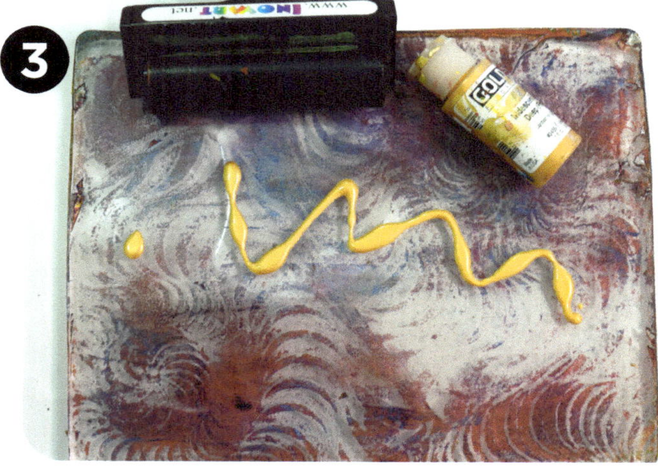

Apply a gold metallic over the residual paint.

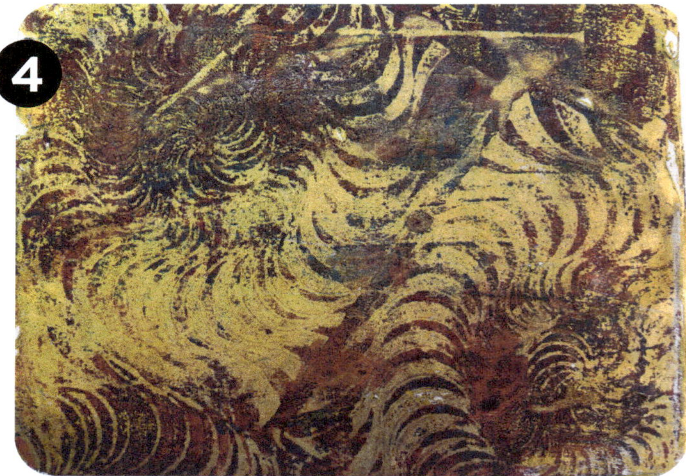

The gold metallic paint and the residual paint are pulled together to create one print, as shown here.

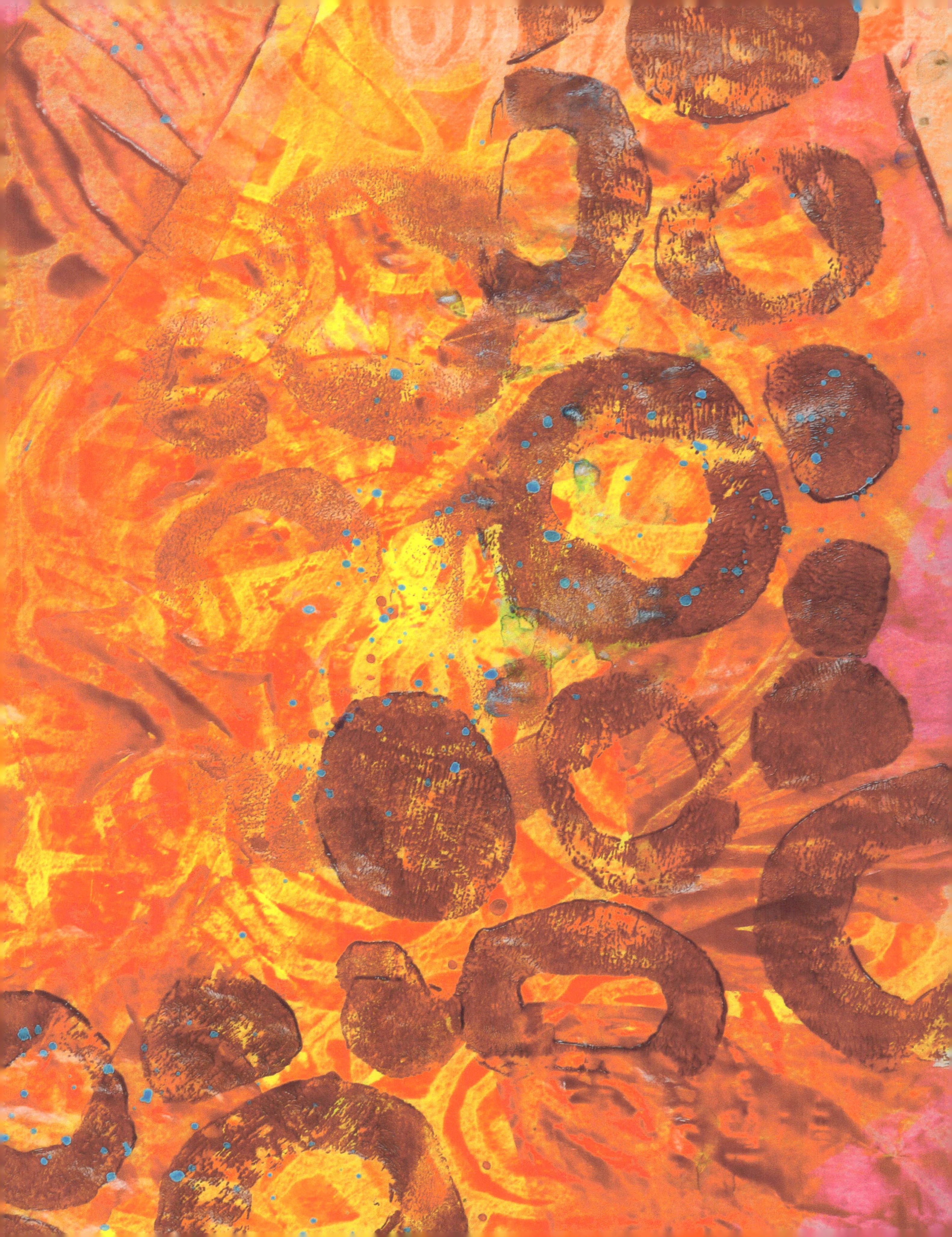

stamps

subtle subtraction

Hand-carved and commercially purchased stamps offer wonderful textures on the Gel Press printing plate. Pressing a stamp into the paint layer removes it subtly, revealing the pattern in a painterly impression. Overlapping and combining stamps with other effects offers more variety and interesting results.

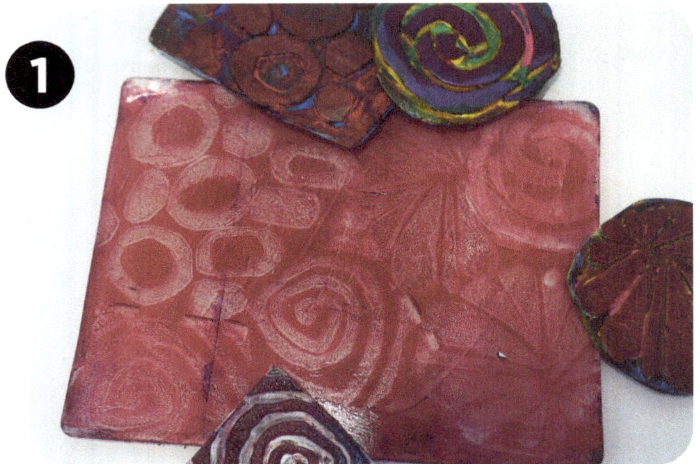

Removing paint with a clean, dry stamp pressed into it will create a subtle pattern on the plate.

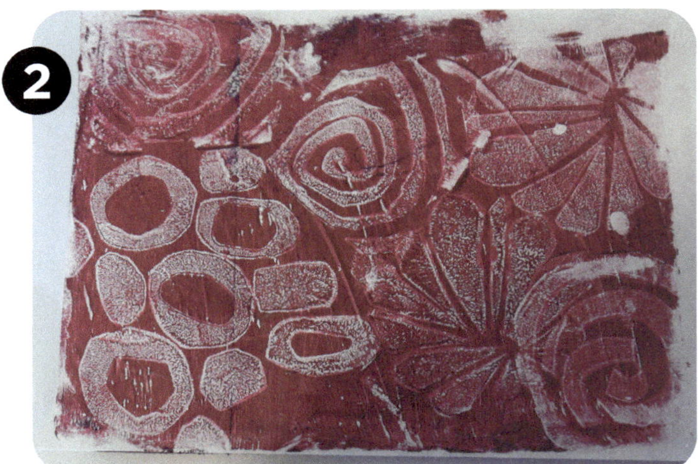

A print on white paper of the stamped plate.

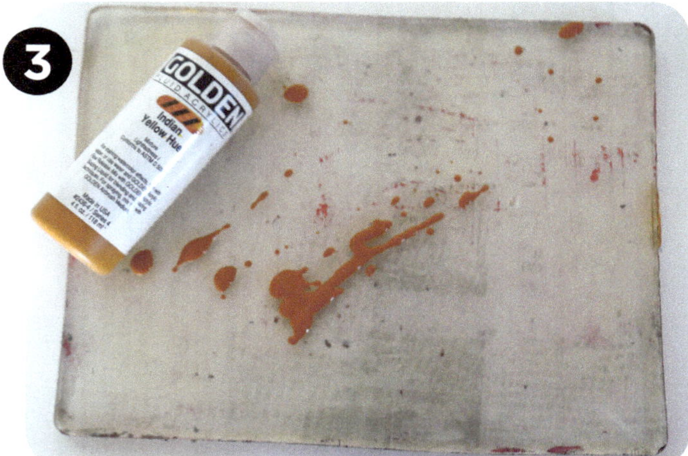

Set up the plate with a thin layer of light gold.

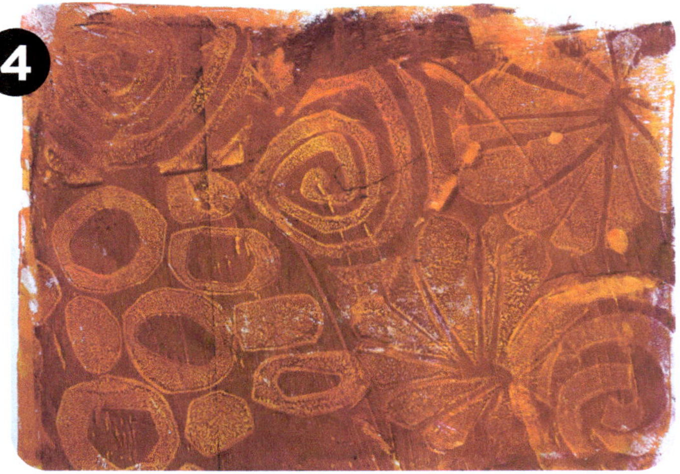

Overprint the light gold onto the pulled red print to tone down the whites.

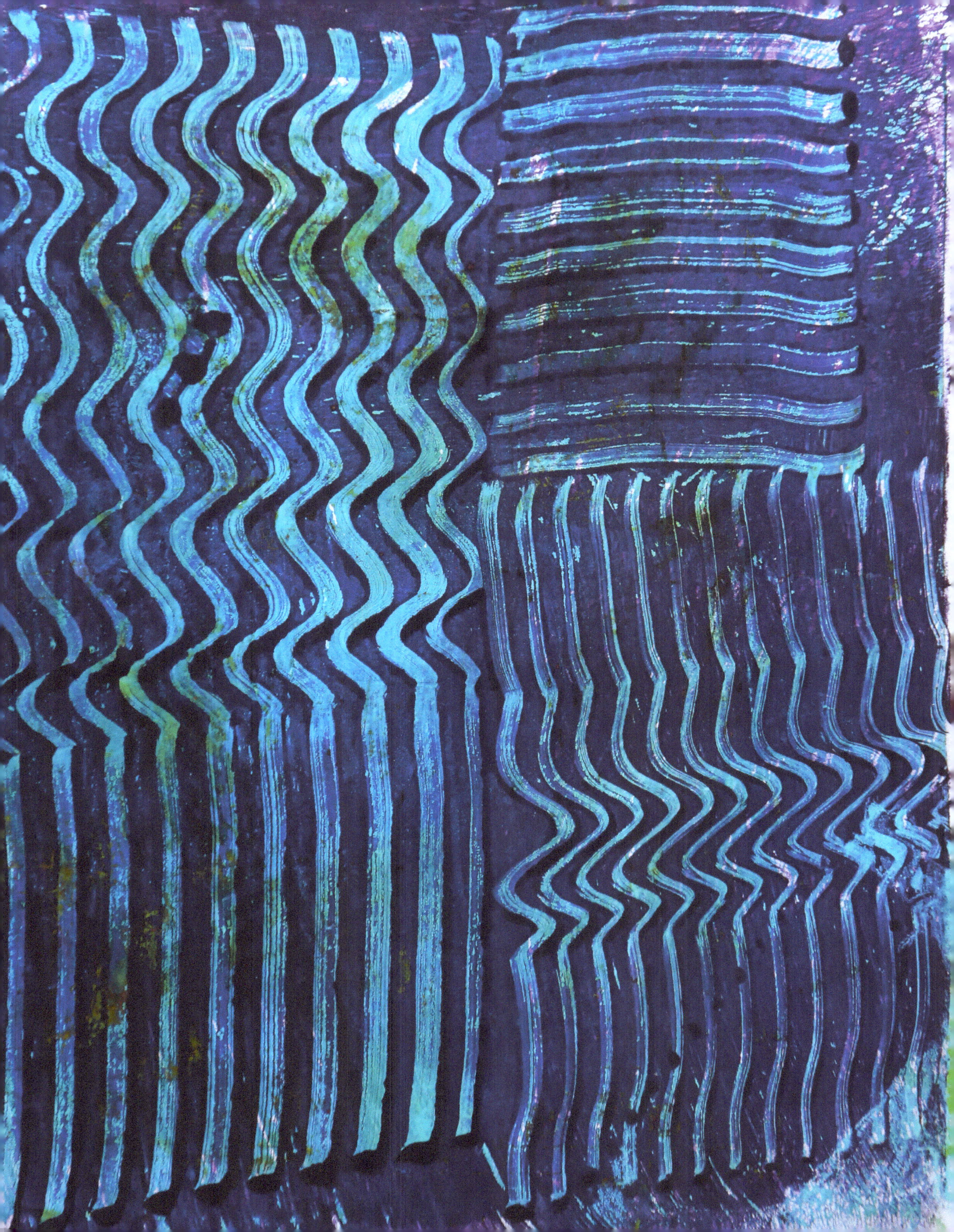

scrapers

catalyst wedges

Princeton makes a line of hand held wedge tools with teeth on two edges. They fit nicely in the palm of your hand and come in many different widths and patterns for scraping. The wedges work wonderfully on the Gel Press printing plate to scrape in straight, wiggle, zig zag or any combination of motions to create interesting patterns scraped out of (removing) the paint.

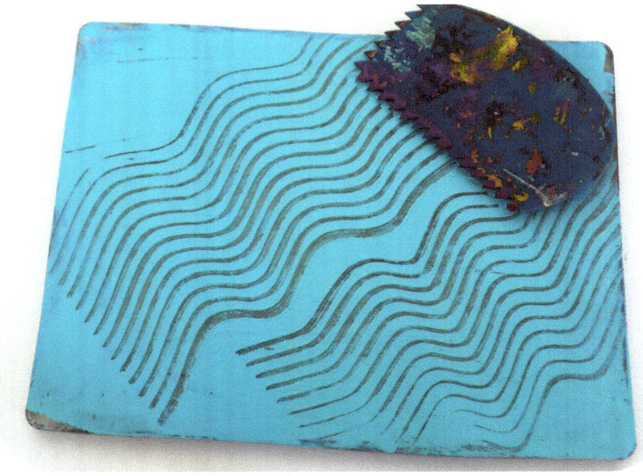

An example of removing paint from the plate with the scrapers.

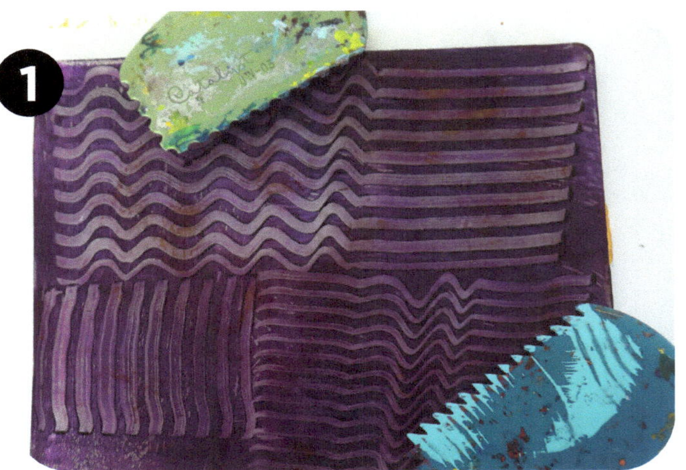

Apply a thin layer of paint with the brayer and scrape through the paint layer with the scrapers.

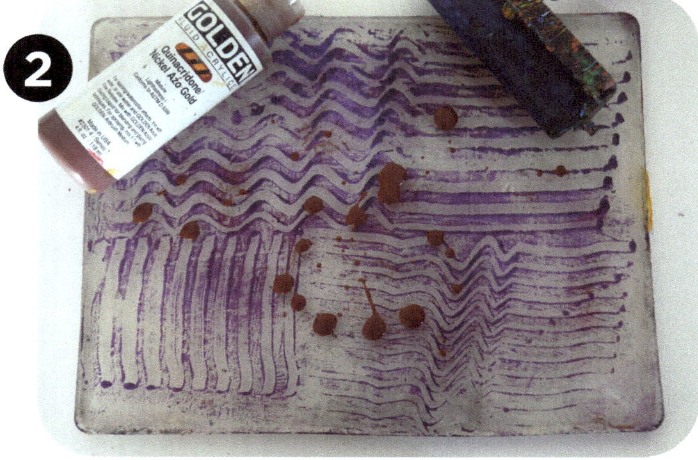

Apply a thin layer of light brown paint to the residual paint after pulling the first print.

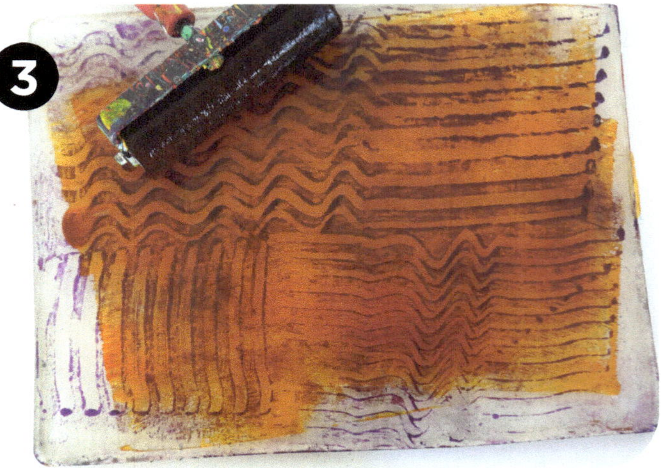

The brown paint and residual paint layer will pull off together for a subtle, painterly print.

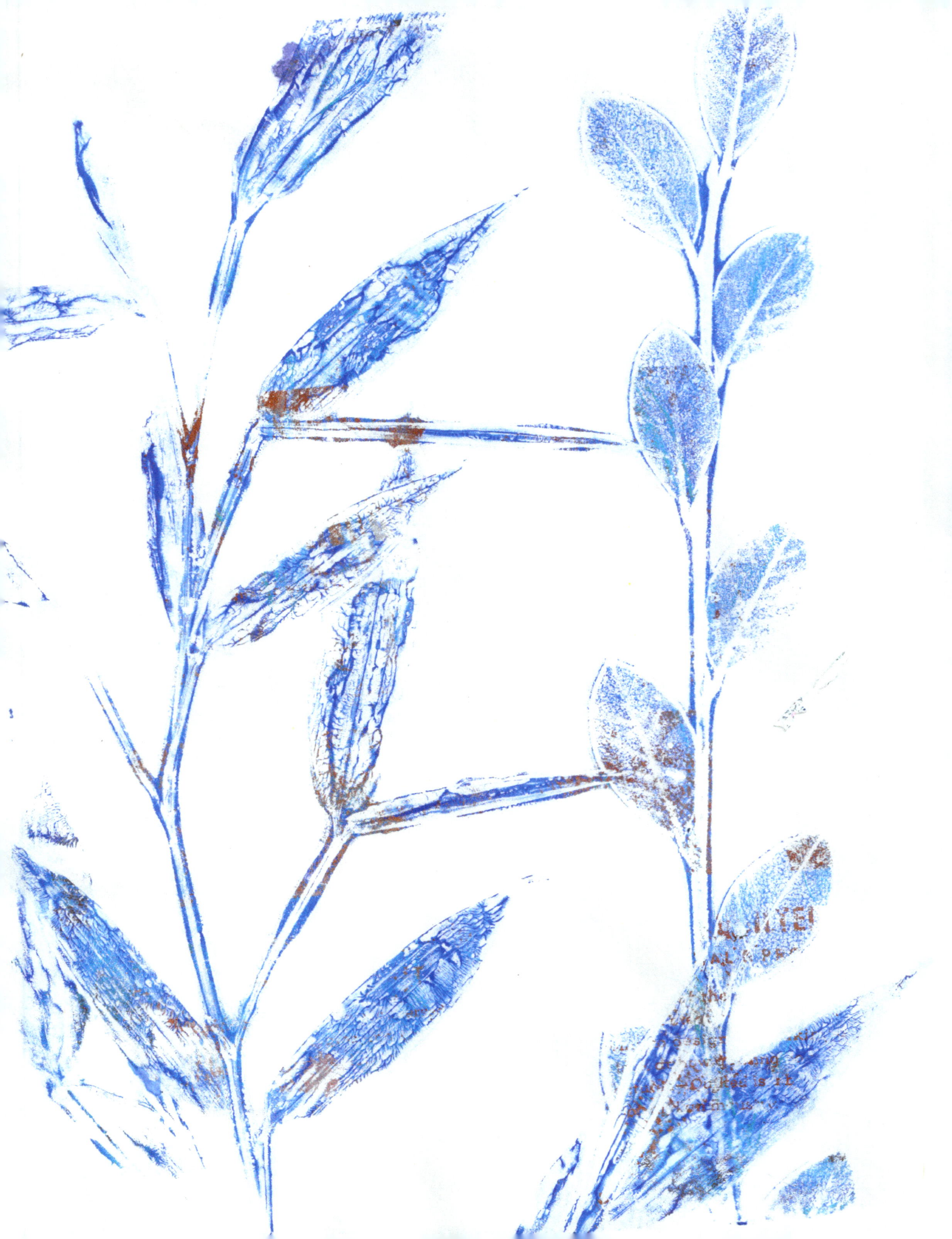

leaves

positive and negative

Freshly picked leaves make lovely masks and positive prints. In Florida we have some HUGE leaves, but a combination of small and medium leaves work just as nicely. Experiment with different types, ferns always offer very interesting shapes.

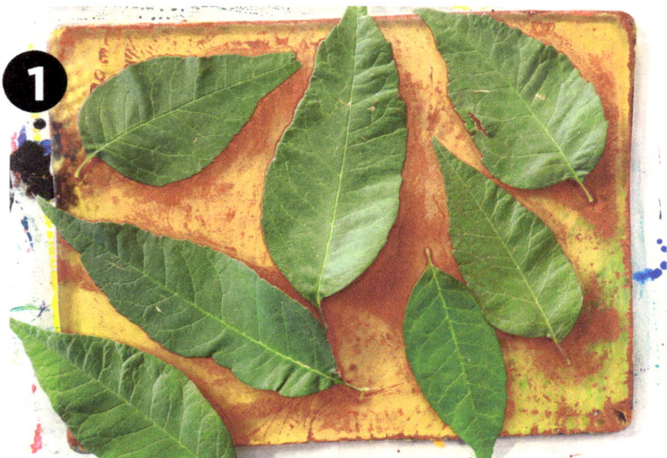

The leaves have trapped paint underneath after the first print is pulled.

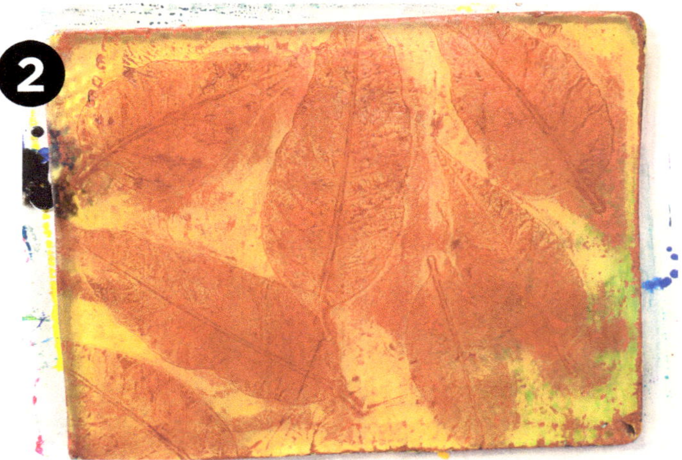

Gently removed the leaves to reveal the ghost print with excellent vein patterns.

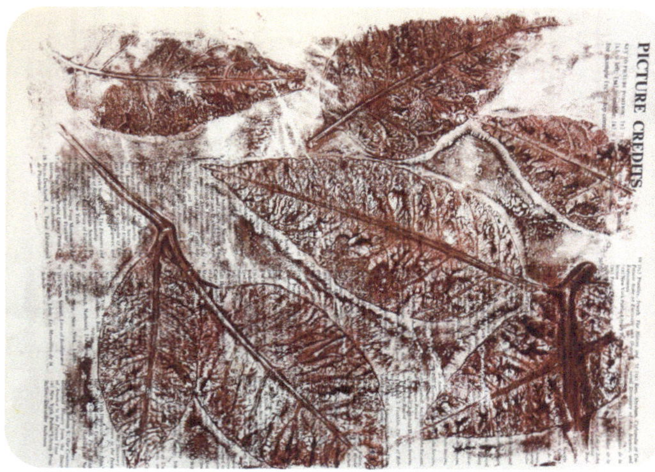

Example of a positive leaf print with trapped paint

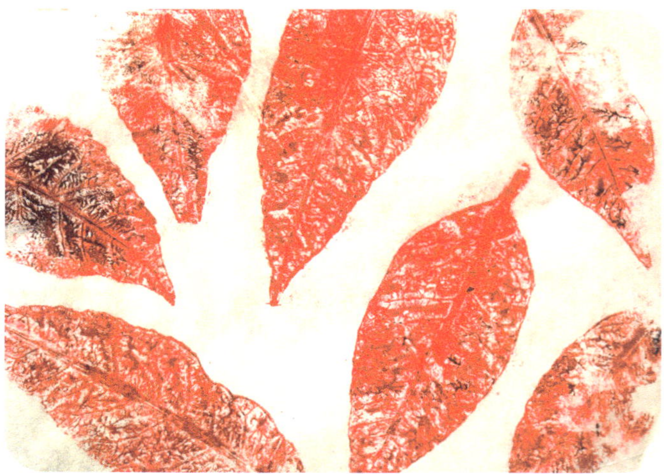

Example of a positive leaf print with trapped paint

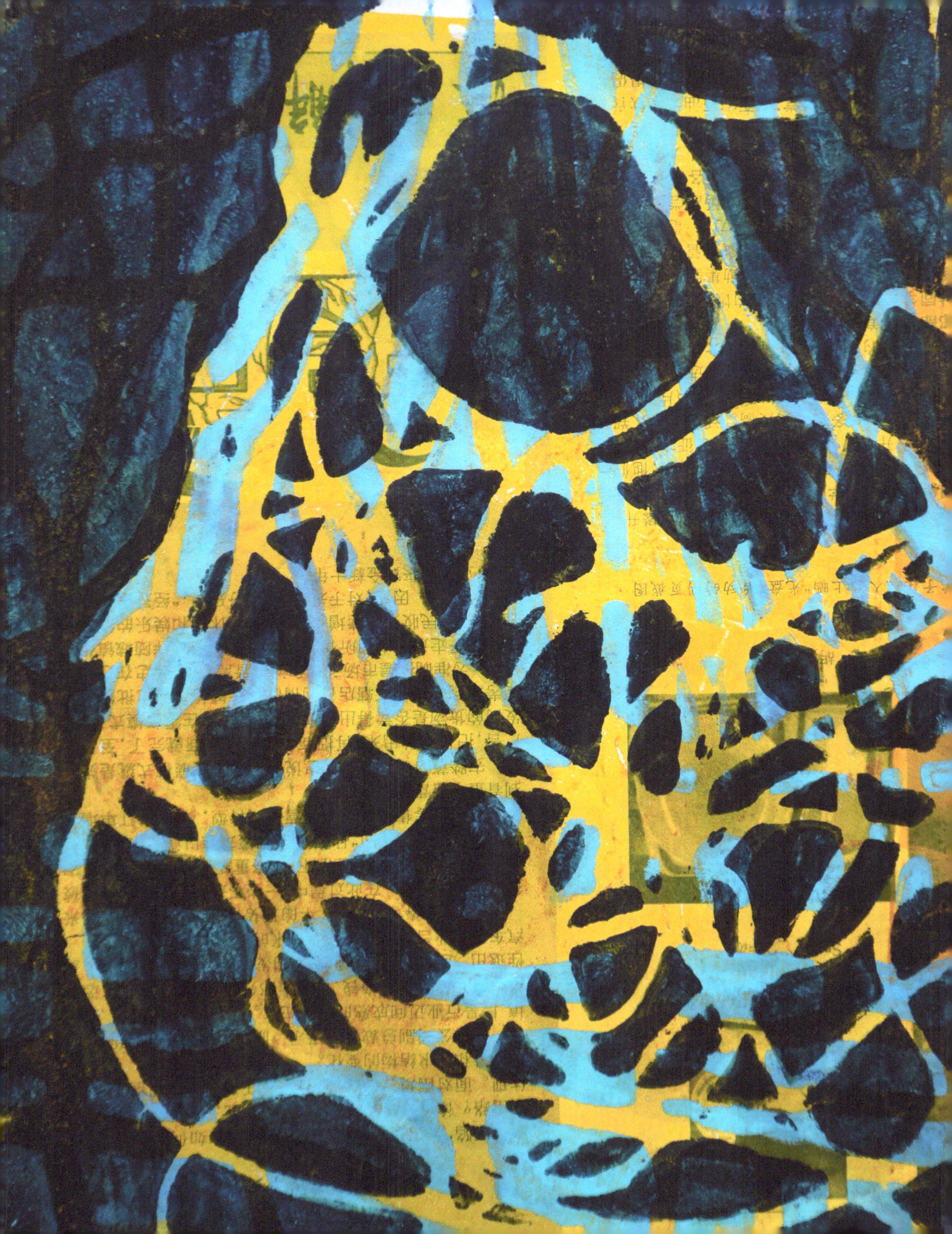

found objects

jute string and layering

A look around your home might reveal some wonderful objects for patterning on the Gel Press Plate. Here I am playing with jute string and taking advantage of adding it on top of some previous printed, lighter layers as well as using the ghost print from it to add on top of another light colored solid layer. Sometimes the most creative art materials are found outside the art supply store.

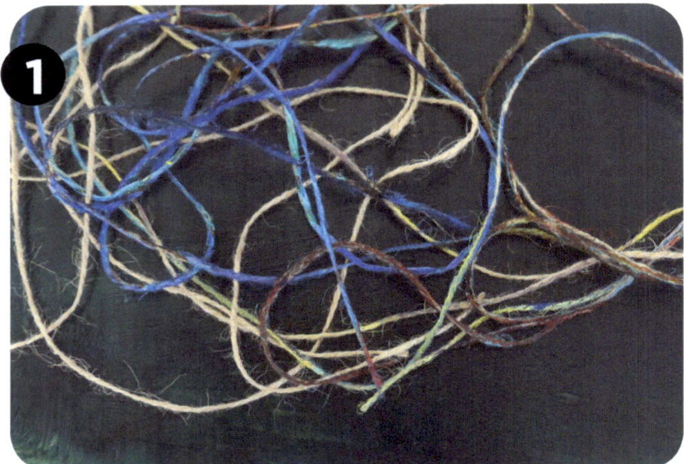

Jute string has a slightly fuzzy edge, it's thin enough to yield detailed line patterns.

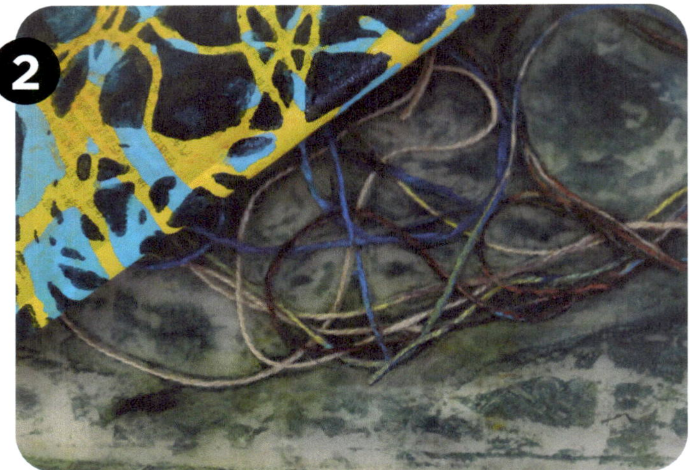

Pulling a print of the string on top of a prepared sheet.

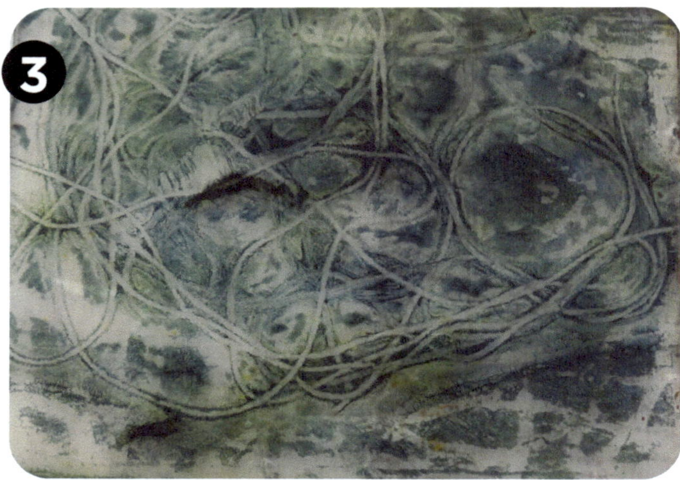

The ghost print after the first print is pulled, and the string is removed from the plate.

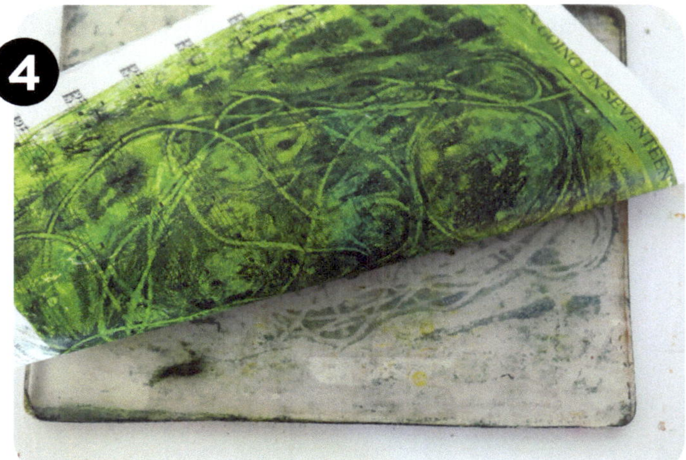

The ghost print applied over a light colored solid that was ready and waiting in the wings.

gel plate
found objects

mark making and imprinting patterns

Marks can be made in the plate from any blunt object. I like to try writing with the eraser tip of a pencil, the end of my paint brush, a credit card corner, or my finger. All of the marks you make into the paint will transfer to the print when you press it into the paper, some more subtle than others. There are many interesting patterns in unusual places, like the bottom of your shoes, tile samples, jar lids, flip flops, and plastic containers. Think beyond the commercial art supply rubbing plate, the possibilities are endless!

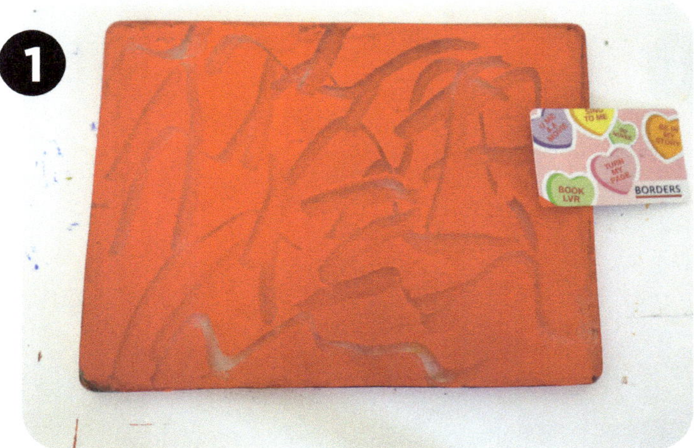

Using the corner of a gift card to make marks.

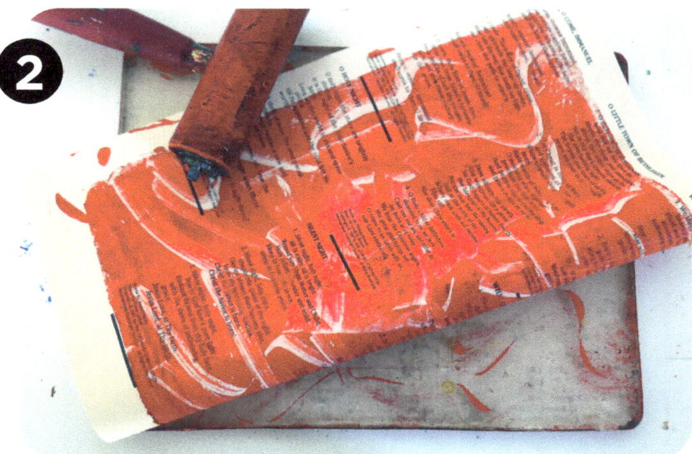

Pulling the print from the gift card pattern.

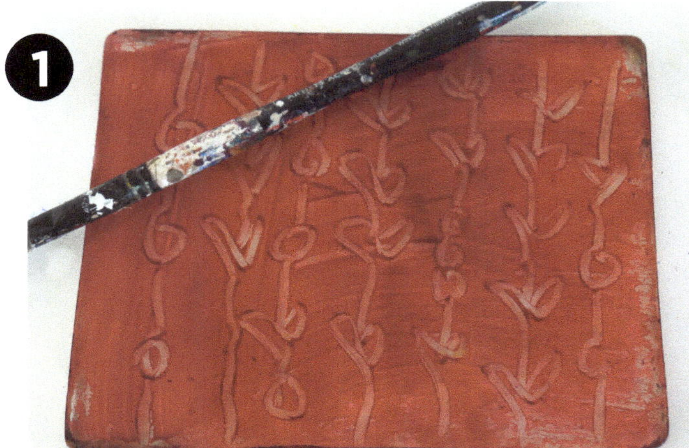

Drawing into the paint on the plate with the end of a paintbrush can yield spontaneous patterns.

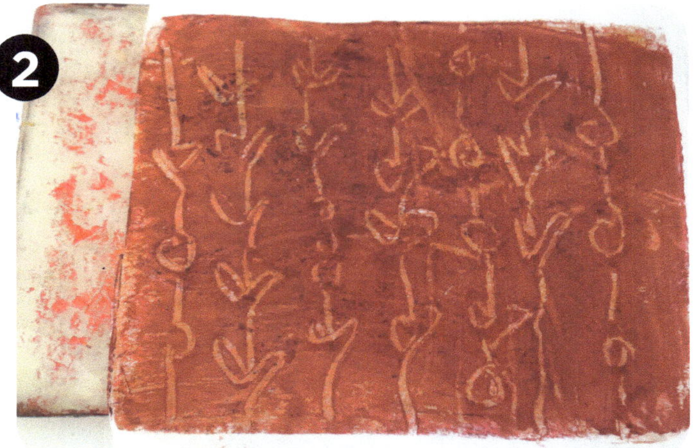

The print from the paintbrush marks. Note that the print is the mirror image of what is on the plate. Something to remember when writing letters.

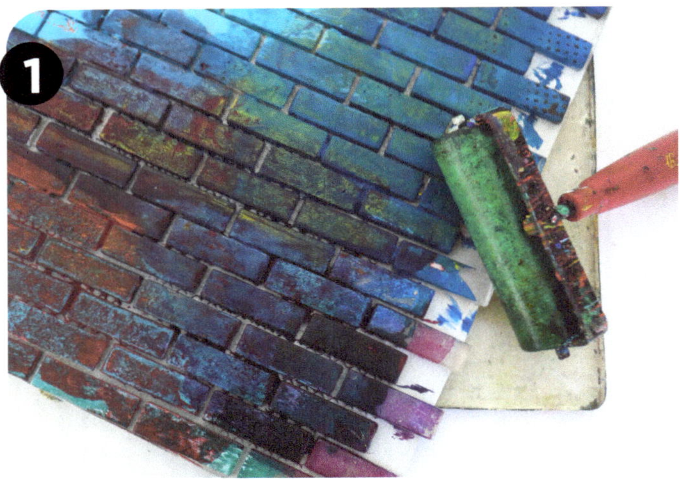

Tile samples from the hardware store in 12x12 sheets come in many different patterns.

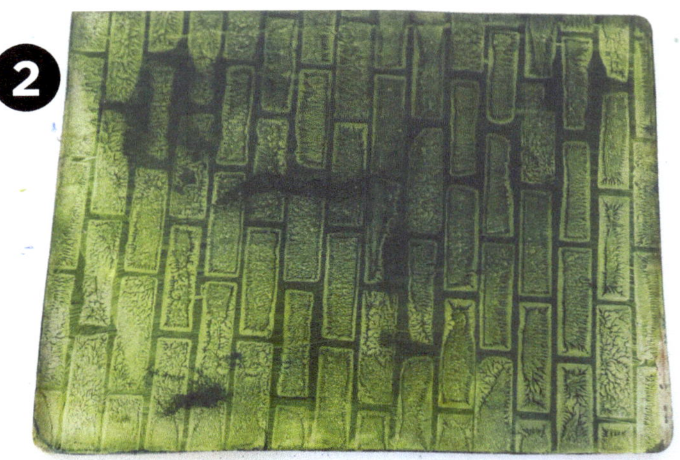

Tile can press into the paint on the plate to create subtle patterning.

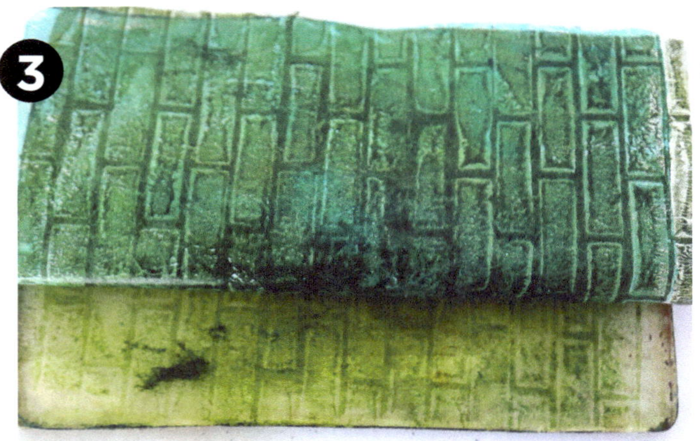

The print over a prepared light colored solid gives a two-tone subtle tile pattern.

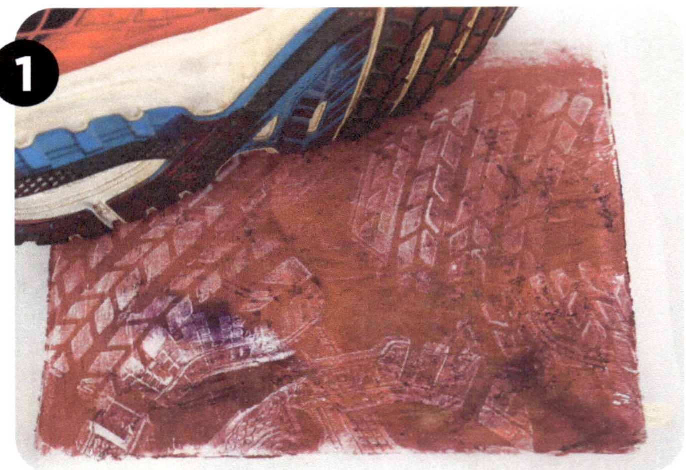

The pattern from the sole of my running shoe.

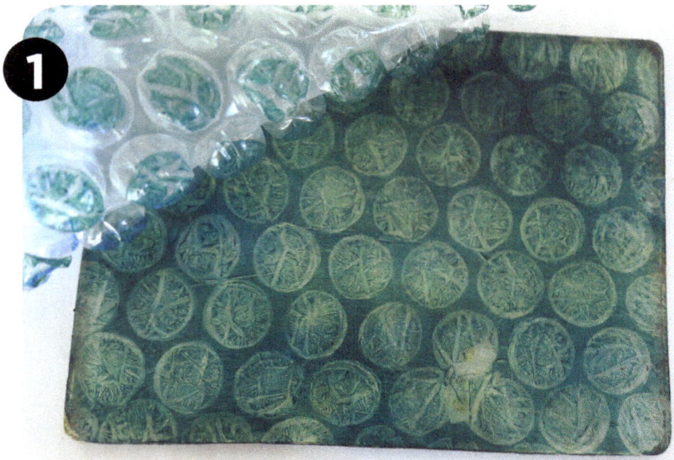

Bubble wrap from packaging comes in different sizes.

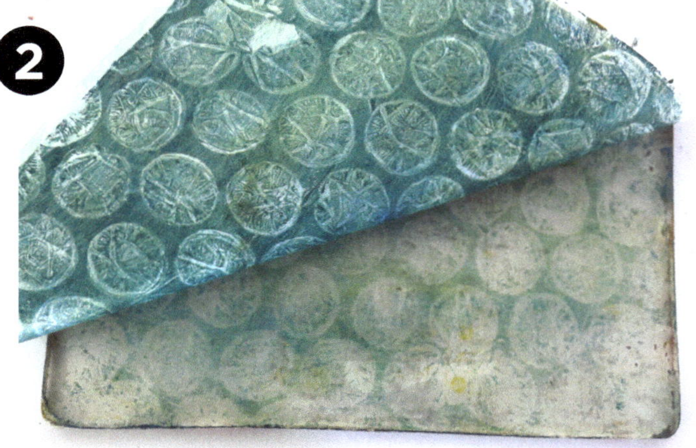

The print over a prepared light colored solid gives a two-tone subtle bubble pattern.

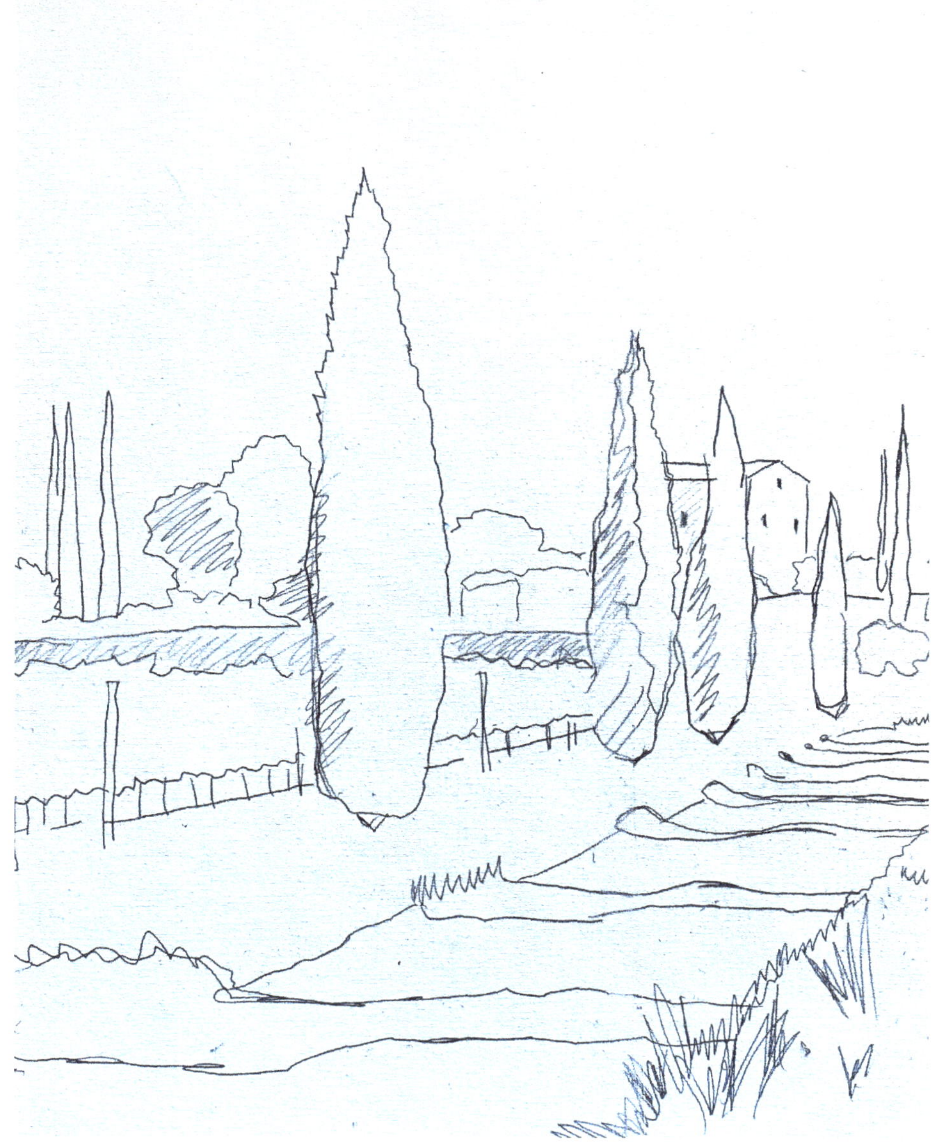

Transferred sketch with graphite paper from my photo of the road our Italian villa sits on. Paper Paintings annual Tuscany Retreat offers some spectacular landscape photo reference

SKETCHING
in the studio

Work from your own reference photo, a photo with permission, or a copyright free photo found on-line in public domain or websites like **Unsplash.com**. Working in the studio, I transfer the photo image either with graphite transfer paper or freehand drawing.

TIP: A good process for freehand sketching is to work on a piece of newsprint the same size as your substrate to finalize your sketch, and then transfer it with the graphite paper to your prepared panel; save all the erasing and redrawing for the sketch paper!

transferring your image with graphite paper

I always start with a sketch before I begin painting in the studio. If you are not confident in your drawing skills you may use graphite paper (shiny side down) underneath your sized-up reference image and basically *trace* your photo with a ball point pen. The graphite transfer paper works like old fashioned carbon paper... It transfers graphite to the substrate from the pressure of your pen! These marks can be erased and edited if needed.

Secure the reference image and the transfer paper with tape at the top so that it does not shift out of alignment. Lift the corner every now and then, to be sure you have not missed any areas of your sketch. My sketch (left) gives me all the info I need to make a good painting.

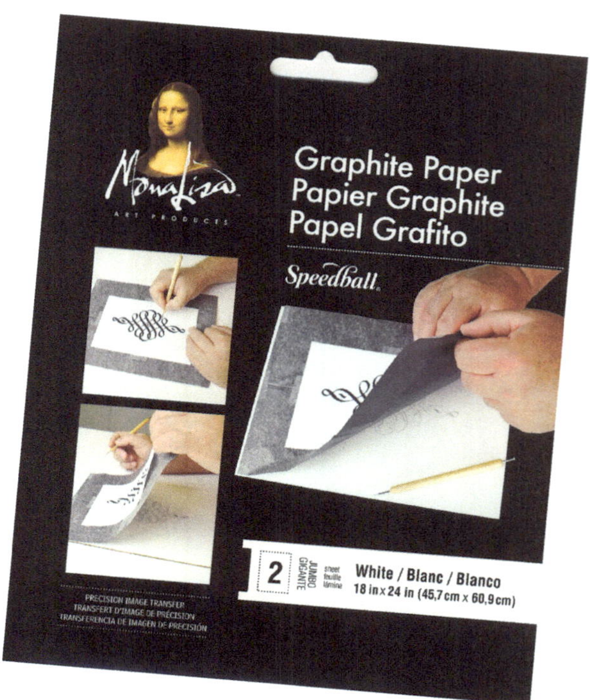

sketching your image freehand

You can always sketch from a photo by looking closely and drawing what you see rather than using the transfer technique. I like the way my drawing takes on unique quality and has a more hand created touch when I draw vs trace. It's up to you how you want to handle your sketch and how confident you are in your drawing skills.

In the video still below (from my on-line Landscape Collage Techniques workshop) you can see that I am sketching with conté crayon on an orange primed background, working form the superimposed photo on the left. I like conté crayon because you can wipe it away with a damp cloth like chalk, no scrubbing with the eraser.

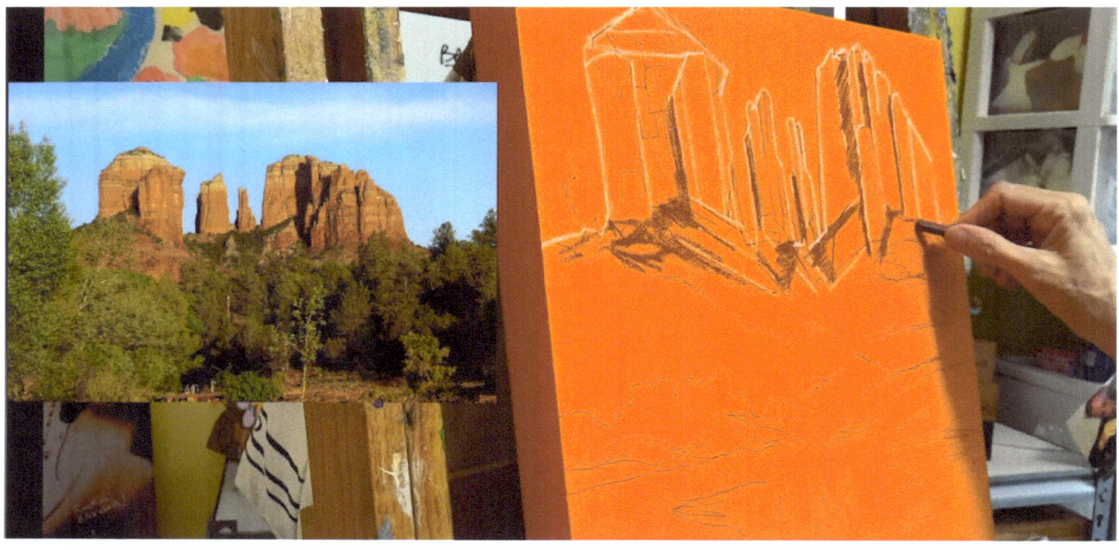

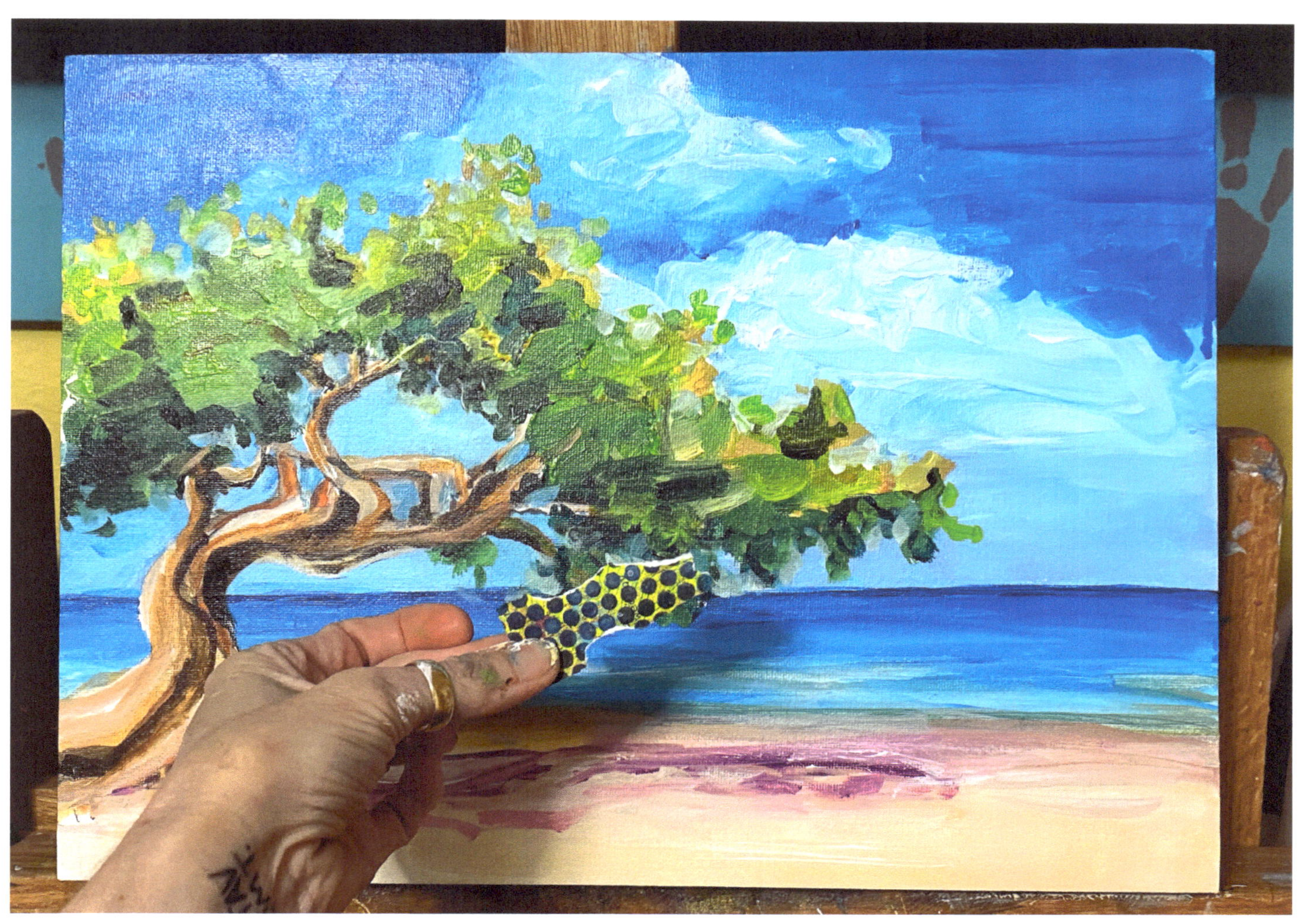

UNDER
painting

In the studio or in the field, I use my under painting process for the same reasons–to block in all my colors so that when I apply the paper over the top, if any spaces are left between bits of paper, the color of the painting is there, rather than the color of the canvas. It is in the under painting process that I work out my values, what is light, dark, and medium tone. I also work out my colors and tweak my composition. It's much easier and quicker to work out these challenges with paint than to have to work and rework collage. Once I get the values and colors to my liking, I allow the painting dry completely.

Don't spend tons of time laboring over your under painting – Do use it as an exercise to help you determine where your values are and what colors you will use in your collage. Think impressionistic, keep your brush strokes loose, but capture the essence of what you are looking at.

I tell my students, *"Don't fall in love with your under painting!"* Do not take this to a level of finish detail that you love so much, you will not want to apply collage over the top.

Landscape Collage TECHNIQUES

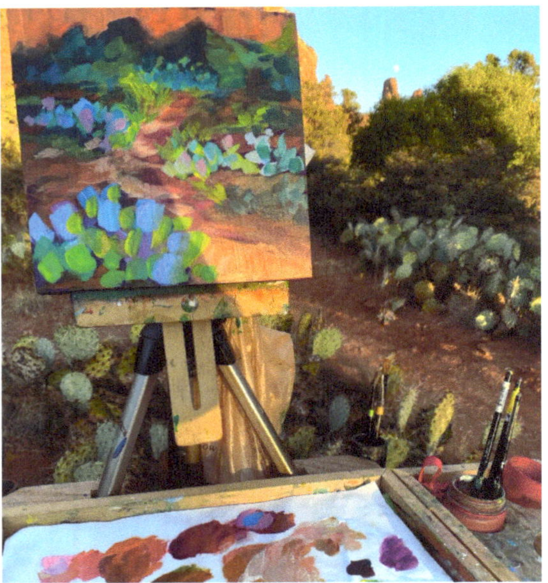

Plein Air under-painting in Sedona

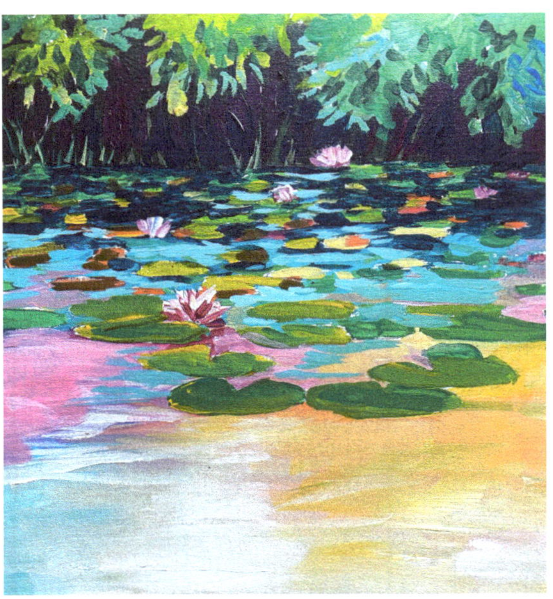

Studio under-painting from a photo

Golden Fluid Acrylic paints

I use Golden Fluid Acrylics for the under painting. Since I have the colors on hand for painting my papers, it makes sense to use the same paints for the under-painting process. I add a bit white gesso to slightly lighten colors or to make them a bit more opaque. Avoid lots of white, however, as it can give your colors a chalky, pastel look. The best way to lighten green is to add yellow, and to darken it, add blue. Experiment with mixing colors this way rather than relying on white and black. I never use black to darken my colors, I either use Van Dyke brown or I look at the color wheel and add the opposite color. This makes for much richer color variations.

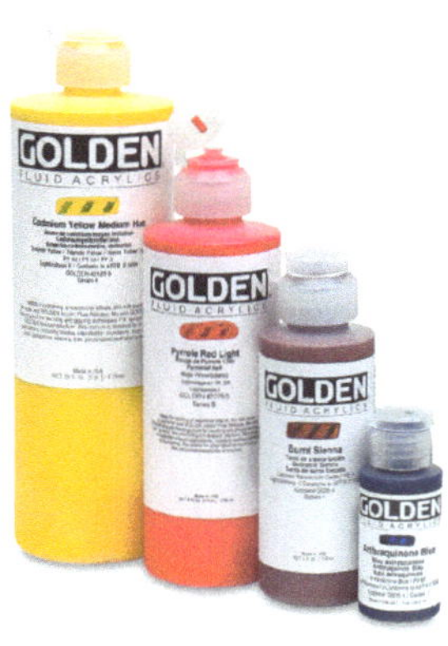

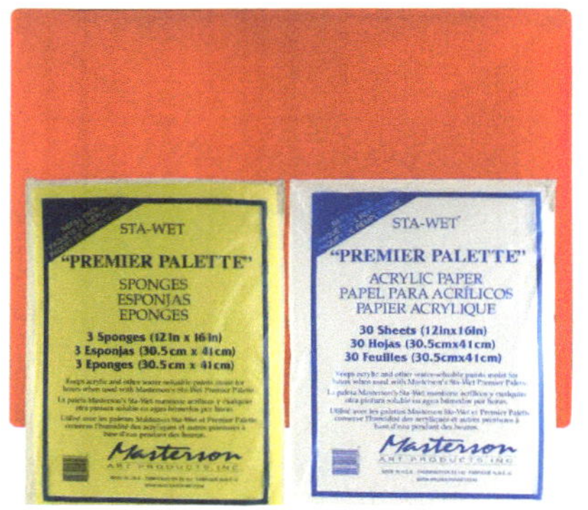

Sta-Wet Palette by Masterson

The Sta-Wet palette is a wonderful way to preserve and conserve your expensive Golden Paints acrylics. This system is basically a big plastic box with an airtight fitting lid. Inside the box is a thin sponge that is used to keep a sheet of palette paper that sits on top of it wet. The moisture keeps your paints wet all day with the lid off, you can work away (or walk away) and never have your paint dry out!

With the lid on, the box will keep your paints wet for up to two weeks. You'll never waste paint again because when you are done with the palette, you can save the sheet you mixed your colors on and use it as a collage paper sheet. The paper is highly absorbent and glues down quite nicely.

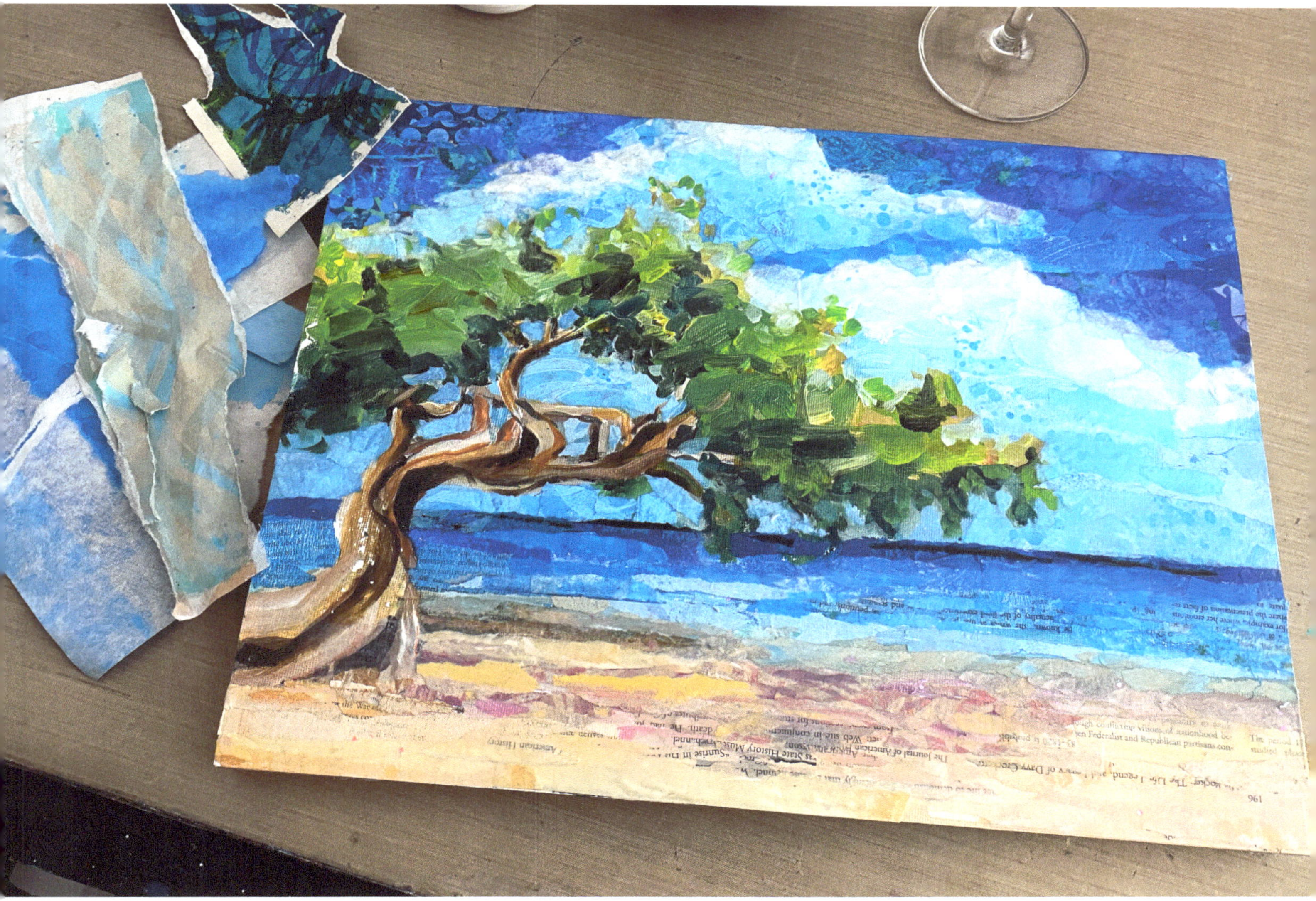

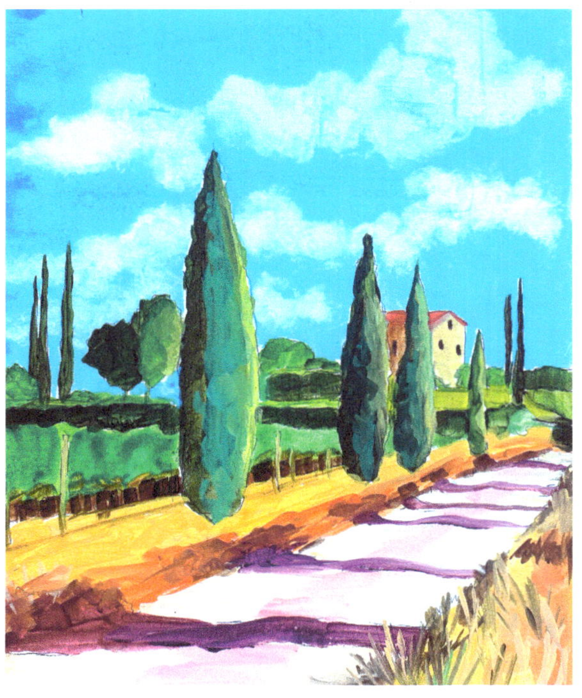

getting it right!

The under-painting is your road map for collage, the more time you spend and the better you establish color, value, and composition, the easier gluing paper on top will be. Don't think that you can "fix it with collage" spend time here to get it right.

Here are some examples of underpaintings that I created for my Landscape Collage Techniques online workshop.

The *Divi Divi Tree* (above) is in progress with some collage having already been added to the sky and sand. the *Tuscan Villa* (left) is a full color underpainting with spicy arbitrary color in the purple shadows and an enhanced blue cloudy sky.

The *Red Rock Crossing* (right) is on my easel as an under-painting that really focuses on the reflection, which is abstract and playful. This piece started out as a freehand drawing, a combination of multiple photos that focused on both the water relection and the red-rocks.

     Landscape Collage TECHNIQUES

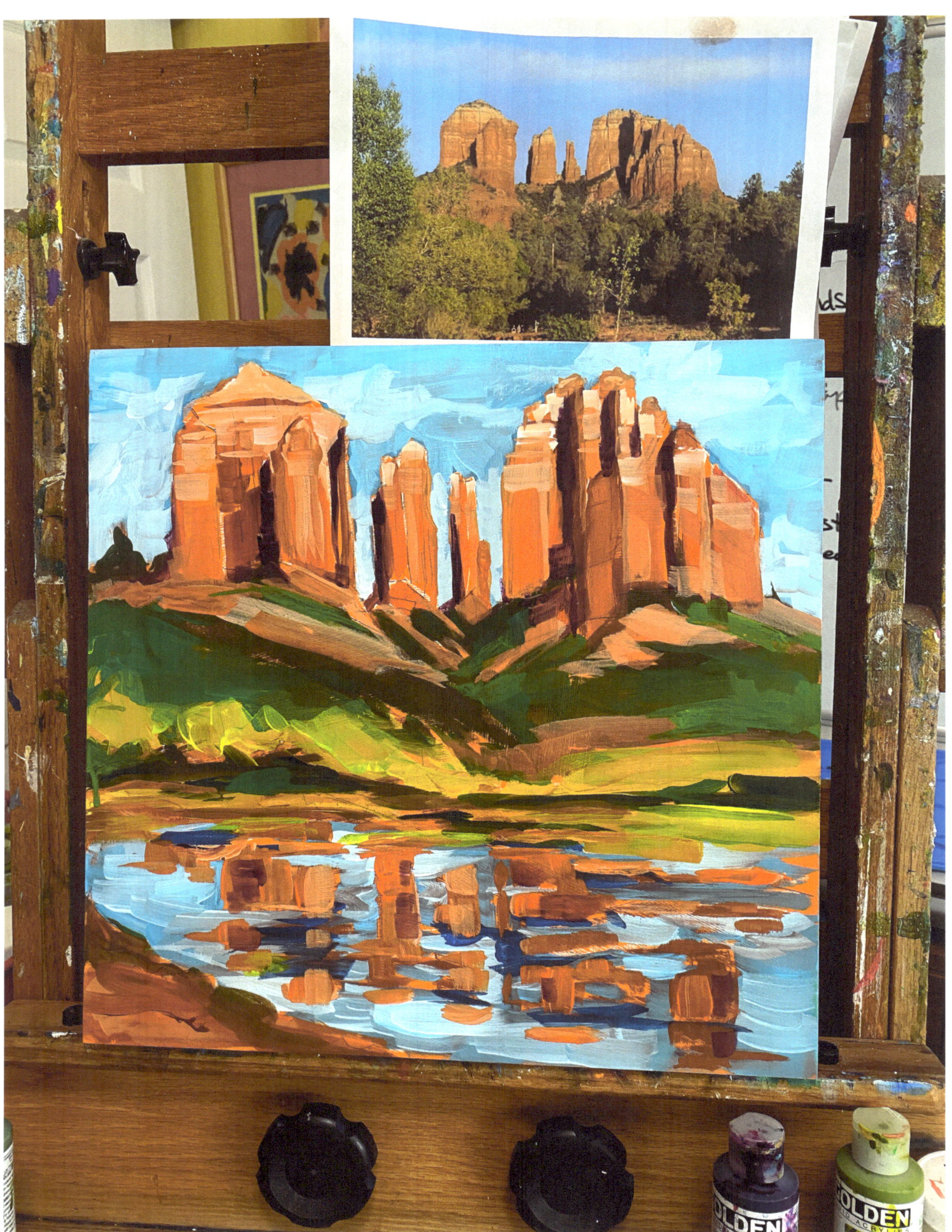

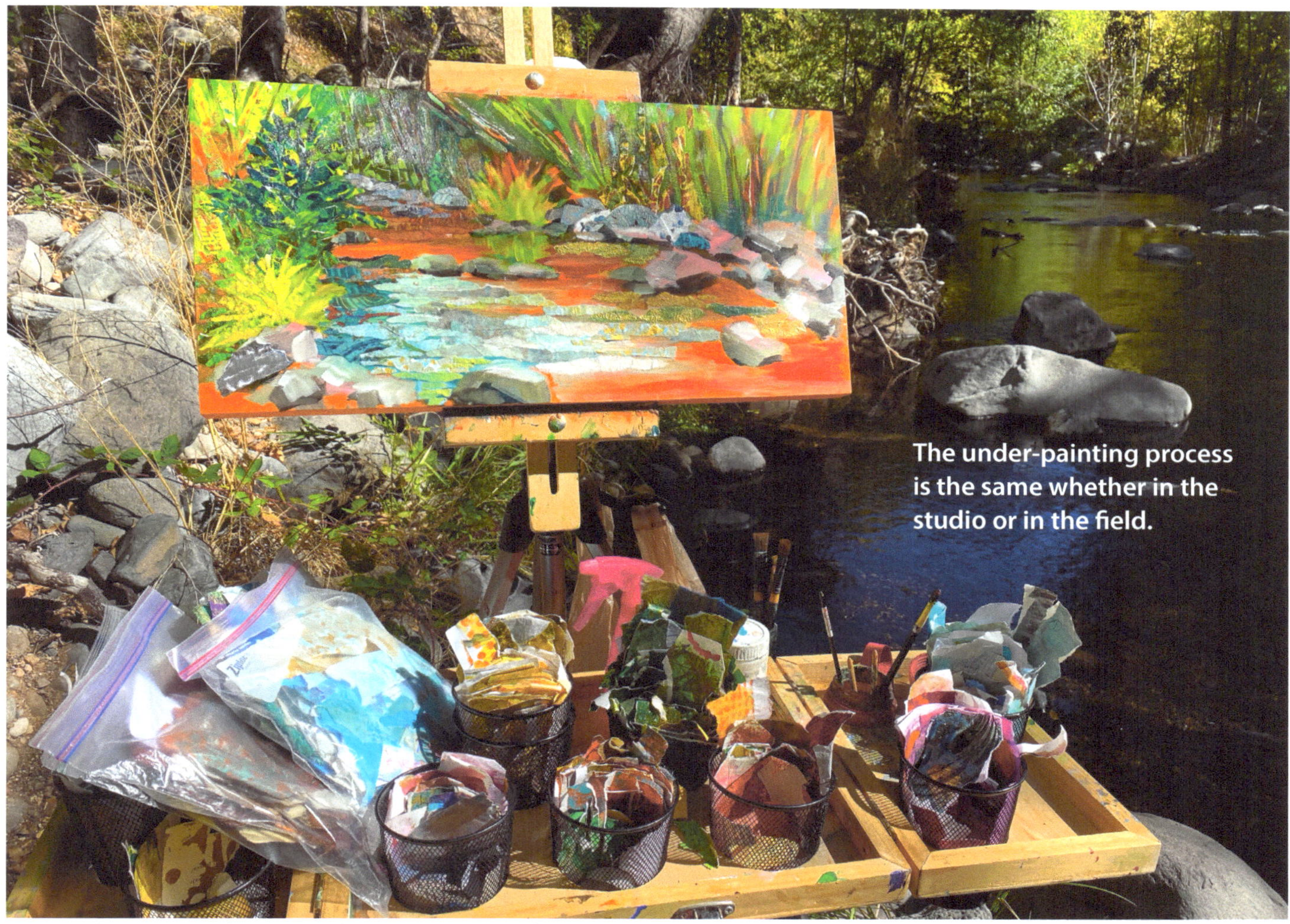

My St. Hilaire System Plein Air easel setup on the bank of Oak Creek in Sedona

SKETCHING
and painting
on location

When you are painting en Plein Air you have to work quickly to combat the elements. As soon as the sketch is quickly mapped out, begin blocking in the color, start with the shadows, then the medium value shapes, then the light shapes. After you get the big shapes blocked in, look at your scene again and go back in with a little more detail; refine the shapes and the colors, while constantly looking at the scene. Keep it loose and impressionistic.

Painting en Plein Air is not for everyone. There are a lot of factors to deal with like wildlife, hiking, uneven surfaces, heat, cold, sunburn, windburn, bugs, etc. BUT it can be very rewarding to connect with nature in this way, to spend time outdoors and remember what it was like to be a kid. When I paint outside I am not waylaid by the typical distractions and I get to spend hours in nature. I really haven't done that since I was little growing up in western Massachusetts!

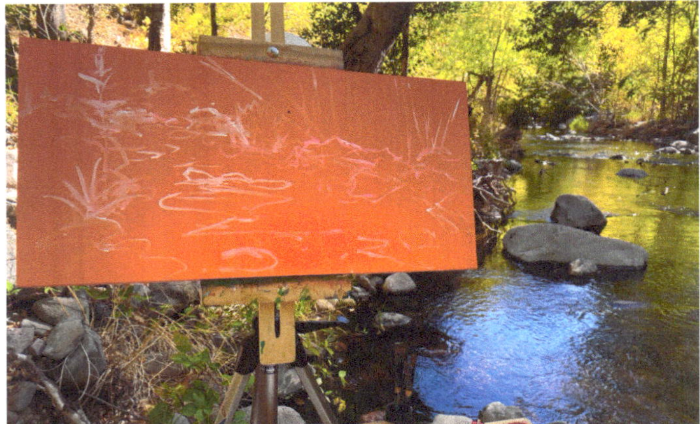

Look at the scene as much as you look at your painting

I start with a watered down white painted sketch using my smallest longhandled round brush. I keep it loose, I hold the brush way out at the end and stand back from my easel. I look at the scene just as much, if not more than I look at the canvas. I prefer to work on a colored gesso background, this is why I use white to sketch. White is preferred also because it will not contaminate any of the colors you paint over your sketch.

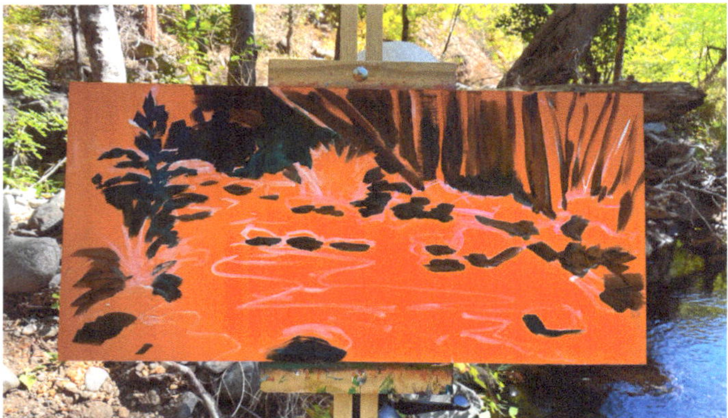

Blocking in the shadows with large shapes

The concept behind colored gesso is to let it peek through your finished artwork. Orange peeking through green offers some wonderful opposite color vibration that can really bring life to your work.

I am drawing in big shapes, not small details. I am looking closely at the proximity of each shape to the other, and checking it with the scene. The smaller details come after you establish the big shapes.

Once you get the sketch worked out, it's time to look closely at the shadows in the scene. I squint my eyes and look through my lashes, this helps make the darks and lights more obvious, then I begin with a medium sized flat brush and block in all the dark areas.

The next step is establishing the medium values. You do

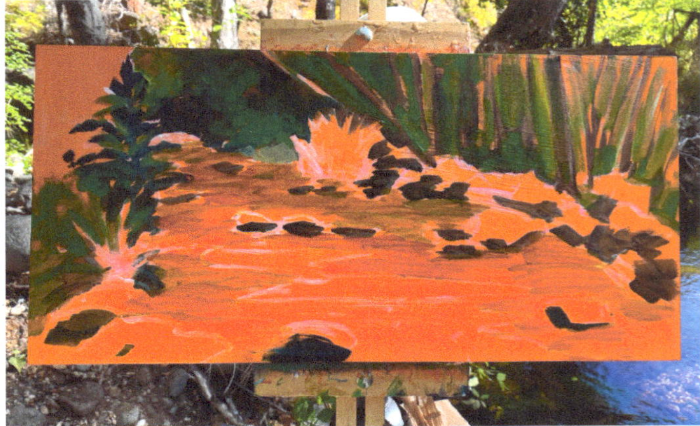

Blocking in the medium areas with large shapes

have to work quickly when painting outside as the light and shadows change fast. The quicker you can block in, the better advantage you have of finishing your under-painting before the light changes.

You'll have to practice working quickly, it's not going to come natural if you are used to working in the studio. Give yourself permission to experiment. *Although the under-painting process is basically the same, working in in the studio offers you more time than working in the field.*

Adding the lights, highlights and details is your final step in the under-painting. You are always looking and editing and changing your painting in progress to make it the best it can be. Don't be afraid to make changes from your original plan.

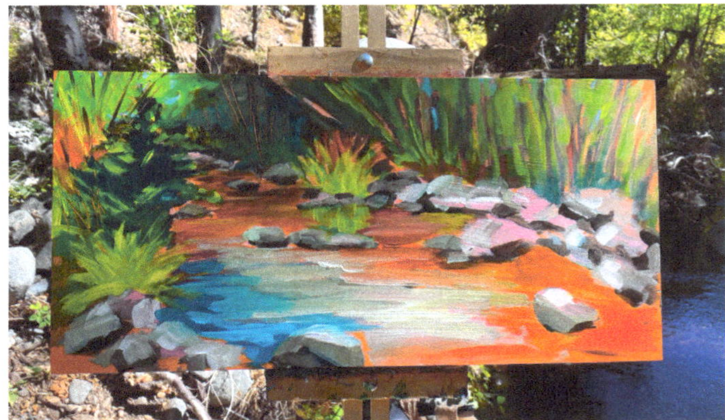

Adding the lights and the details

If you paint en Plein Air, you have to know that people ARE going to talk to you, look at what you are doing, ask you questions and sometimes even block your view as they tell you stories or show you photos of their own work on their phone. It takes a strong person to be able to keep on painting under these circumstances! I am not trying to discourage you, just prepare you for what's out there on the other side of those studio walls!

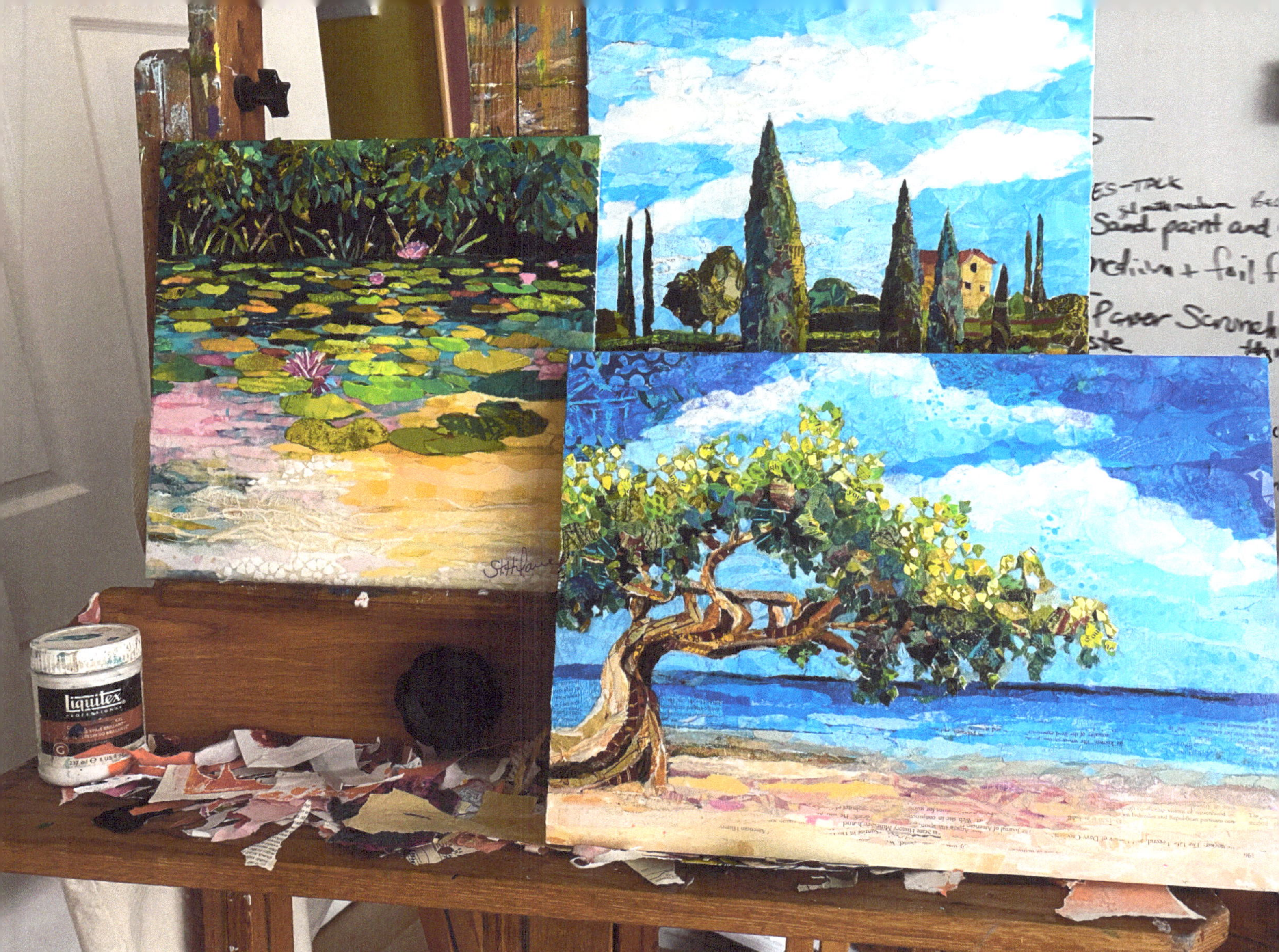

COLLAGE
application

My pieces of paper are torn, I never cut with scissors. I treat each piece of paper as a *brush stroke*, therefore I do not want any hard edges.

Consider making your shapes end organically, rather than having them cut off abruptly like a piece of tape. An organic end that trails off naturally will visually flow into the next piece–just like a brush mark. We are painting with paper, so you want to follow the shapes, sizes, and direction of marks that you intuitively created in your under-painting.

I apply the glue to the board, place the torn paper into the glue, and apply more glue over top with pressure from the brush to make the paper lay down nice and flat.

Follow your under-painting in color and value, hold up your papers and be sure they are the right match before tearing and gluing them down, I call this *auditioning*. Once you start auditioning, you may find that you do not have enough colors or values in your paper palette, because someone once said…"*You can never have enough paper!*"

Landscape Collage TECHNIQUES

vary the shapes and sizes of your paper brush marks

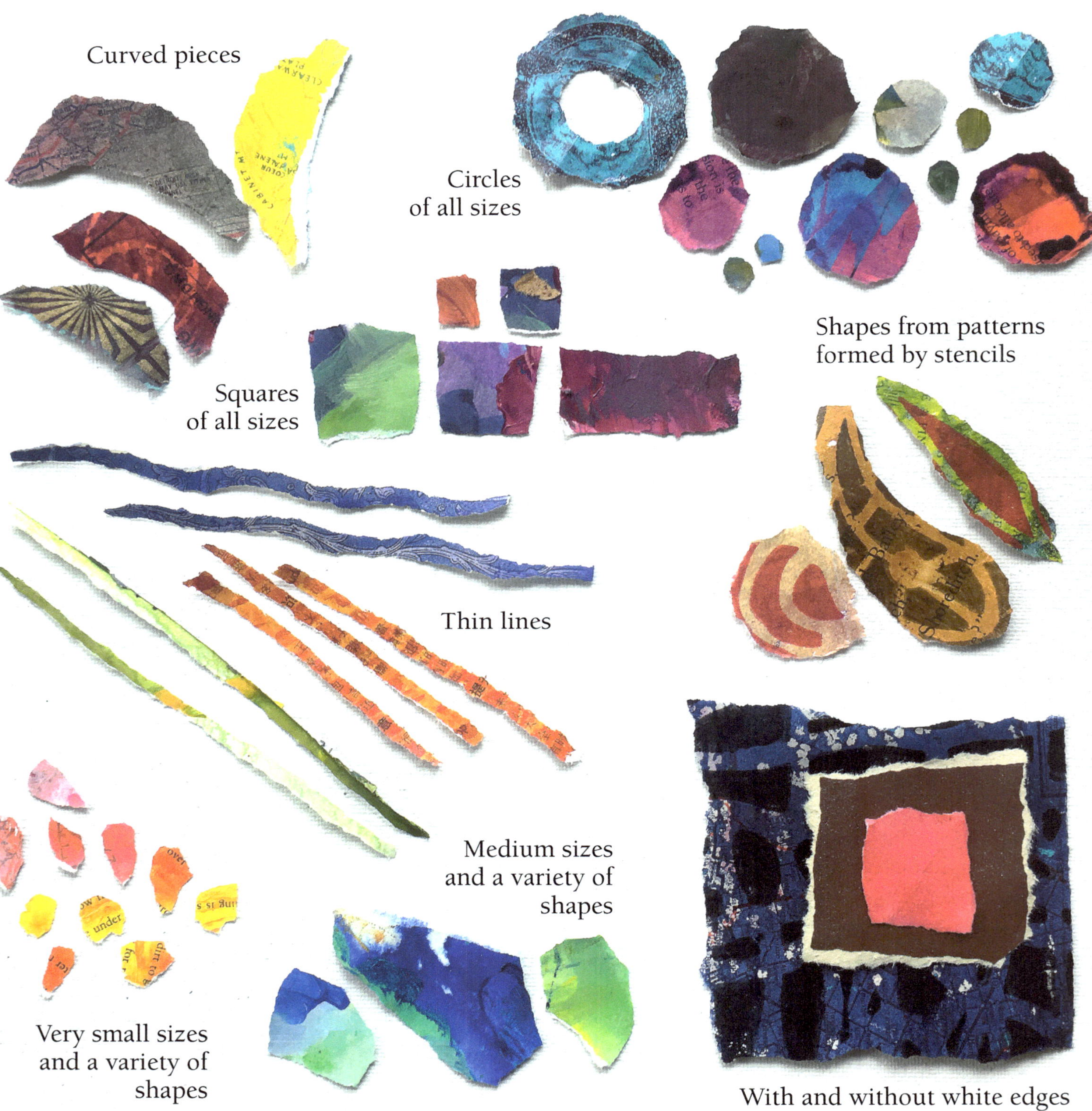

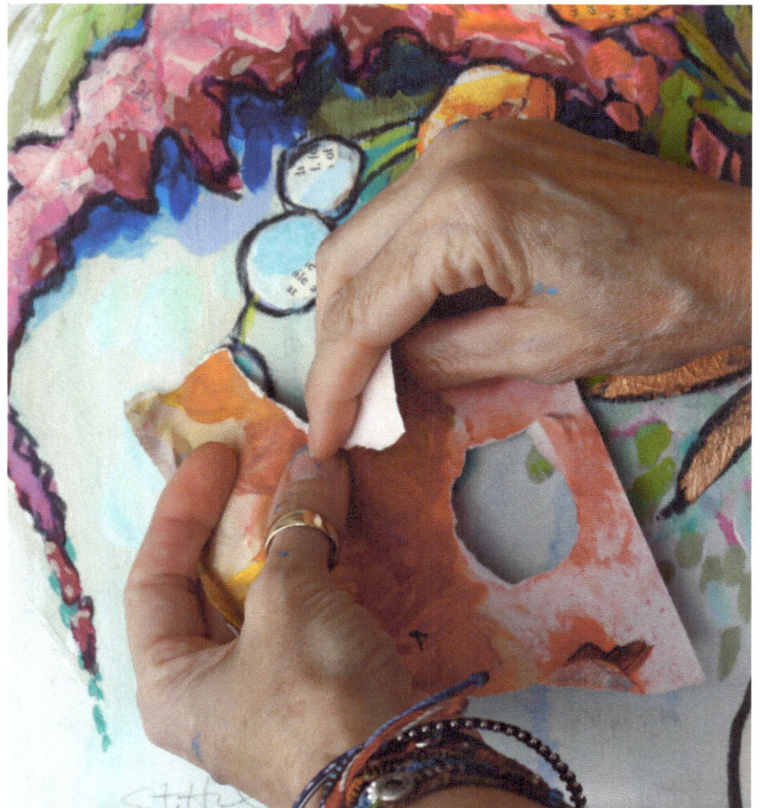

Eliminating and embracing white edges with tearing techniques takes a little bit of practice. Pulling the paper up toward yourself with your dominant hand eliminates white edges.

eliminating white edges

1 Pull up, with your dominant hand, toward you to create the shape that you want

2 The white edges will be left on piece of paper in your non dominant hand

Eliminating white edges requires pulling the paper UP while ripping– as you pull in an upward motion, the white edge is left behind. Practice pulling UP while ripping and rotating the paper so that you are always tearing in an upward motion. This takes a bit of getting used to–I suggest practicing on some scrap papers to get the hang of it.

embracing white edges

1 Consider using the white edge of a paper for a highlighted edge on a stem

2 Consider using the white edge of a paper for the rim around petals that stack on top of one another

3. To achieve a white edge, turn your paper colored side down and follow the same steps from above

directional patterning

1 Sheet music lines need to follow the form of the subject

2 Type and text needs to follow the form of the subject

3 Patterns need to follow the form of the subject

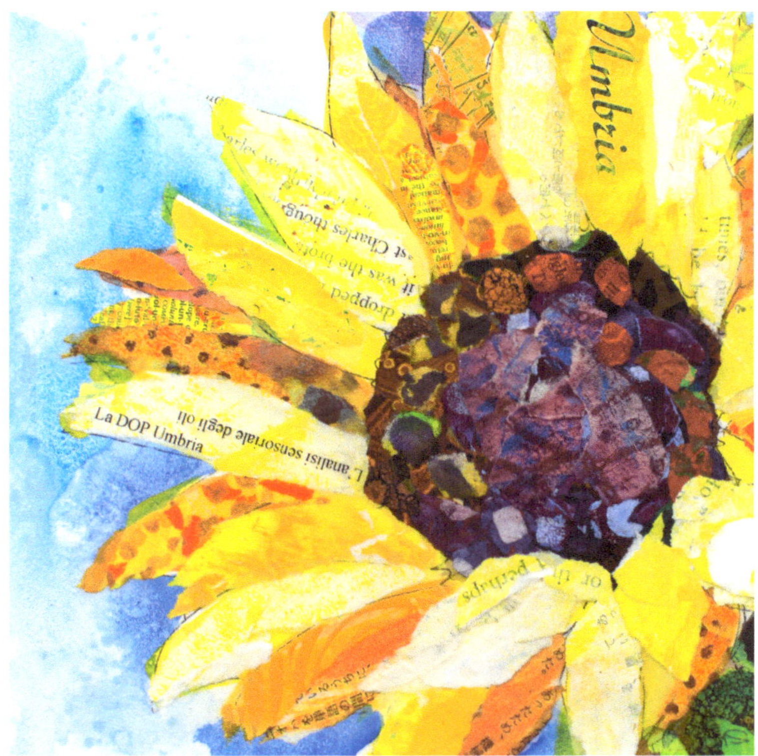

A bold pattern needs to go in the same direction as your brush stroke, here you see the text goes down the length of the petals.

Landscape Collage TECHNIQUES

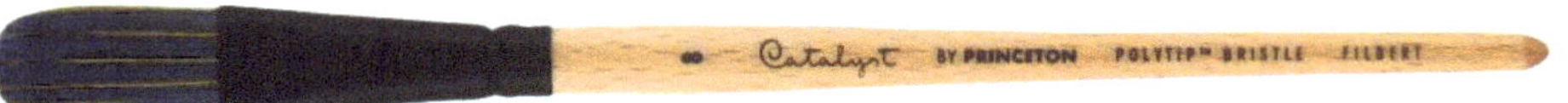

Link on my Amazon art supply resource page

applying the glue

1 Apply a thin layer of glue to the board with a 1-inch filbert style brush

2 Place paper, one piece at a time, into the glue

3 Press the paper down with the glue brush, applying enough pressure to get the paper to lie flat, and applying a thin layer of glue over the paper at the same time

4 Bring the glue in from all sides of the piece of paper, making sure there are no loose edges–brush off all excess glue

5 Examine the art to be sure there are no erroneous lumps of glue, it dries hard and is not removable

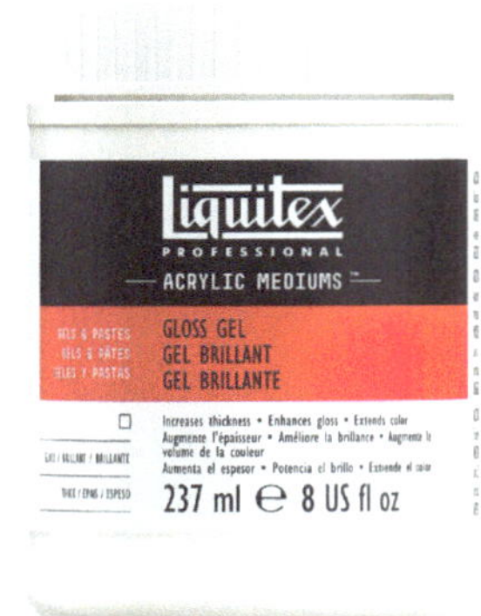

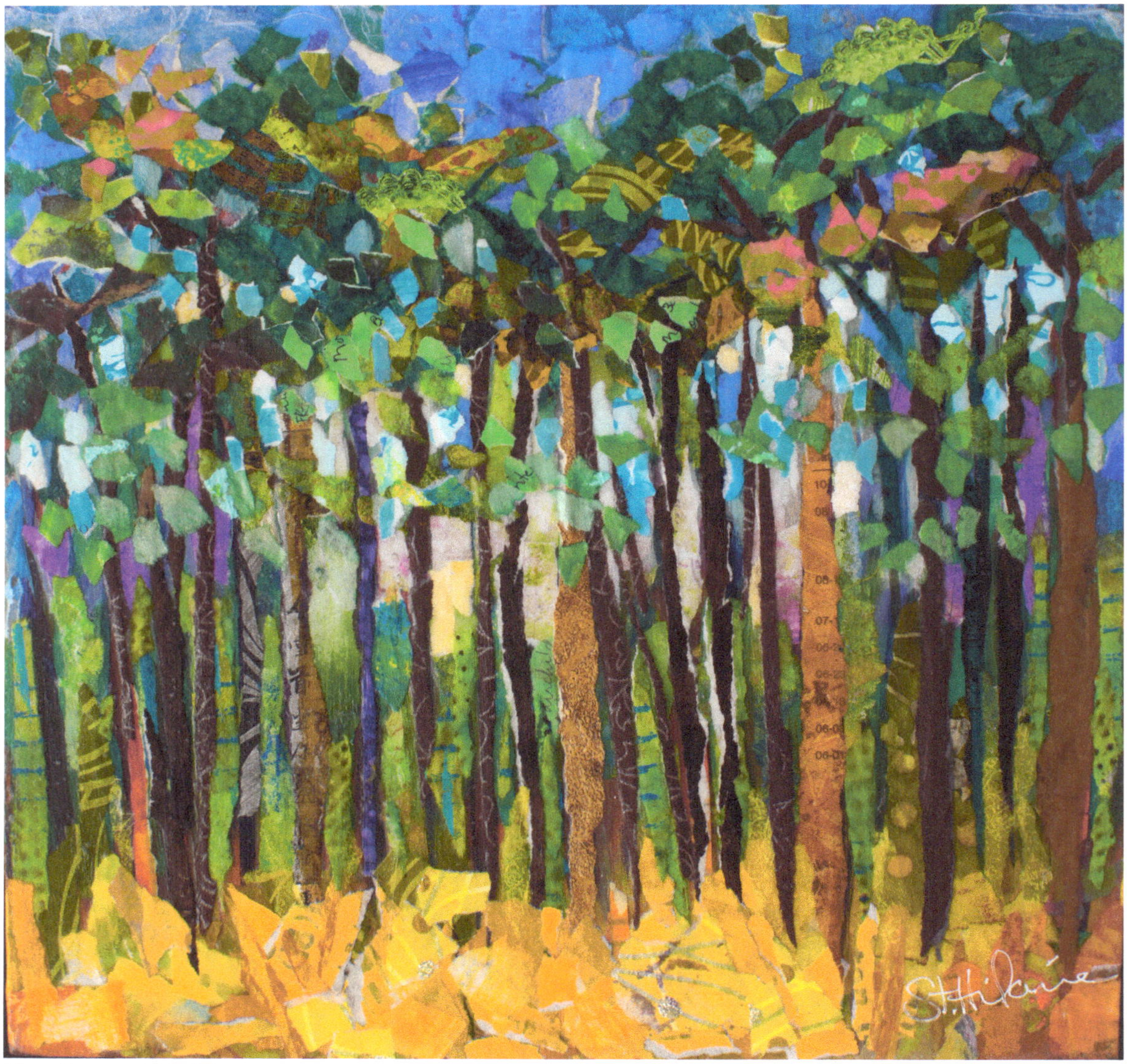

Pine Forrest / 10x10

working back to front

(Right) Evaluate your composition and determine what is farthest back and what is closest to the front. Apply collage in that hierarchy, working from back to front. In the piece to the right I started with the sky, then the pink rock formation, then the greenery in front of it. In the stream I started with the light colors in the water, then the darker colors, then the rocks in the lower right. Among the trees I start with the trunks, then the foliage over top, then the foliage that overlapped down into the edge of the stream.

Carefully consider what is behind and what is in front in your landscape before you begin collage application. If you make a mistake you can always overlap again with a new piece of paper; collage is a very forgiving medium that way.

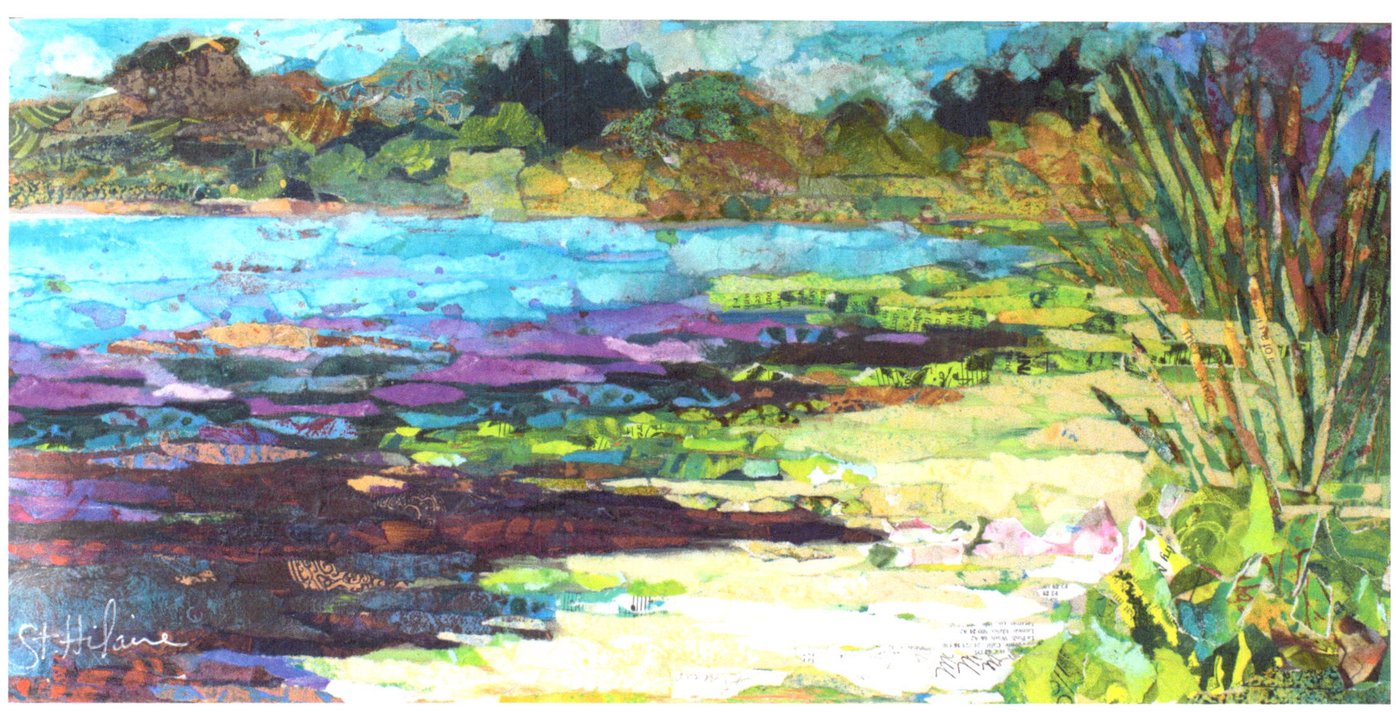

applying paper brush marks

Painting with paper is just like painting with a brush, you must carefully tear each piece of paper, allow it to end in an organic shape, and apply it in a way that follows the form and volume of the subject in the same way you used your paint brush in the under-painting.

You intuitively followed the form of your subject with your brush marks when you painted. In other words, you would not paint a round object with straight horizontal strokes, you'd paint it with curved marks. Think of your torn paper as paper brush marks and glue them down in the same direction and in similar shapes.

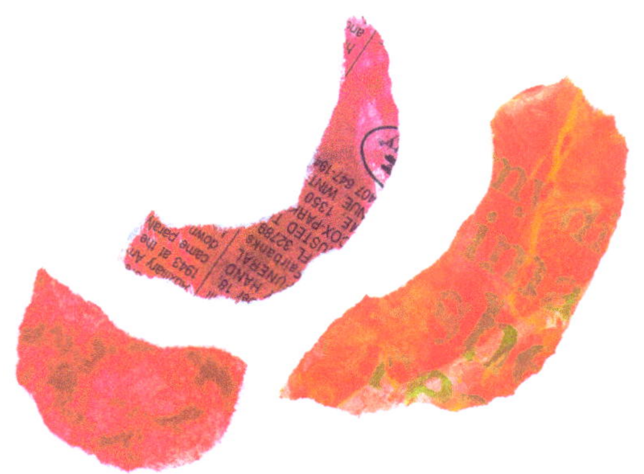

Paper brush marks should be torn to end organically vs. with straight edges like tape.

   Landscape Collage TECHNIQUES

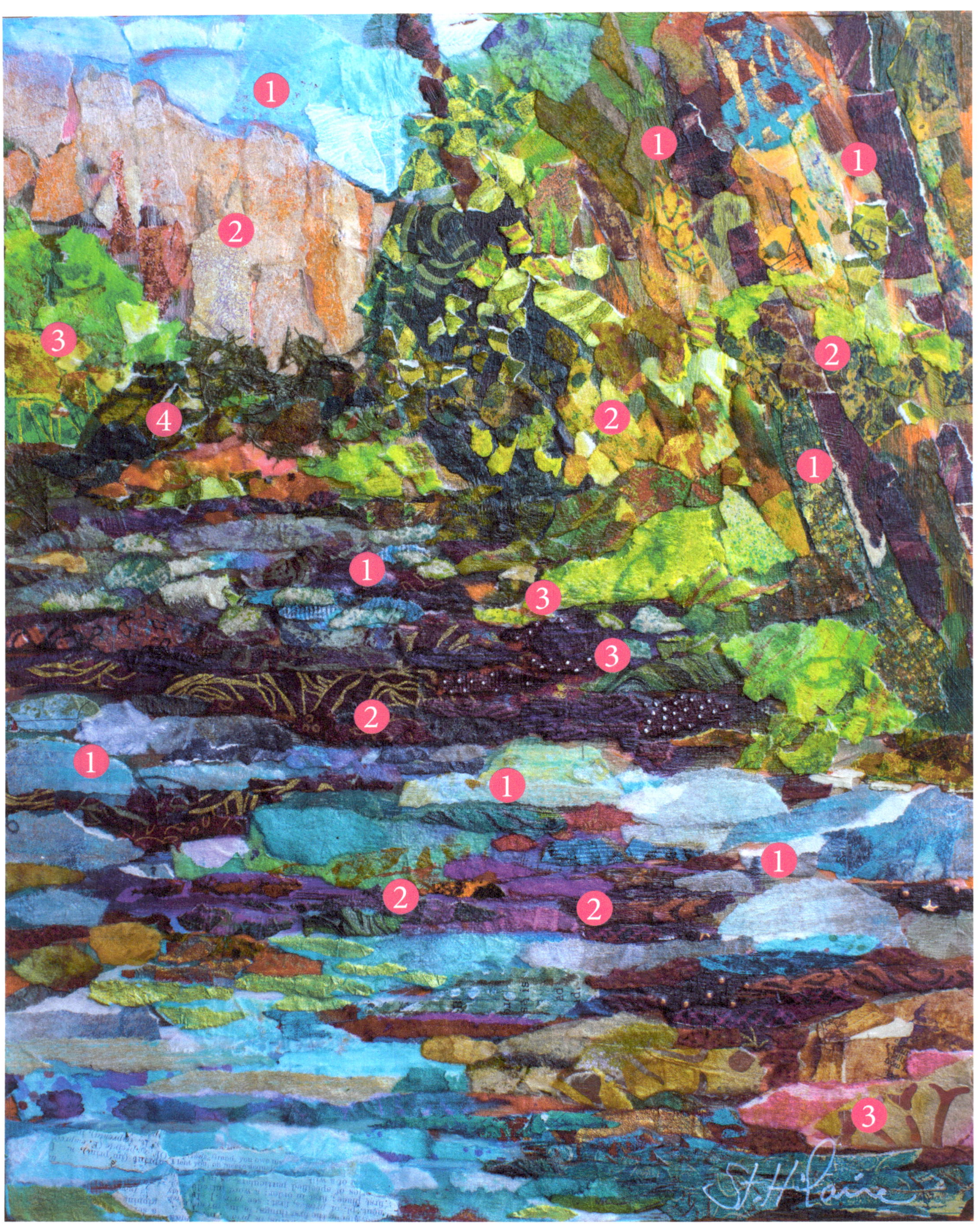

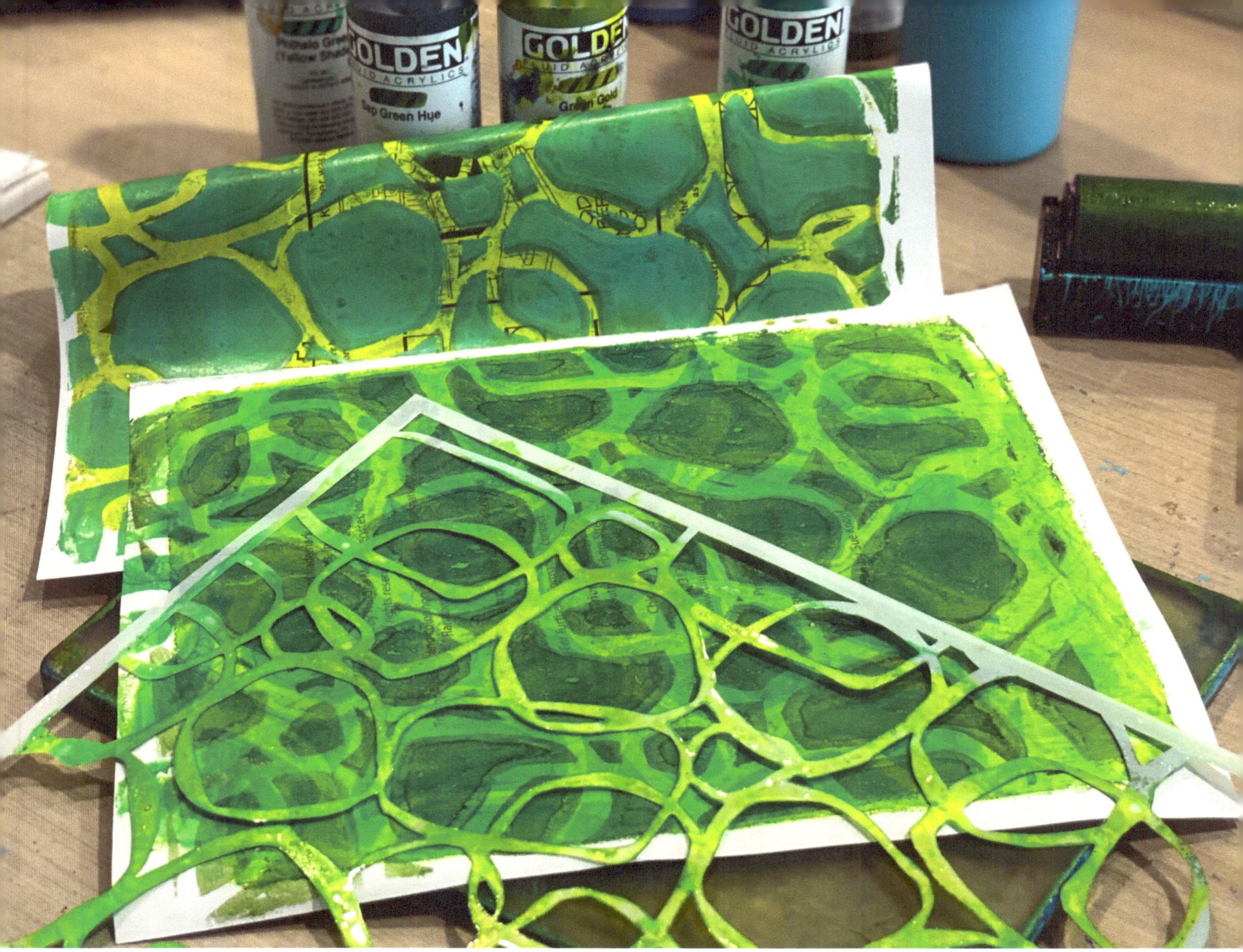

transitional papers

Helping the eye blend from one color to the next

Creating collage papers that transition from one color to the next help the eye blend. Here I am suggesting dappled sunlight by using a transitional paper that goes from light green to dark green.

Transitional papers also help the collage change colors in a manner that suggests a soft blend. The base of the red-rocks in Sedona (as demonstrated in *Thunder Mountain* (right) has vegetation that is green. Transitional collage papers that include the red-rock orange and green help to achieve that soft blend.

Creating transitional papers means laying down one color on your gel plate as a solid, and then patterning it with a second color through stenciling and stamping. Layering these colors back and forth a few times, this creates a transitional paper.

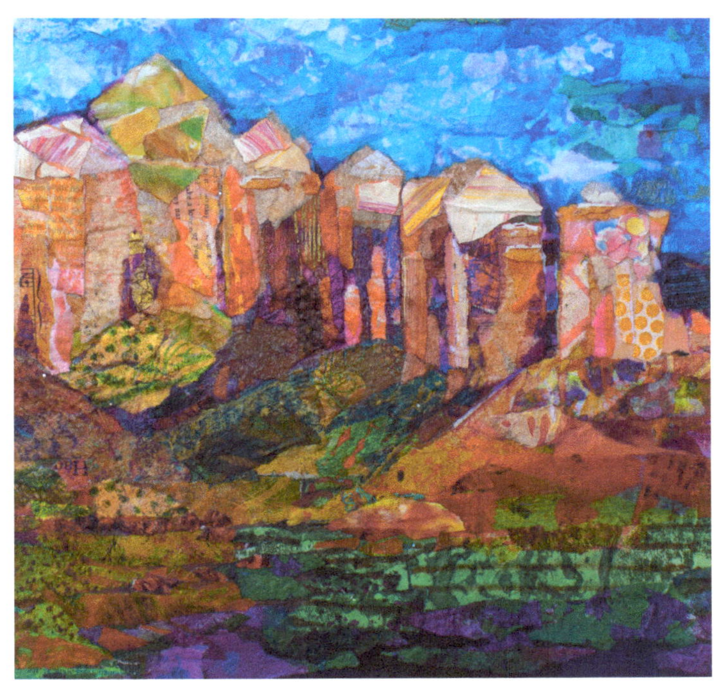

Thunder Mountain (detail) / 12x24

Landscape Collage TECHNIQUES

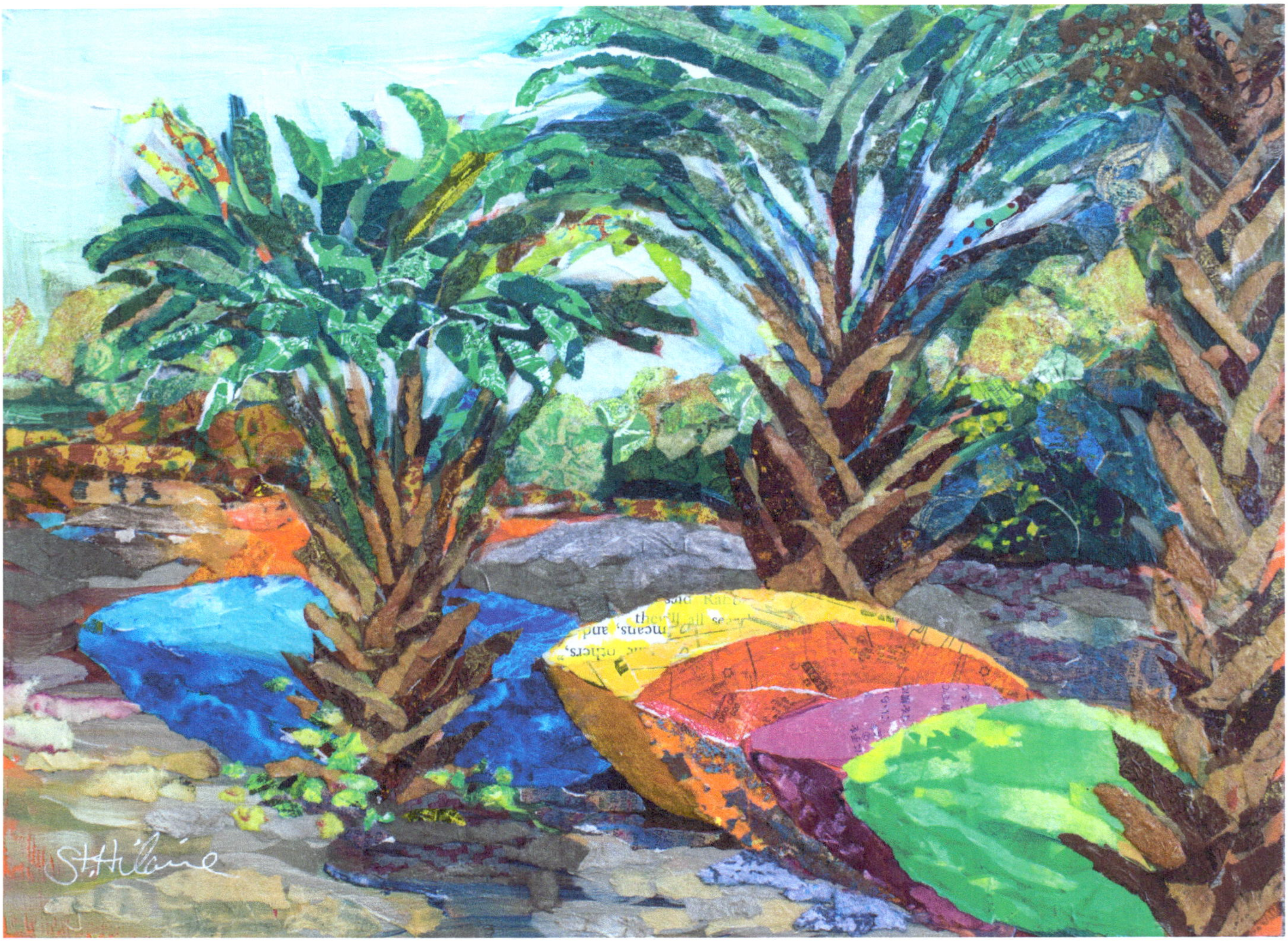

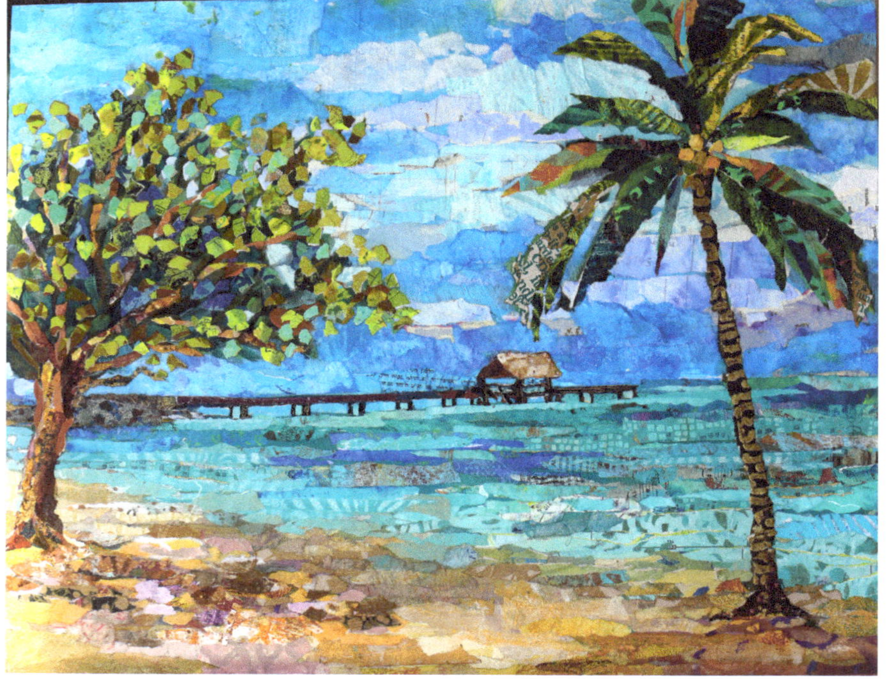

Transitional layers of green help to give the dappled light effect in the palm fronds by incorporating light, medium, and dark all on one collage paper.

Tobago / 20x16

Where the water meets the land is a blend of both colors and that's when you need transitional papers. Transitional papers help the eye blend from one color to the next. Not only does this transition occur where the water meets the land, but it occurs where the shadow meets the lighter sand as well.

SIMPLE *shapes*

Landscape collage is about simplifying your view. You cannot represent every tiny element of what you see with your eyes in collage, you will have to edit out some details and reduce others to basic shapes—think about the impressionists, this is an impressionistic medium.

As you prepare to sketch, either from life, photos, or graphite transfer, think about editing the scene to make it more simple, and reducing complex shapes into simpler shapes that give the impression of the object versus precisely rendering every tiny detail. You have to break what you see down to its' most basic form. Alays ask yourself, *"How can I capture the impression of a scene with few details?"*

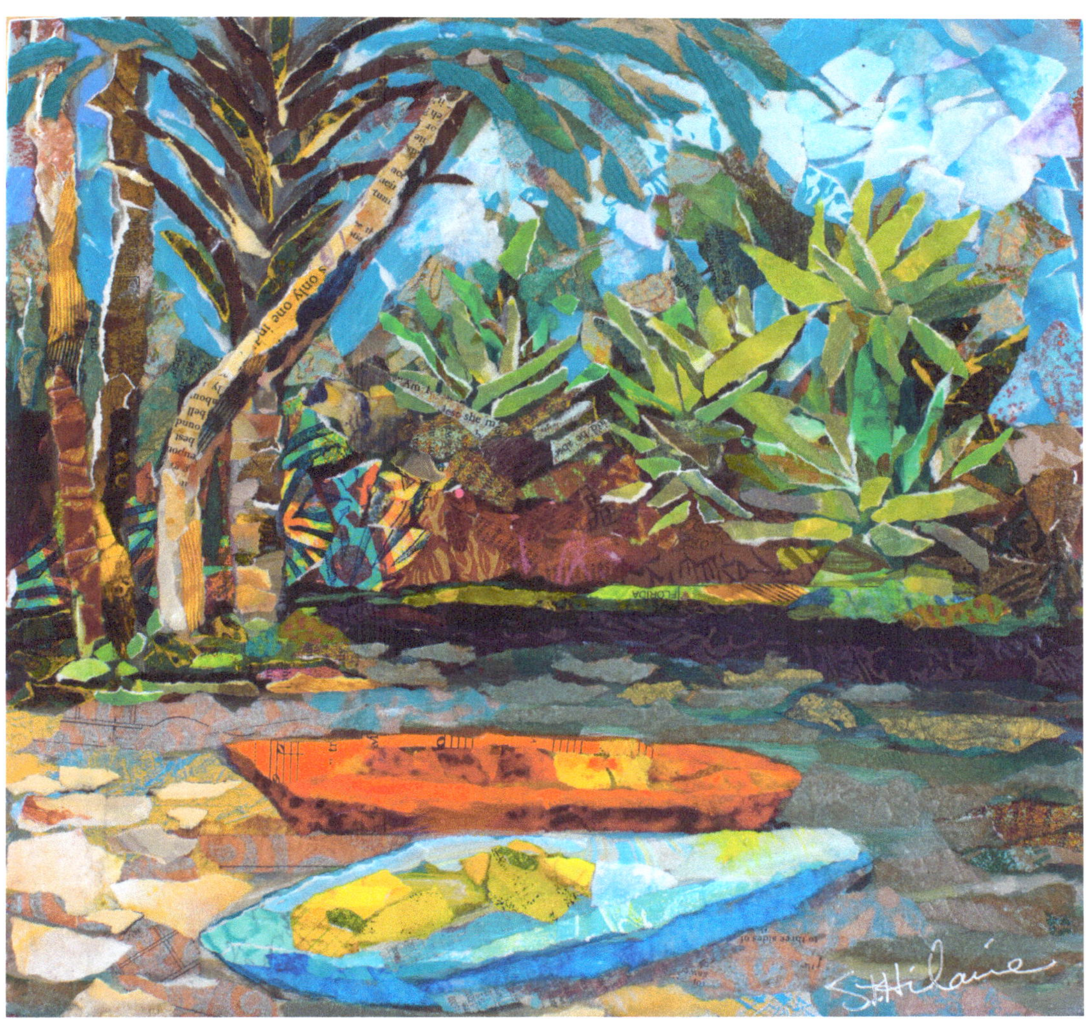

Up The River / 10x10

In this collage I have reduced the palm fronds to basic shapes that suggest palms and go in the direction of palm fronds without rendering every strand. I also edited many palms out to represent them with a few individuals. The kayaks and the life jackets are very basic shapes that suggest detail versus precisely rendering.

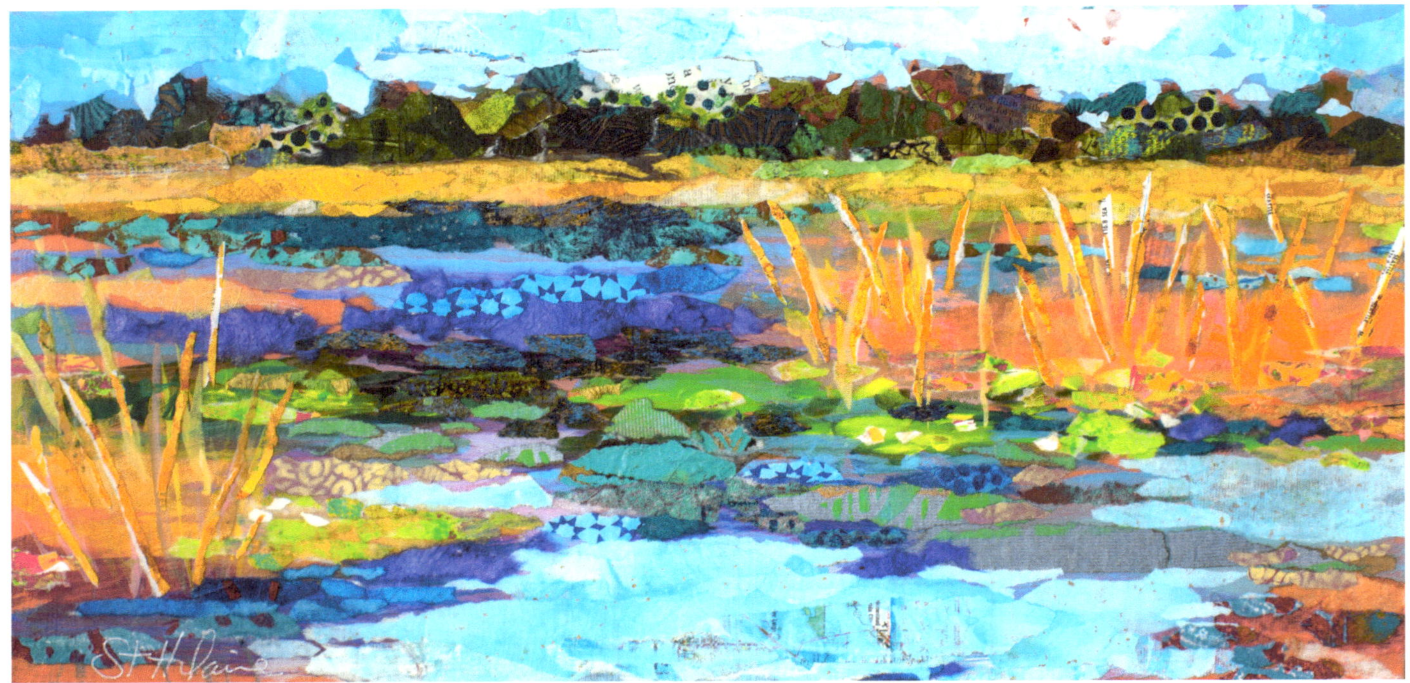

Wekiva Meander / 24x12

I have simplified the tall grass into clumps of color and then added a few upward slivers of paper to suggest large clusters of grass. Also you can see that I have reduced many lily pads to a few lily pads and simplified them into basic oval shapes. Note the tree line in the back does not have any individual trees, they are edited down to an indication of such with a variety of greens and a basic shape along the horizon.

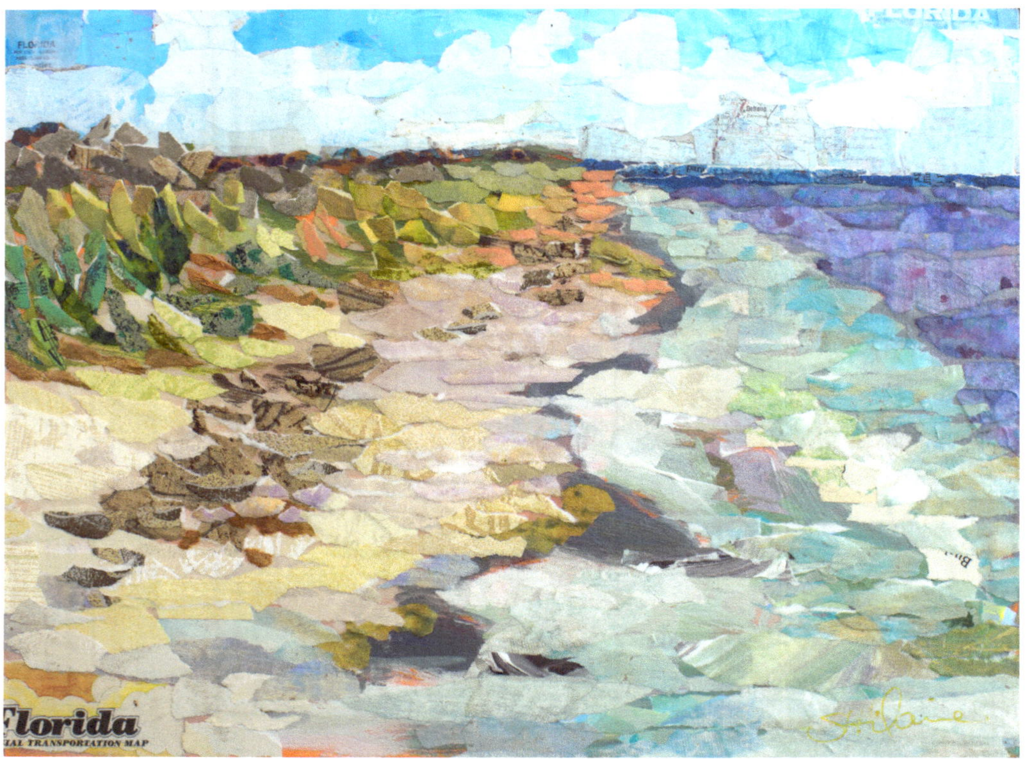

Beach Day Morning / 9x12

I have simplified the vegetation on the sand dunes into sweeping green papers as well as the frothy edge of the waves into sweeping white and light blue papers. Note that the clouds on the horizon are simple pale blue/white shapes without a lot of detail.

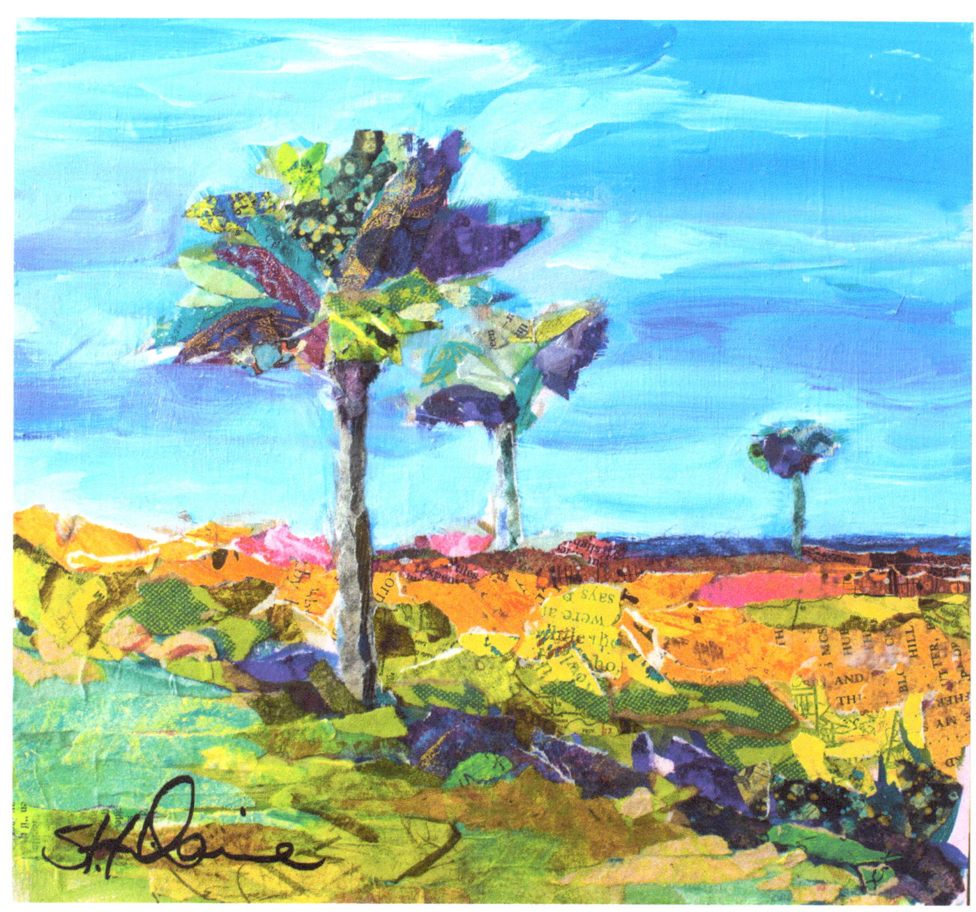

We Three / 10x10

Simplifying the palm fronds into very basic shapes with lots of color–the second and third palm become even less detailed as they disappear into the distance. Note the simple shapes that makeup the grass and vegetation in the foreground and below the trees.

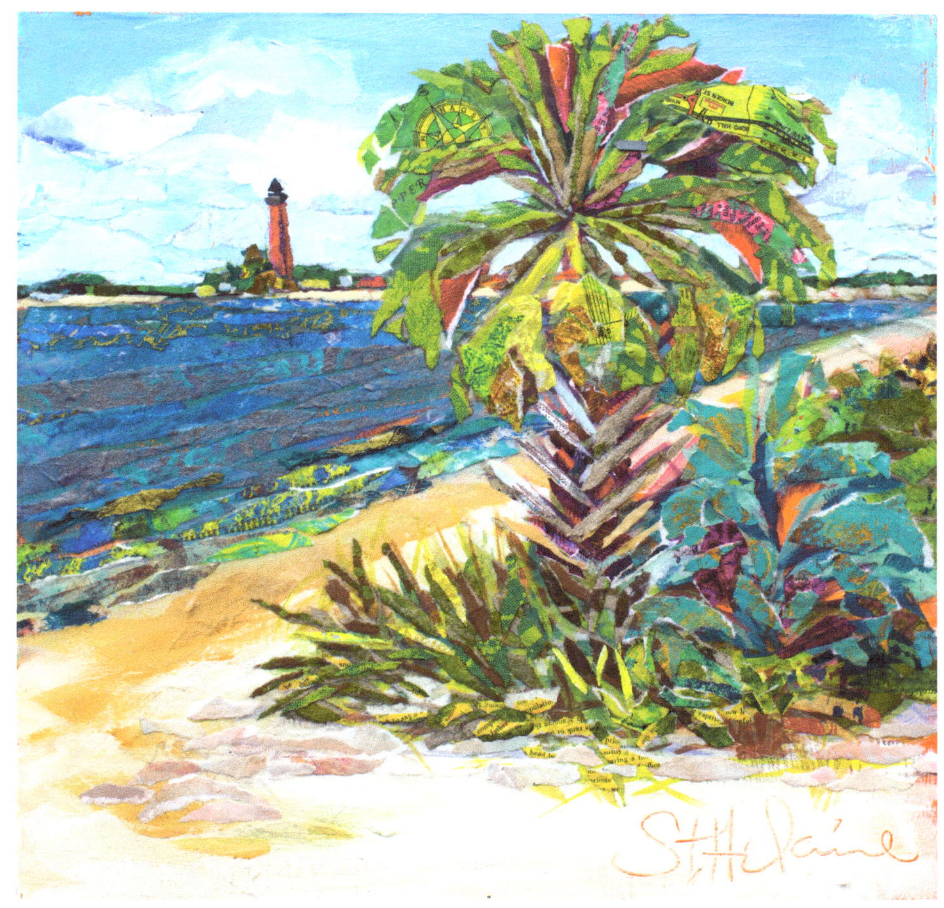

Around the Bend / 10x10

Another simplified treatment of palm fronds and the criss-cross pattern of the base of the palm trunk The waters' edge is created with directional pieces of paper that follow the shoreline and the vegetation below the palms is edited down to basic shapes.

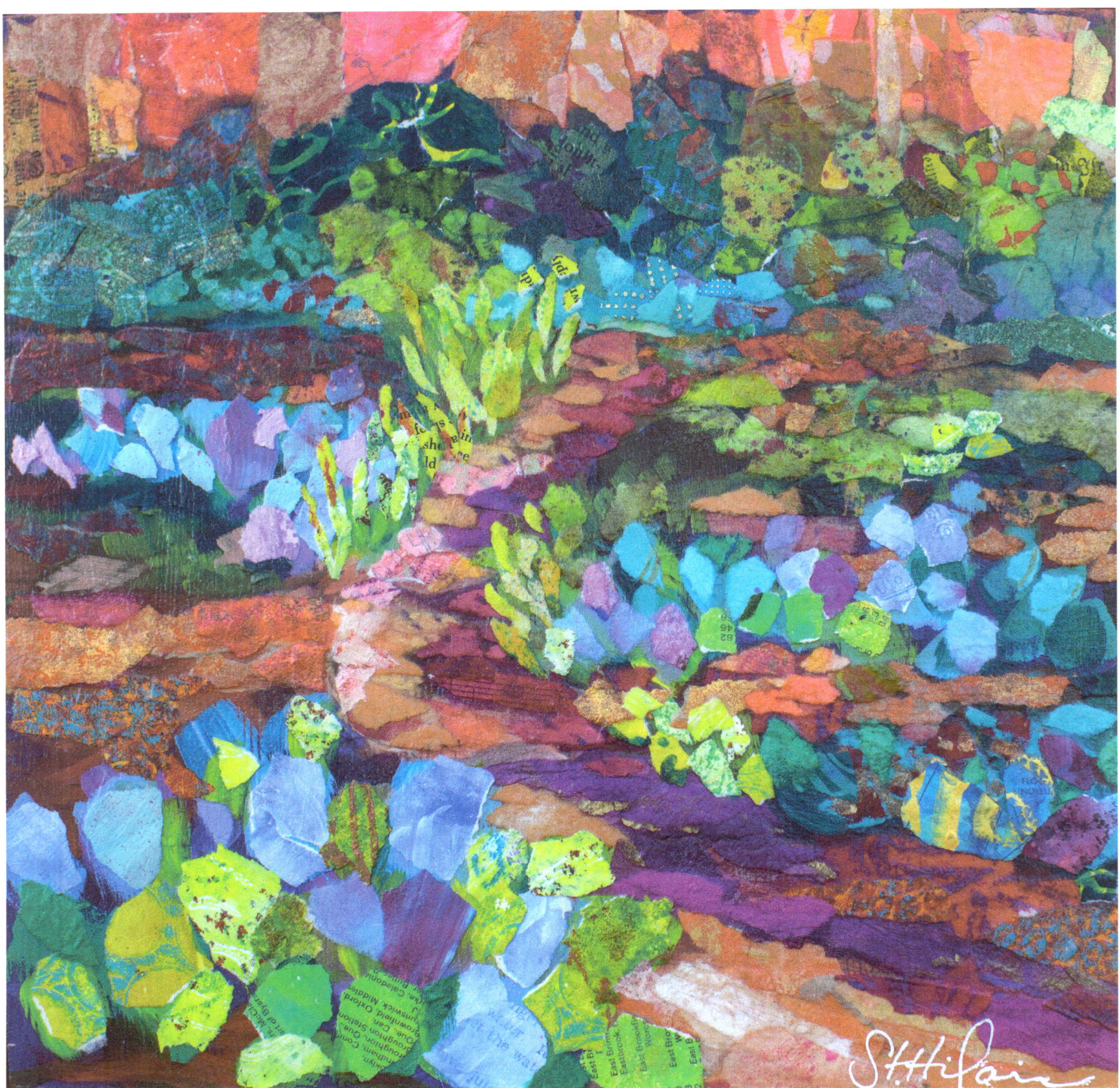

Mystic Trail / 10x10

A simplification of prickly pear cactus clusters. I have reduced the
number of paddles and broken them down into more basic oval-like
shapes. The cactus are slightly more detailed in the foreground and
far less detailed in the background at the end of the path. Reducing
detail in the distance allows your landscape elements to receed; sort
of like an out of focus photograph.

 The purple paper along the path represents cast shadows from the
vegetation on the right hand side, they are simple, elongated shapes.

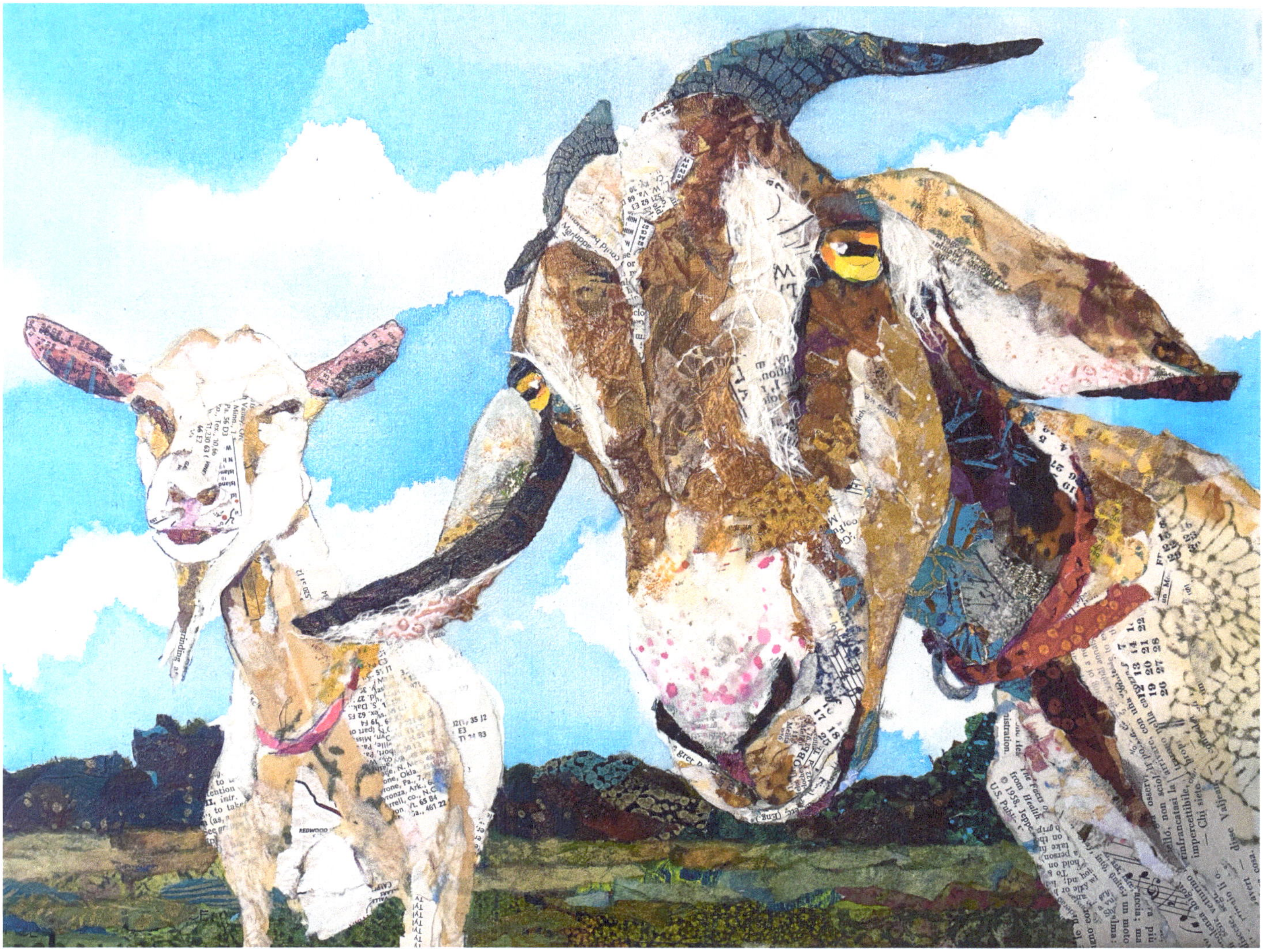

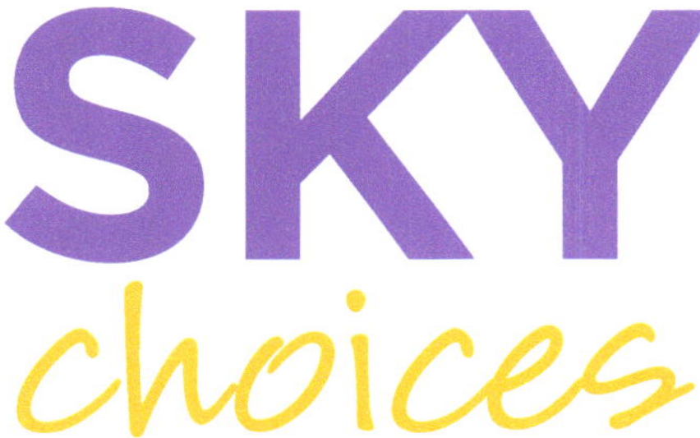

Carolina Goats / 16x12

SKY
choices

painted or papered?

Sky blue is so very pale that sometimes its difficult to create collage papers in such a light hue. I use Manganese Blue and Titanium White in my sky papers, but even then sometimes they come out too dark. Often I choose to leave my sky painted, like the one with the goats above. This sky was painted with Fluid Acrylics on Fredrix Mixed Media Canvas Board, I applied the paint VERY watered down and used a paper towel to blot out the clouds while the blue was still wet. A simple technique that yields beautiful painted clouds.

In the collage on the right, I chose to collage the sky with pale blue papers and plain white Sushi-Gami rice paper over the blue. This particular roll of rice paper tears with wonderful organic edges. It's slightly translucent, allowing the blue hue of the paper (or paint) it overlaps to show through. The combination of the rice paper clouds and the blue collage paper makes for a very nice soft sky effect. You can find this paper on my Amazon list, Amazon.com/Shop/Paper-Paintings-Collage-Artwork

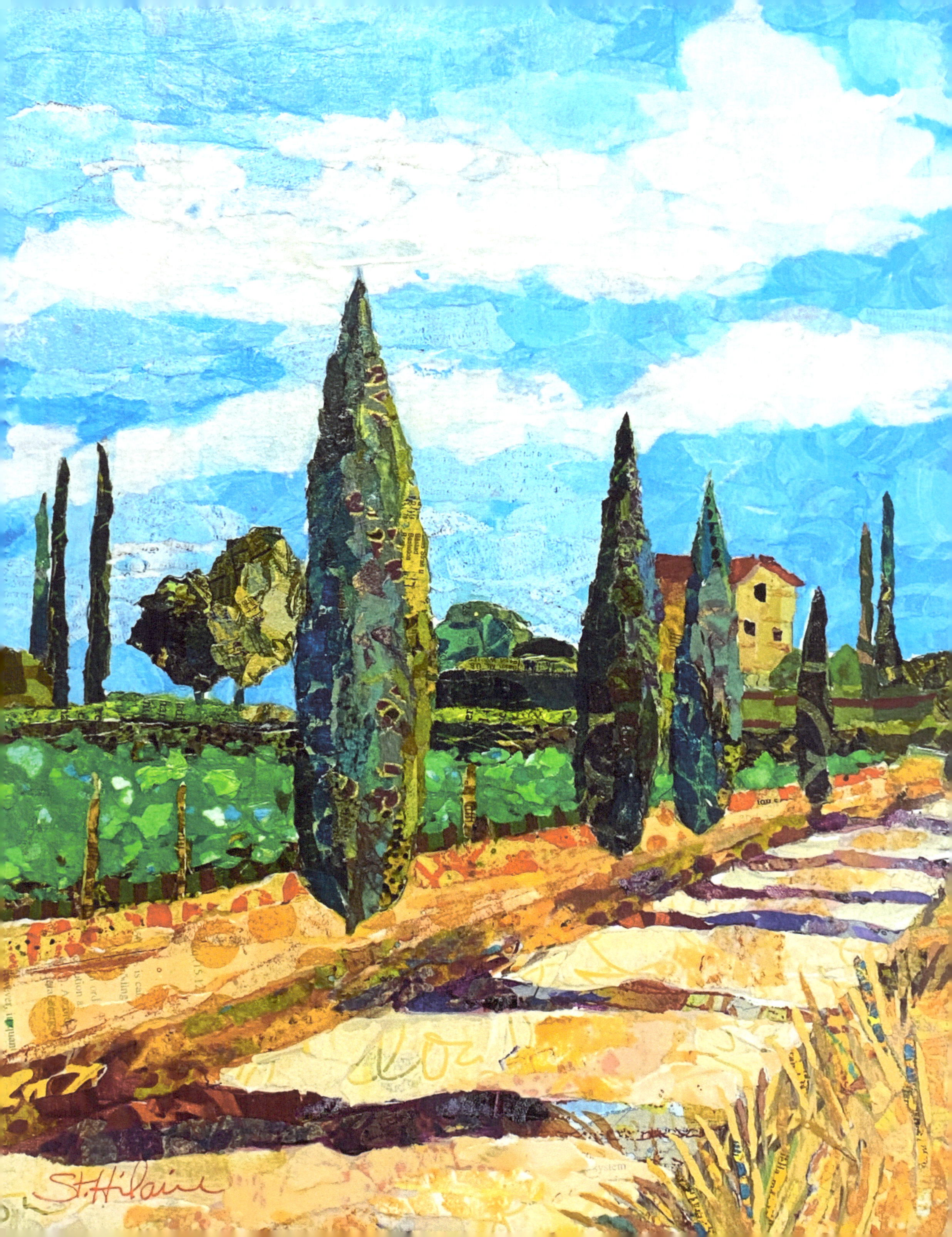

St.Hilaire

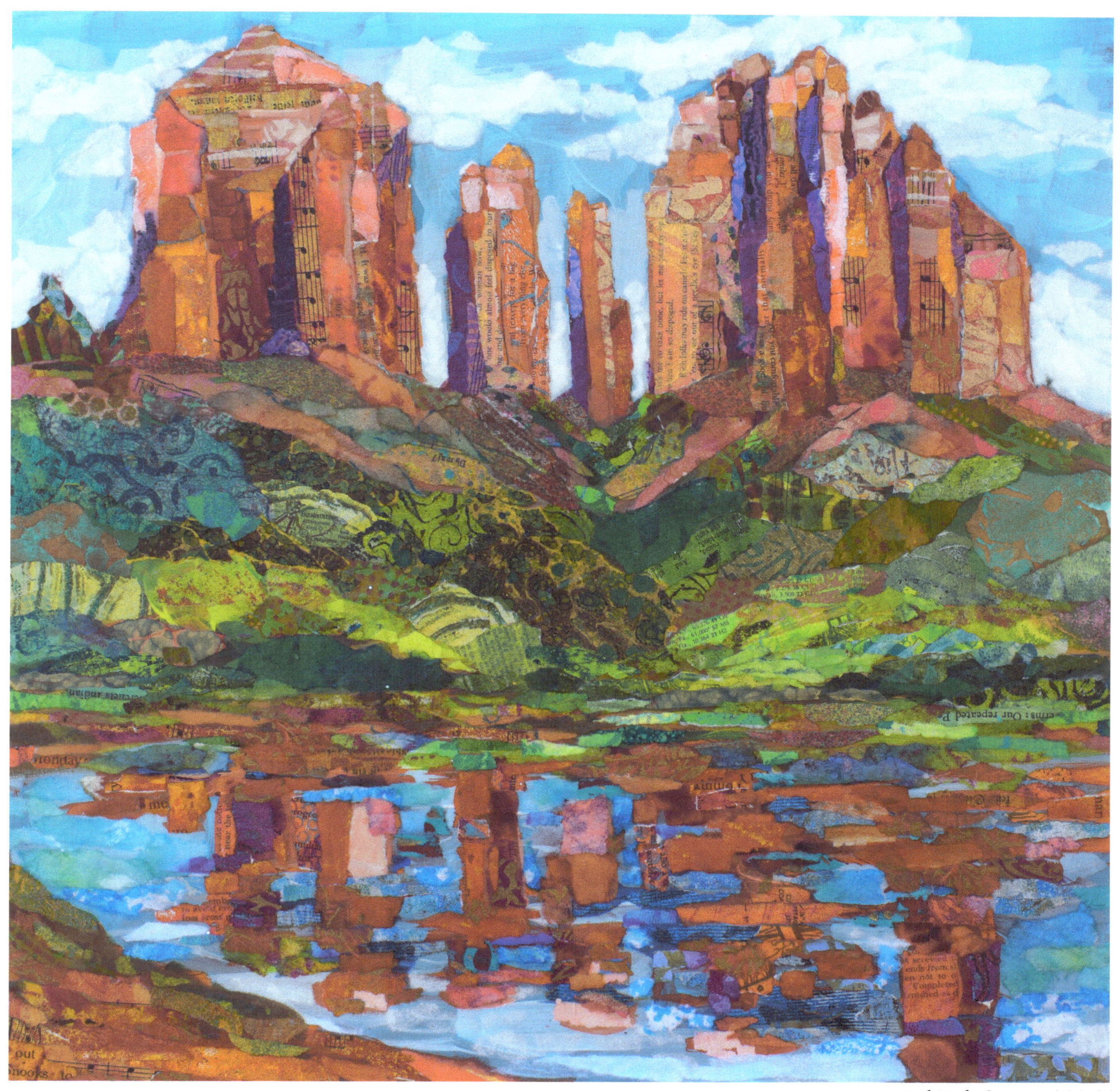

Red Rock Crossing / 14x14

WATER
in collage

Horizontal pieces lay flat and vertical pieces raise up. Always paint water
with horizontal paper brush marks to create a surface that lays down.

   Landscape Collage TECHNIQUES

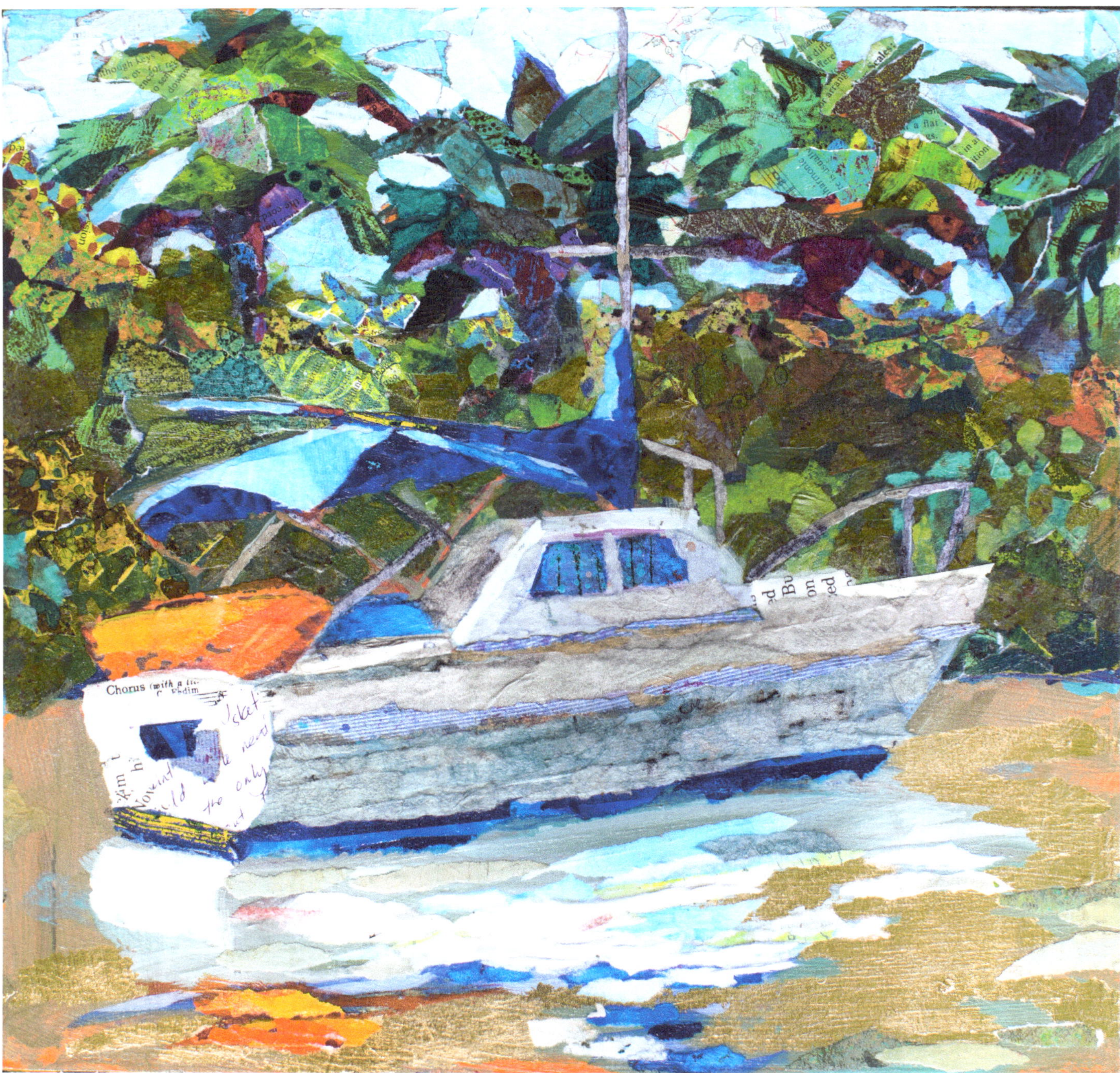

Adrift / 16x16

rendering reflections

Water provides wonderful opportunities for abstraction in landscape painting. Working with reflection and refraction may seem daunting, trying to get it "right." For me, it's my favorite part of collaging the landscape, I prefer scenes that offer me the opportunity to play with reflections.

It's important to just think about it in terms of shapes, creating something that gives the impression of what you see. Look closely at how the edge of the reflected image wiggles back and forth along the horizontal surface of the water, giving the feeling of rippling.

With a little practice, it an be a lot of fun to work with reflection, and refraction in collage, just remember to apply your pieces horizontally!

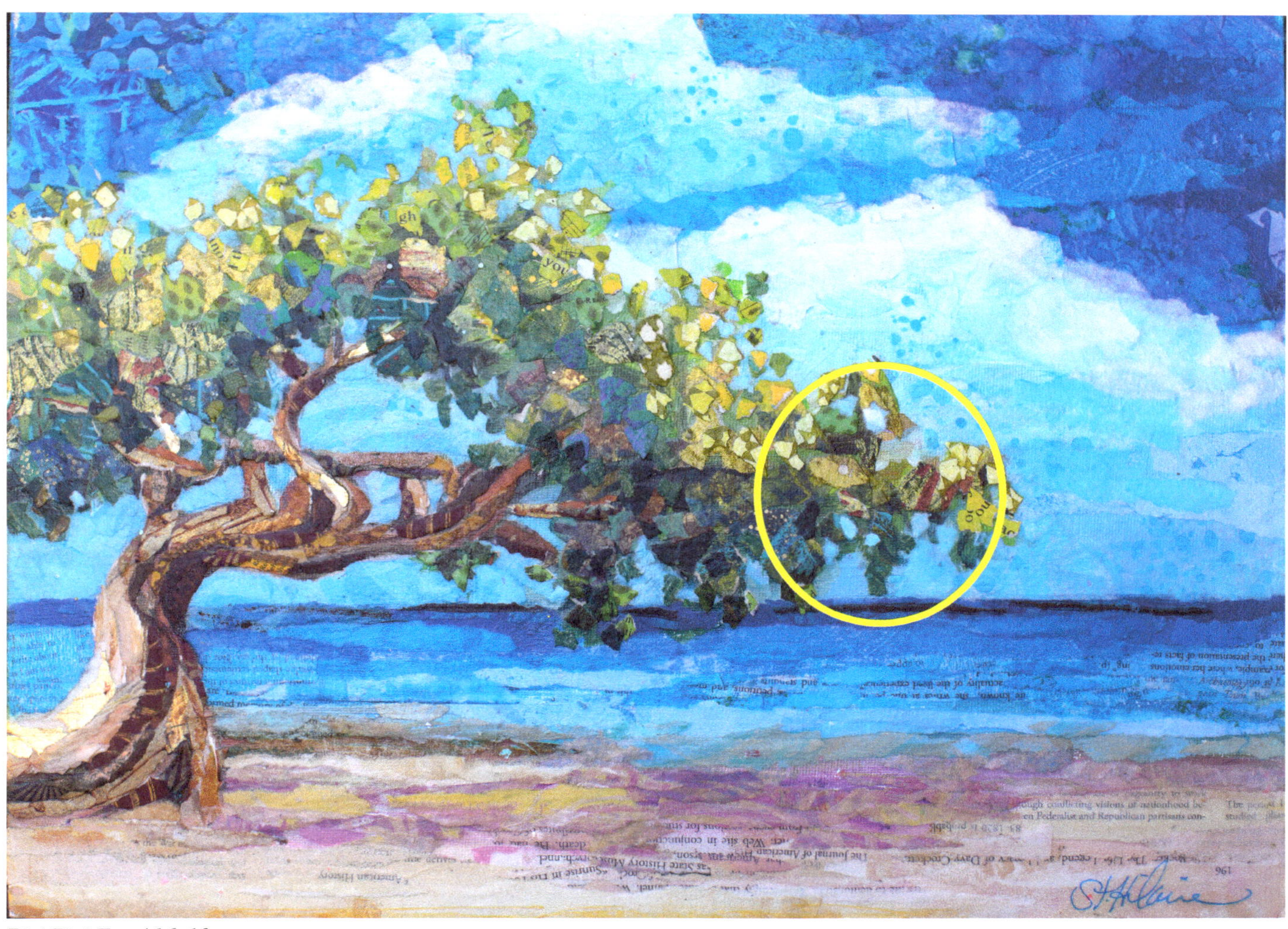

Divi Divi Tree / 16x12

TREES
sky windows

The yellow circle (above) highlights some light blue pieces of collage paper added on top of the canopy in order to open up some sky windows and make the leaf layer look more organic

Opening up around the edge and in between branches of a tree canopy is easy when you use what I call sky windows. Bring back some bits of the sky blue paper over the tree canopy. These bits of blue sky can also provide windows in the middle between branches, giving it a more life-like feel. It doesn't matter that these little openings of sky are going on top of your greenery at the end, when you step back and look you will get the impression of openings.

As with anything else, shading is key to rendering 3-D objects. Note that the *Divi Divi Tree* (above) is light at the top, then gradually down to medium, and dark underneath. You'll also see the same full range of values on the tree trunk as it is affected by the light.

Beach Tree (right) is an example of the addition of arbitrary color. Use your artistic license to spice up the colors in your composition, don't always be locked into what you expect to see—local color. You can see that I have infused red, blue, orange into the tree trunk as well as the canopy. Giving the water a more sea green color is me using my artistic license to spice up the color palette and add life to the scene!

Landscape Collage TECHNIQUES

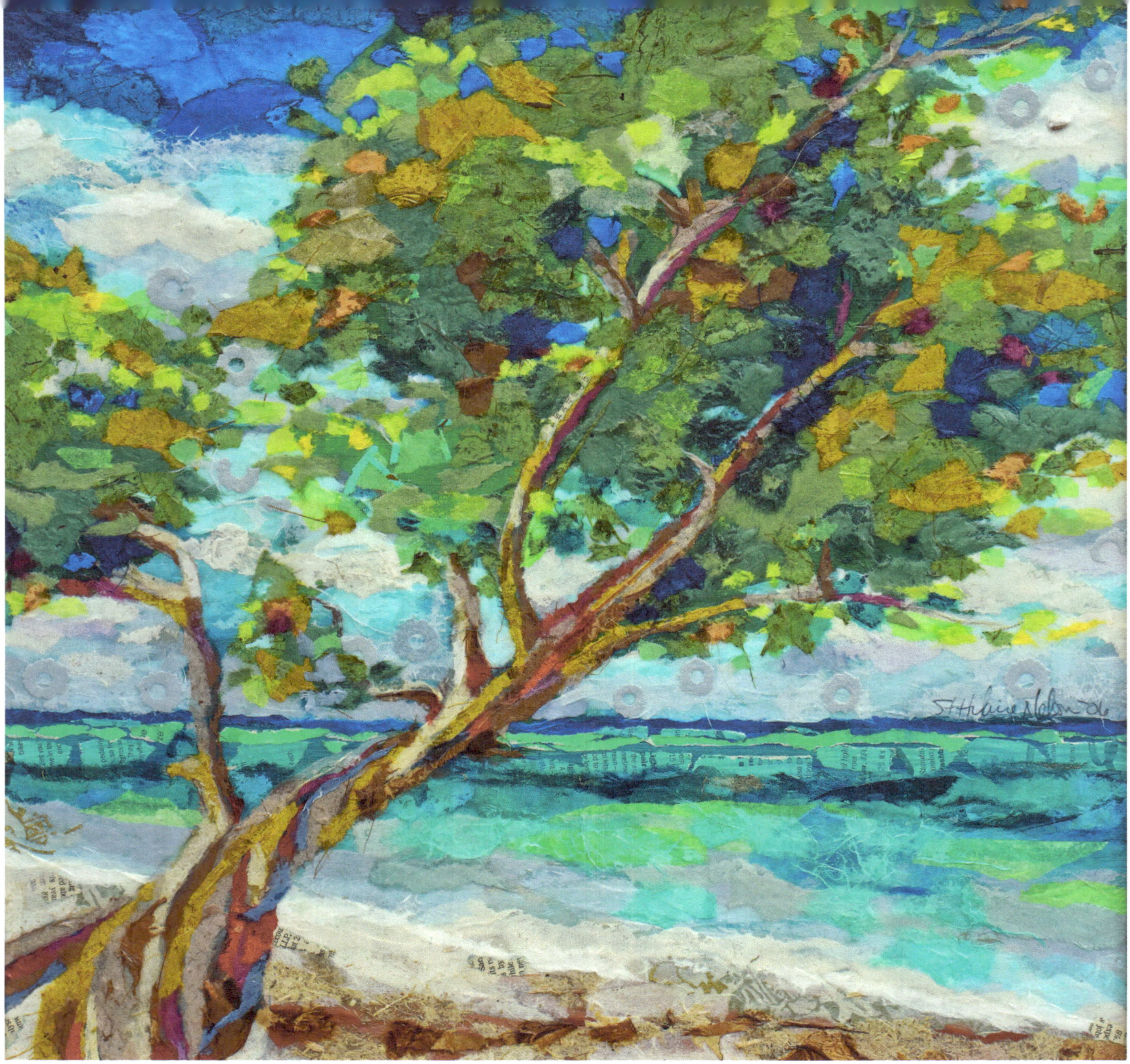

Beach Tree / 16x16

When you have clouds behind your tree, your sky windows will be the color of the clouds, or the color of the sky as it appears directly behind the tree. Be mindful to match the colors for more believable results, in a sky that gradually goes from light at the top to dark at the horizon line, you have to pay close attention to the value as it appears directly behind your tree canopy.

Note the transitional paper I use for both tree shadows on the beach. In *Divi Divi Tree* (left) that paper is purple plus the sand color in order to create a soft edge on a purple shadow. In *Beach Tree* (above) the transitional paper is brown and sand color in order to create a soft edge on a sand shadow.

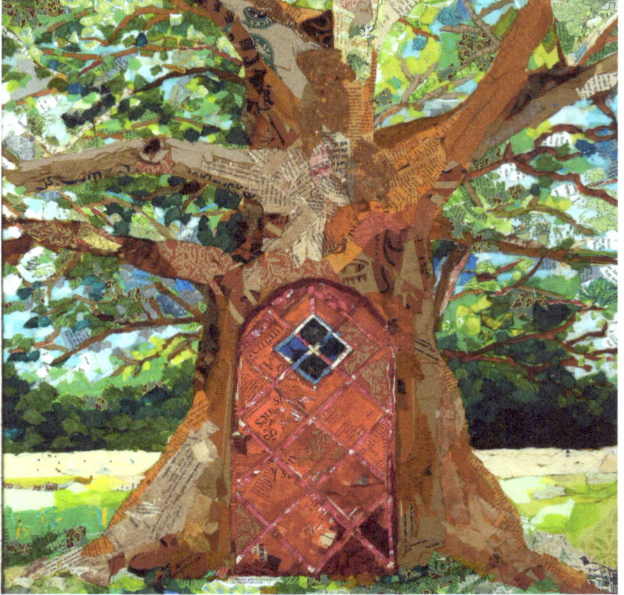

Enchanted, 24x24 (right) The ultimate combination of artistic license, arbitrary color, sky windows, and shading

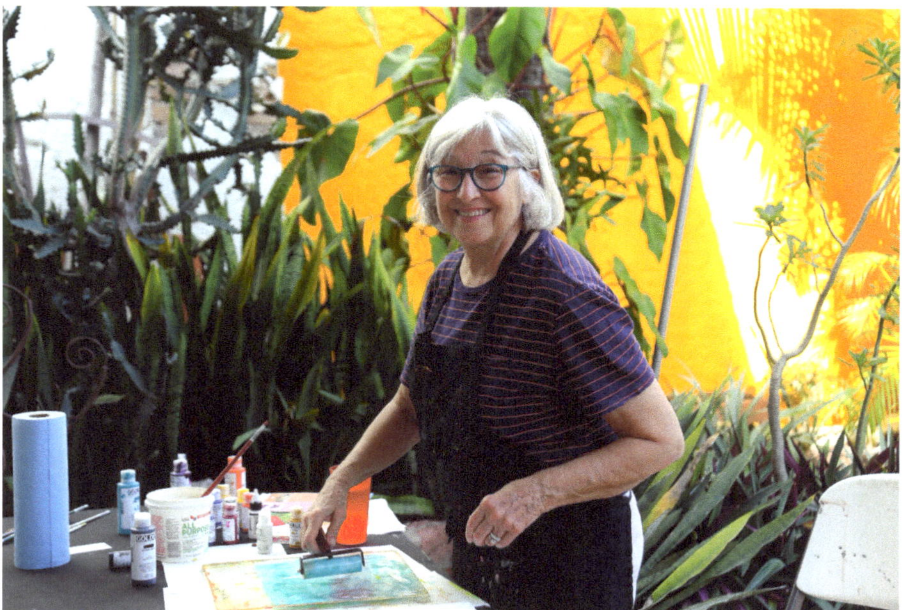

Once you've finished having FUN with the process, it's time to hang your art

finishing
TOUCHES

signing your work

Once your landscape collage is finished, and you are happy with it, it's time to prepare for hanging!

Be sure that your signature is legible and clear, so that in the event someone wants to learn more about you, they can look you up on-line.

Sign *on top* of your varnish because the surface will be smoother. Use any pen that you prefer, just make sure it indicates that it is permanent or waterproof, and fade proof or light-fast. These are important properties when signing your beautiful work of art. If these properties are not listed on the pen itself, do a little research on-line to be sure. I like Micron pens which come in many colors, they meet all the criteria.

Color, thickness, size, are all personal preference. Practice signing legibly with different pens on paper until you get something you are happy with.

Pens need to be "juicy" once they start to dry, toss them and get new.

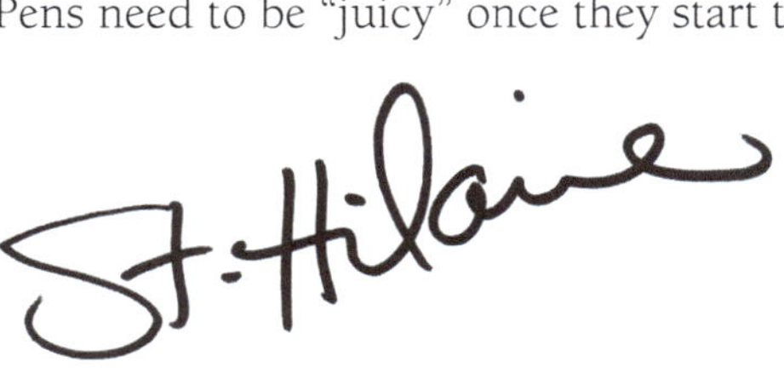

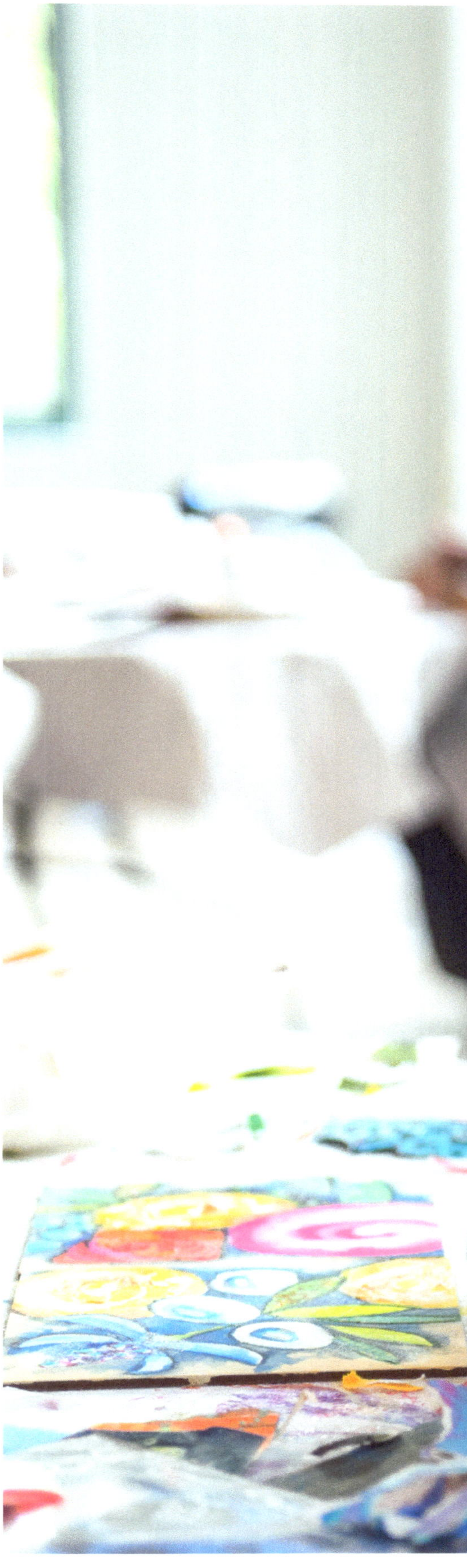

Landscape Collage TECHNIQUES

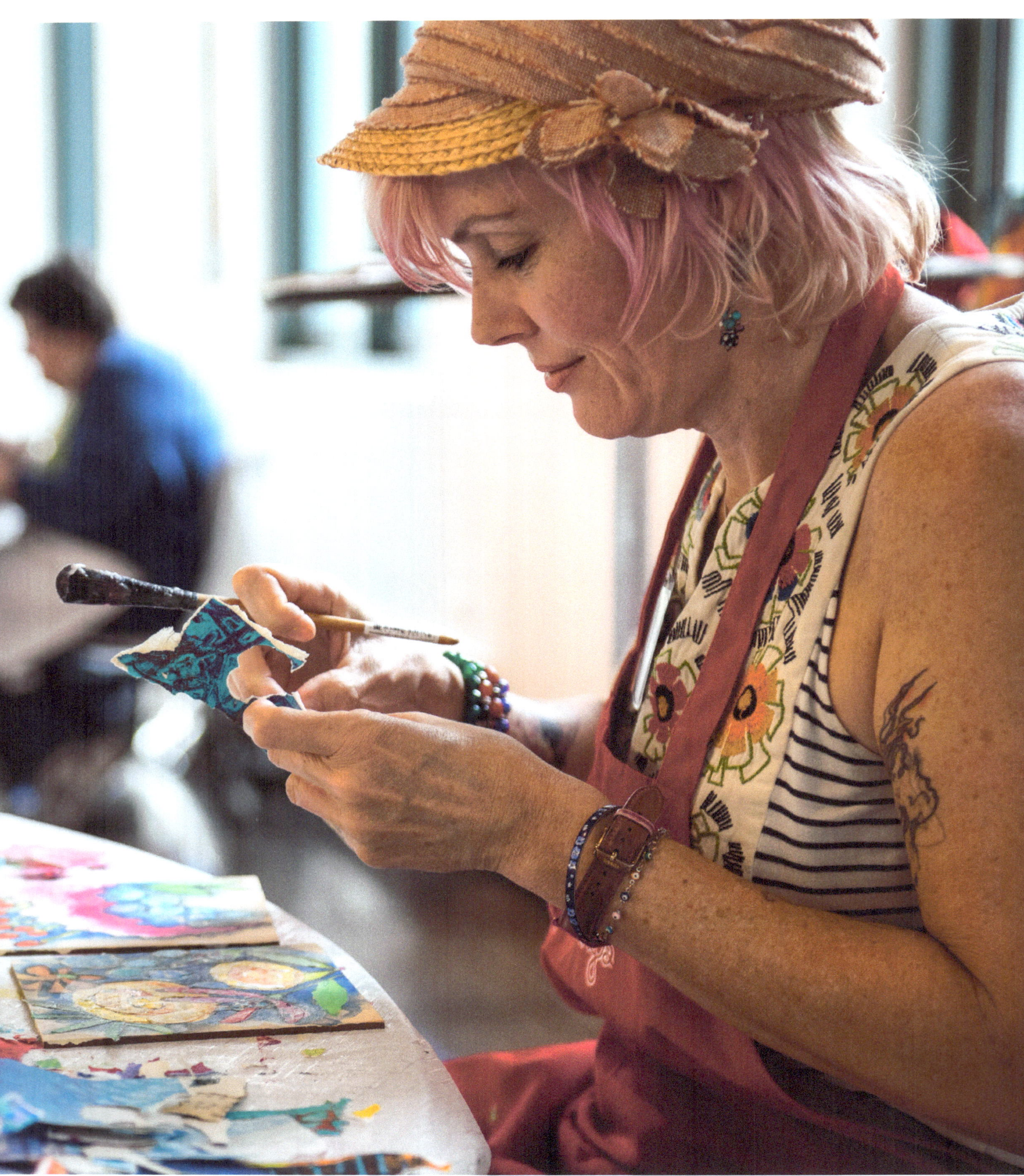

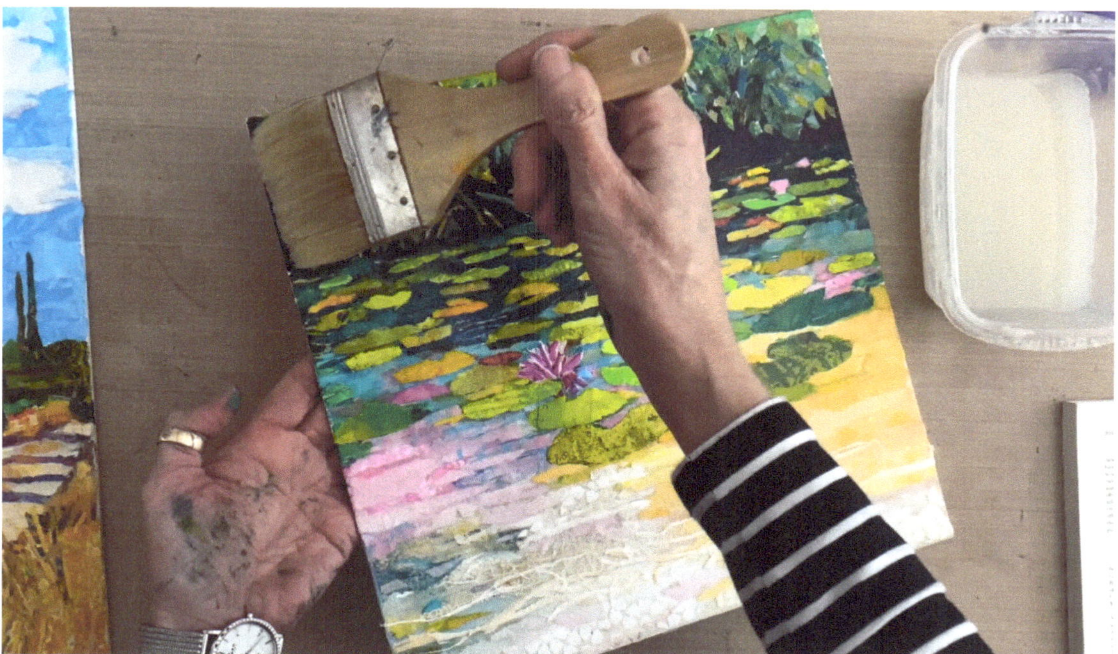
Tip your art slightly to the side in order to look for missed spots

Applying Final
VARNISH

I use Golden Paints brand varnish with UVLS to protect my work. Polymer Varnish with UVLS (Ultra Violet Light Stabilizers) is a waterborne acrylic varnish that dries to a protective, flexible, dust resistant surface over acrylic paint. It is removable with ammonia, and available in Gloss, Satin and Matte.

I typically use a satin finish (personal preference) and only two coats with several hours of drying time in between. Allow your project to dry overnight before applying the final varnish coat. I find that a desk fan can speed the dry time of varnish by circulating room temperature air across the surface; never use heat to attempt to speed dry your varnish, this causes a dry surface with dampness underneath.

Source: GoldenPaints.com

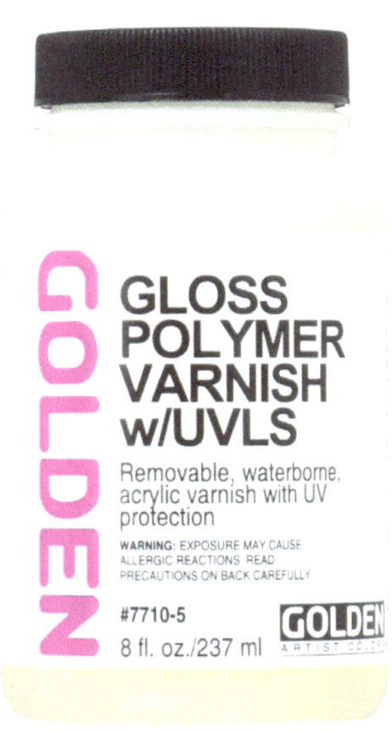

thinning varnish

This reduces the film thickness applied and the chance of uneven application. If applied in a thick state, the varnishes may show brush strokes and trap foam bubbles. The varnishes are thicker for the purpose of maintaining an even suspension of the solids within them. Even slight settling of varnish solids during storage may result in streaking within the dried varnish film.

surface consideration

Take into account the ambient conditions of the work area. Ideally, the temperature should be above 65° F and below 75° F, while the relative humidity is between 50% and 75%. Excessive humidity or cool temperature may result in bloom, a whiteness or opacity resulting from moisture trapped between the varnish and paint layers. If the surface of the piece being varnished is warmer than the varnish applied, the varnish will become thinner in viscosity upon application. This may result in unexpected dripping or sagging, particularly if working vertically. Likewise, if the varnish and surface are relatively cool, but warm significantly shortly after application, the varnish may drip or sag.

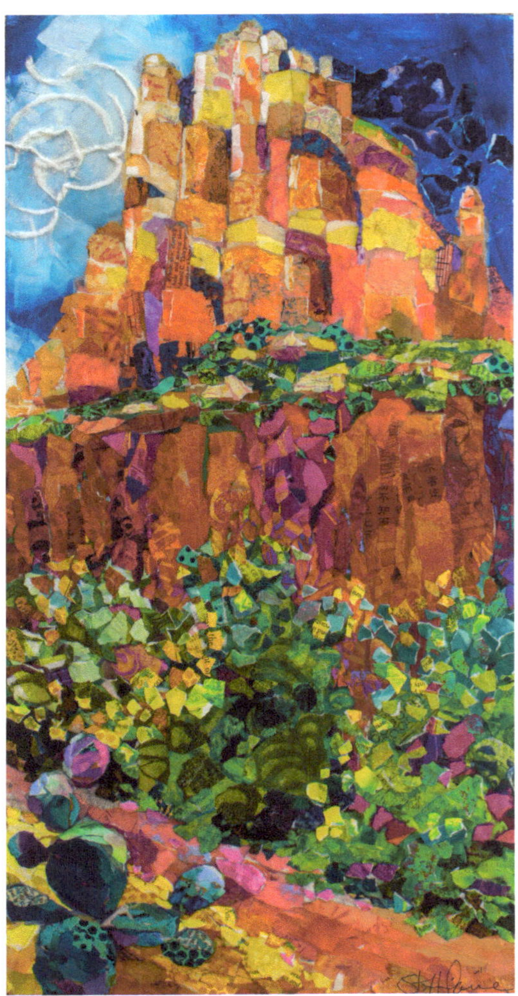

Magic Mountain / 12x24

brush application

Use a high quality bristle brush, such as a wide thin flat color-wash brush. Work from a shallow container to help control brush loading. The varnish solution should wet only the lower 25-30% of the length of the bristles. It is always best to apply the varnish on a horizontal surface in order to minimize running or sagging. Apply two thin coats with sufficient drying time in between, rather than one thick coat of varnish. The latter will take longer to cure, staying soft for some time, and could result in drips or a cloudy film. Apply the varnish in a manner which allows it to be brushed out to the most uniform, thinnest film possible.

two coats

When applying a satin or matte varnish, never apply more than two coats. A thick film of these reduced sheen varnishes will result in film cloudiness, dulling of color intensity, and loss of clarity.

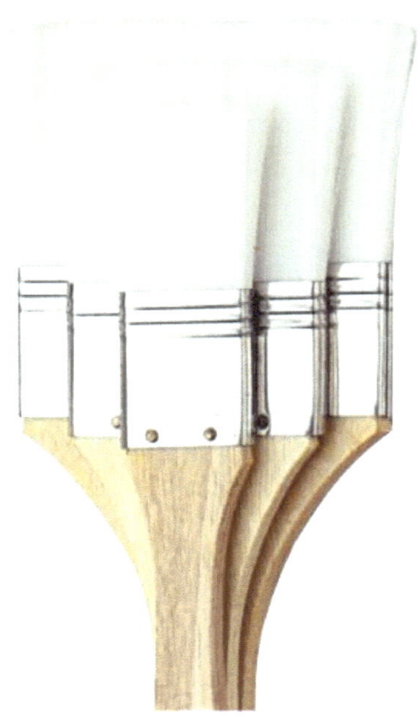

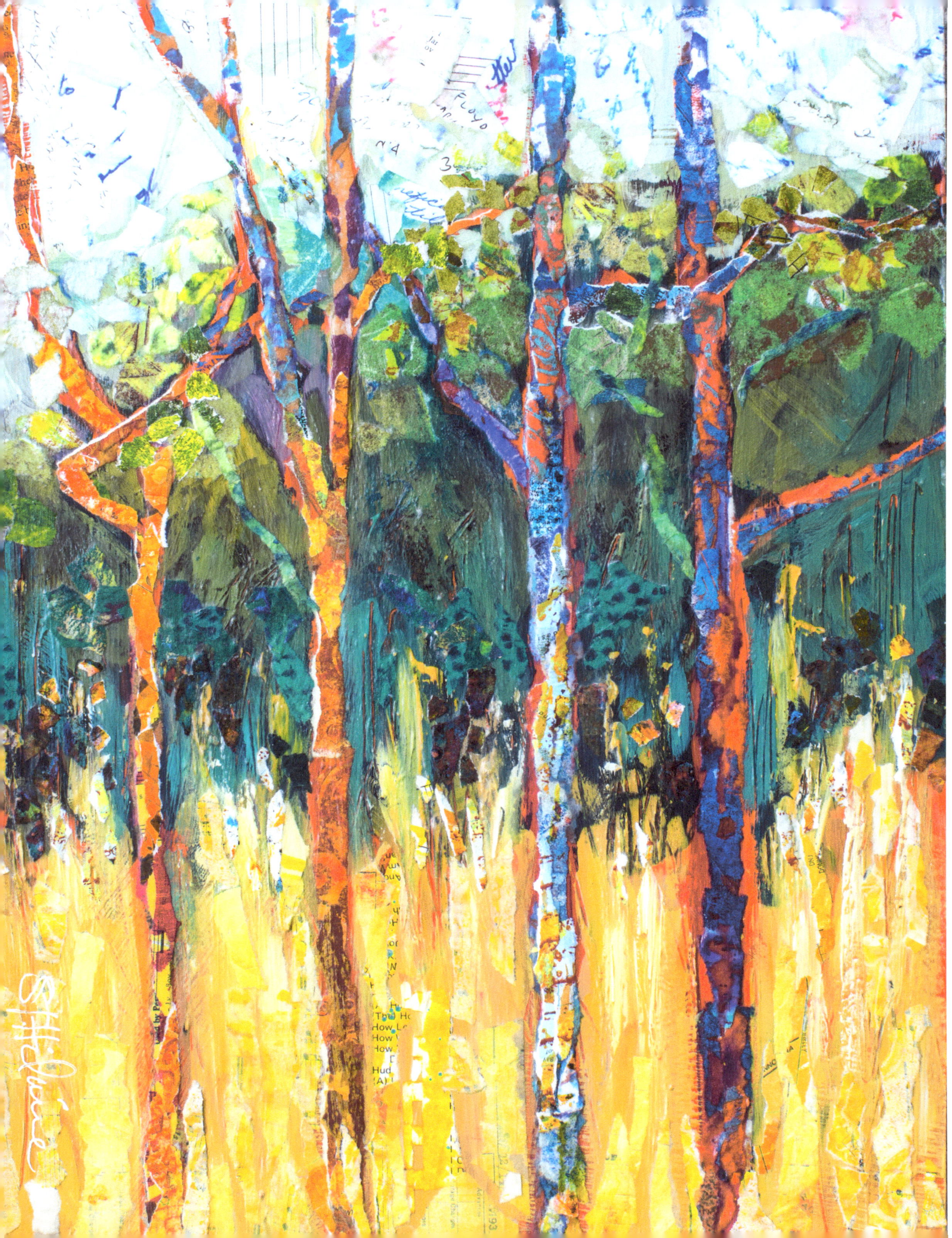

ABSTRACT
artistic license

You don't always have to try to recreate the scene... Sometimes I enjoy taking license to abstract the landscape and break it down into even MORE simple shapes, totally eliminating fine detail and stylizing the look more toward abstraction.

This is easy to do with collage paper! Start laying in a lot of patterns and textures, capturing simple shapes versus fine details. Play with the idea of abstraction, you might just find it to be the happy medium between realism and impressionism.

Family / 12x16 (left) Here i focused on the
vertical feeling of the trunks, the grass,
and the branches; leaving out the rest!

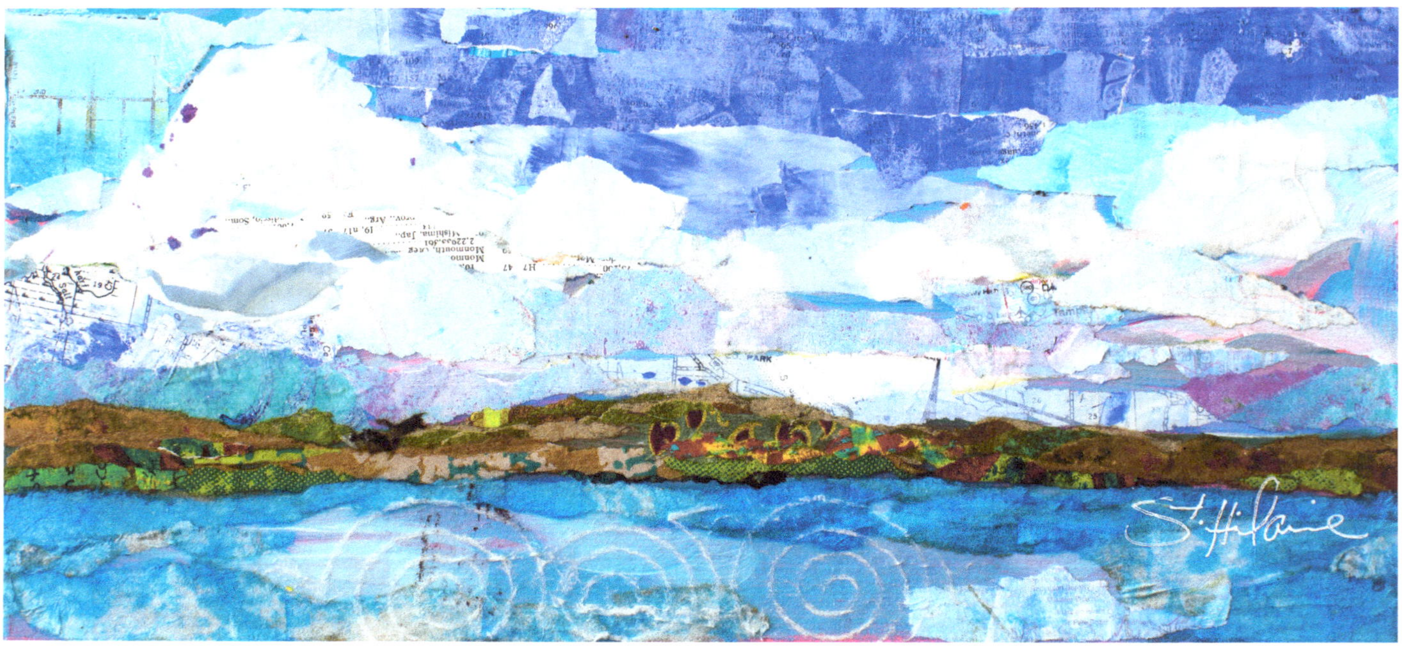

View From Turtle Mound / 20x10 In this piece I really focused on the large shapes of the sky and clouds, simplifying the land and water into simply horizontals

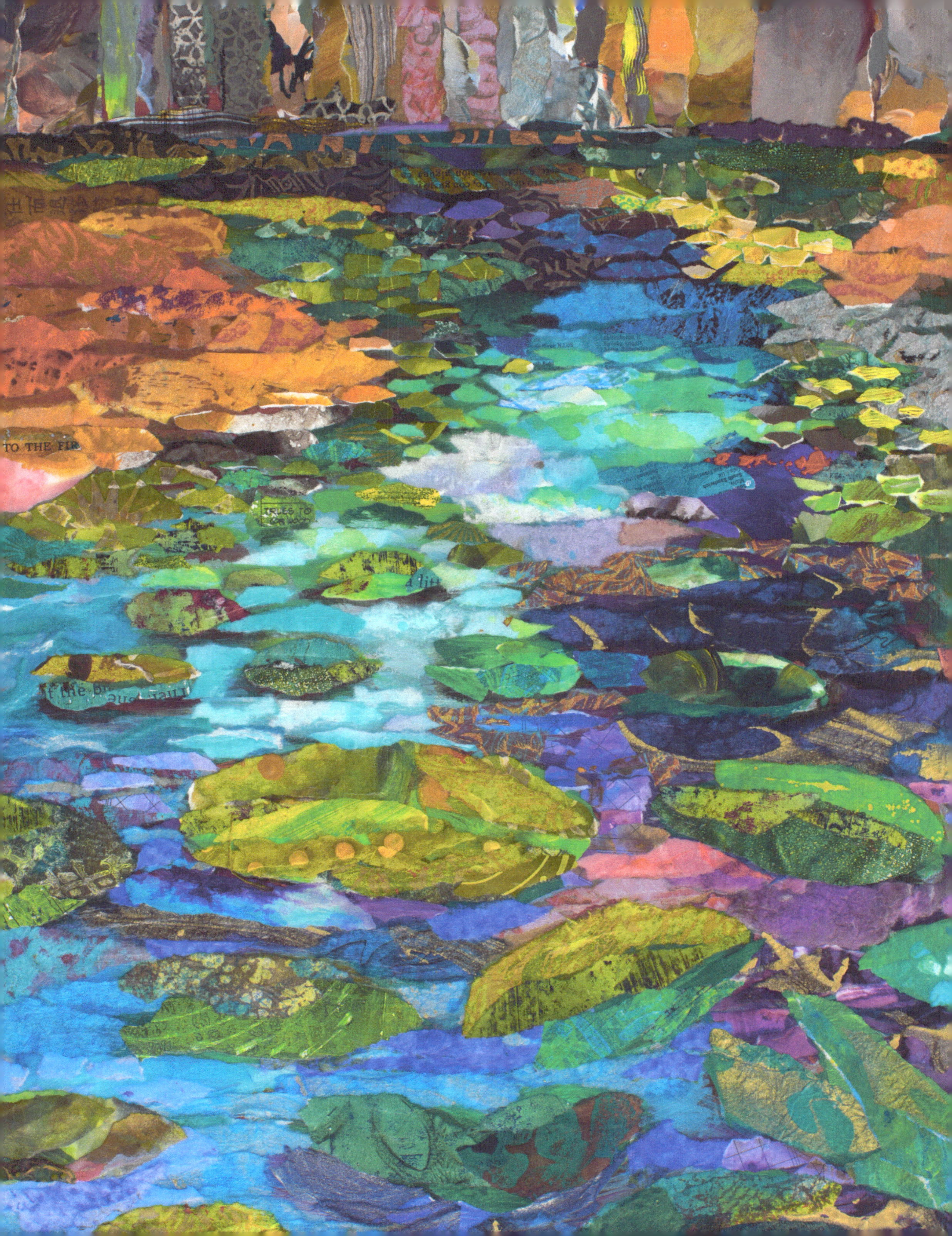

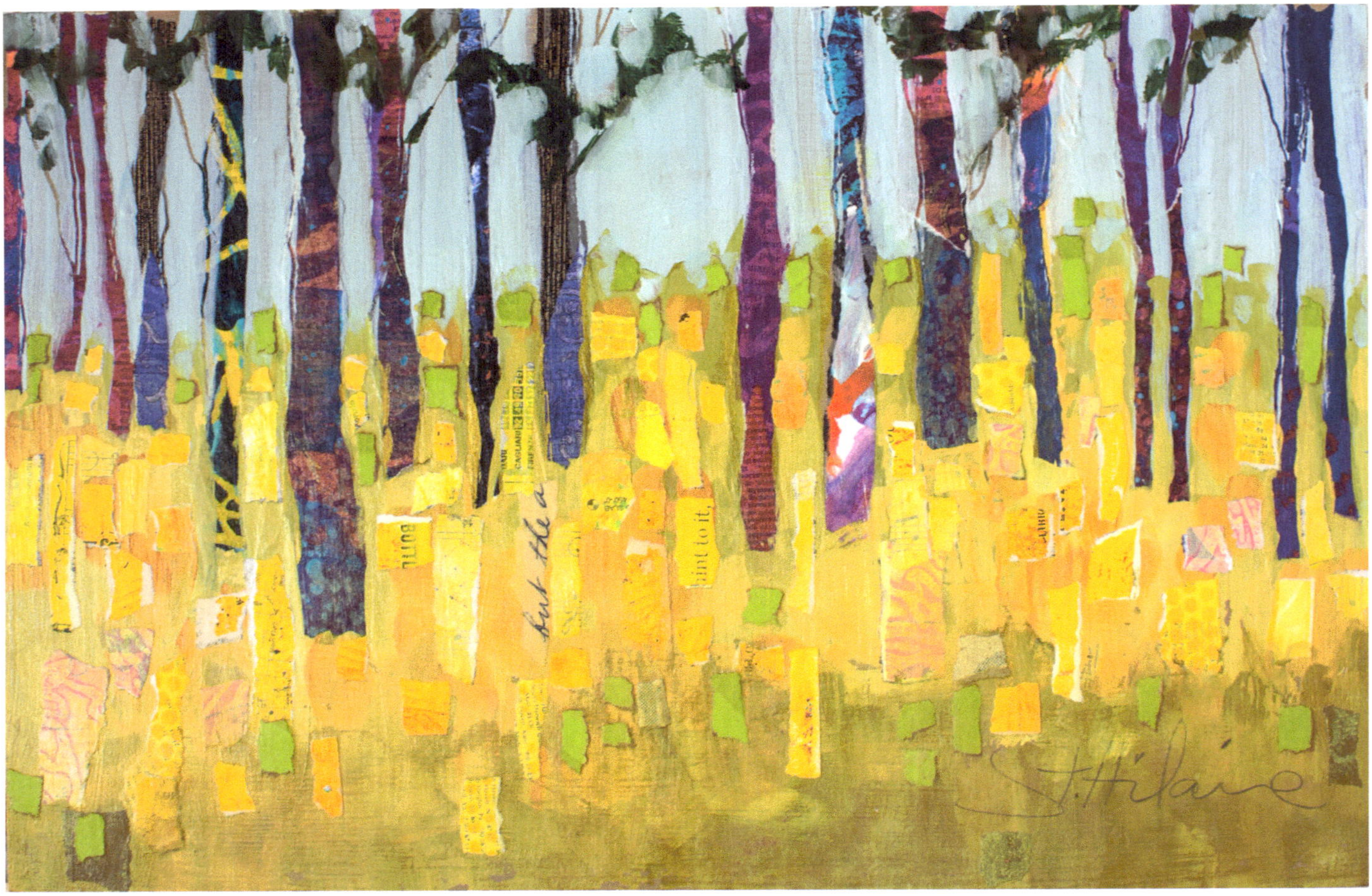

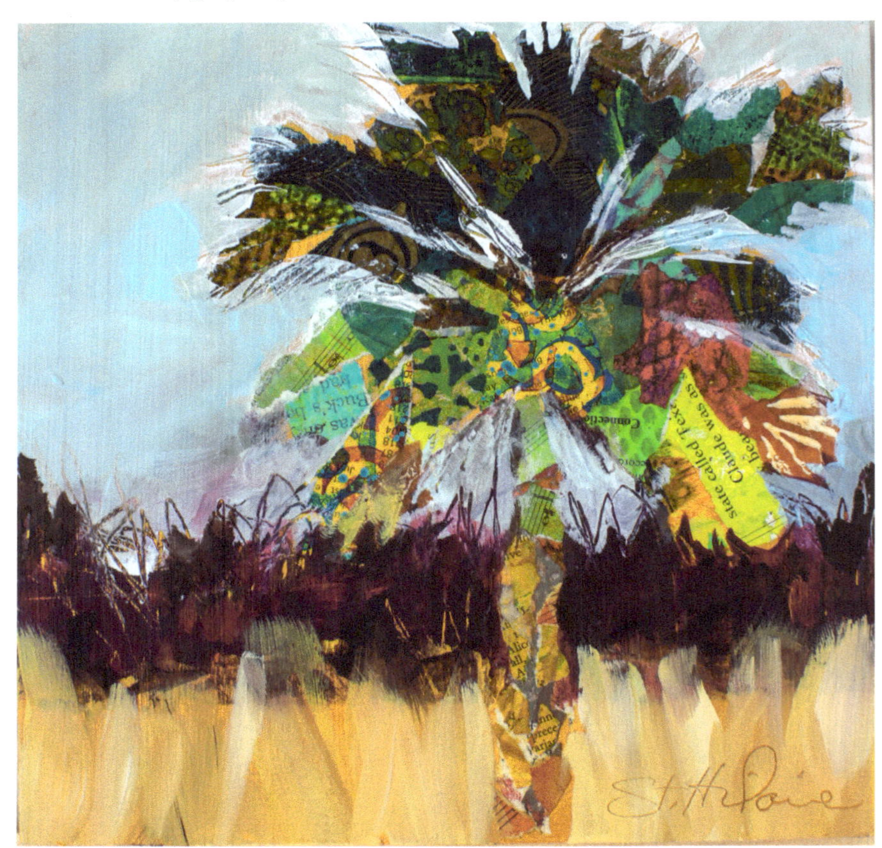

Pine Forrest Trees / 17x11 Pine trees with a Gustav Klimt sort of graphic pattern twist!

Nymphaecae / 11x14 (left)
This piece is about color and shapes more
than anything else, my very FIRST ever
Plein Air Painting created at the Wekiva
Paint Out in Orlando, Florida

Florida Native / 8x8 (right)
This piece is a combination of collage,
mark making, and negative space painting,
breaking it all down into basic shapes.

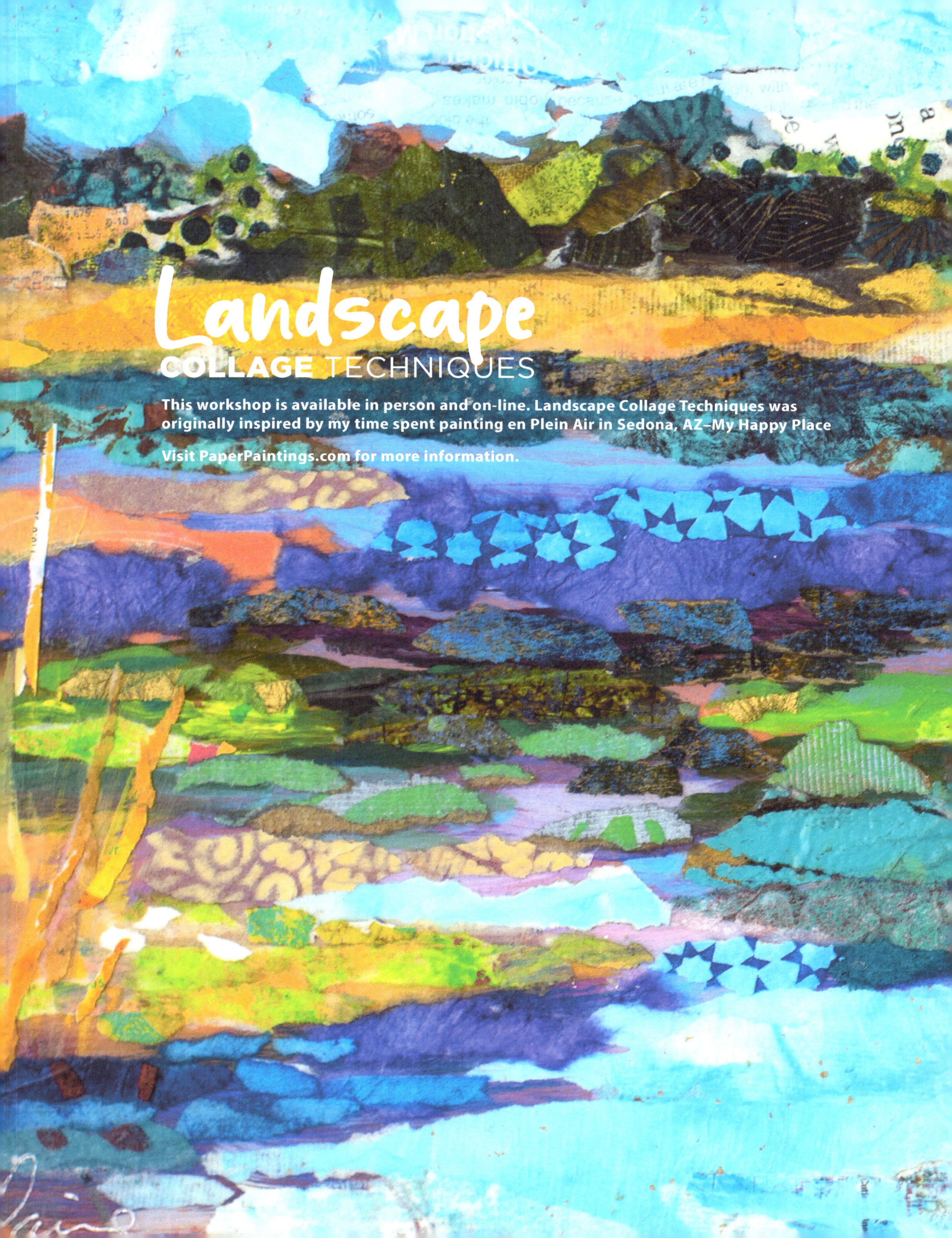
Landscape
COLLAGE TECHNIQUES
This workshop is available in person and on-line. Landscape Collage Techniques was
originally inspired by my time spent painting en Plein Air in Sedona, AZ–My Happy Place
Visit PaperPaintings.com for more information.

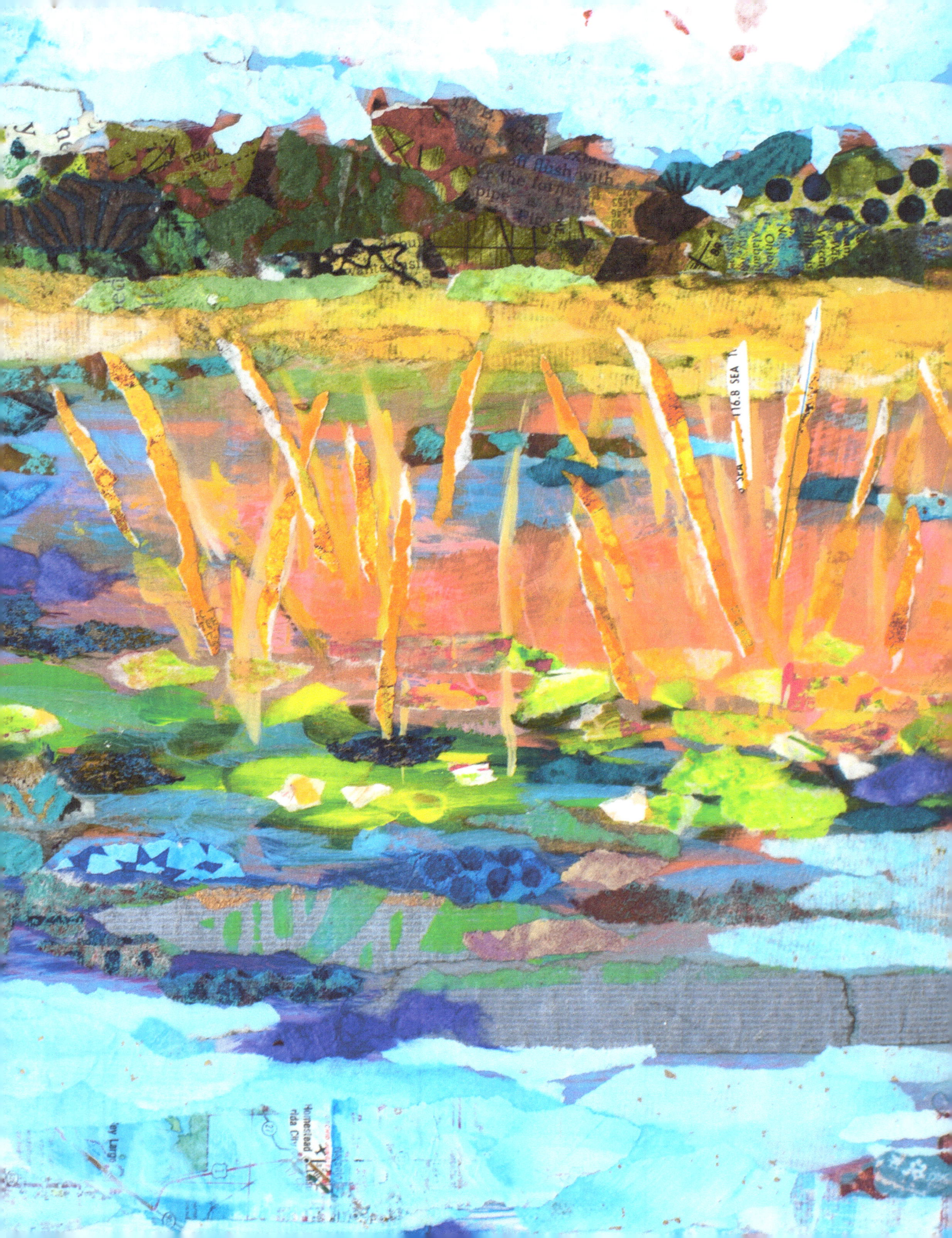
116.8 SEA

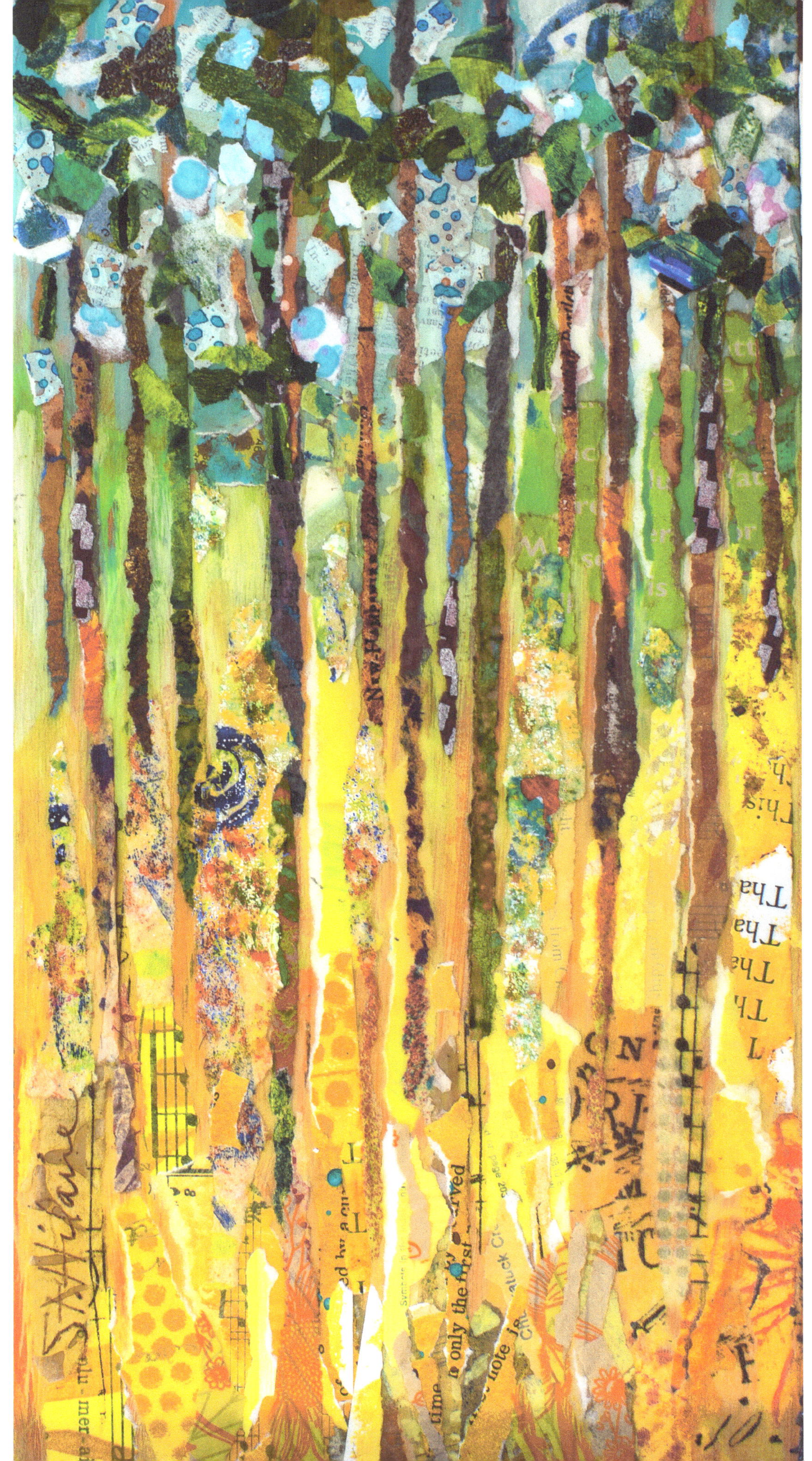

ABOUT THE AUTHOR

What sets the collage work of Elizabeth St. Hilaire apart is her use of unique, one-of-a-kind papers. Her signature collage style utilizes papers colored by hand, in every hue and texture needed to provide a complete paper palette.

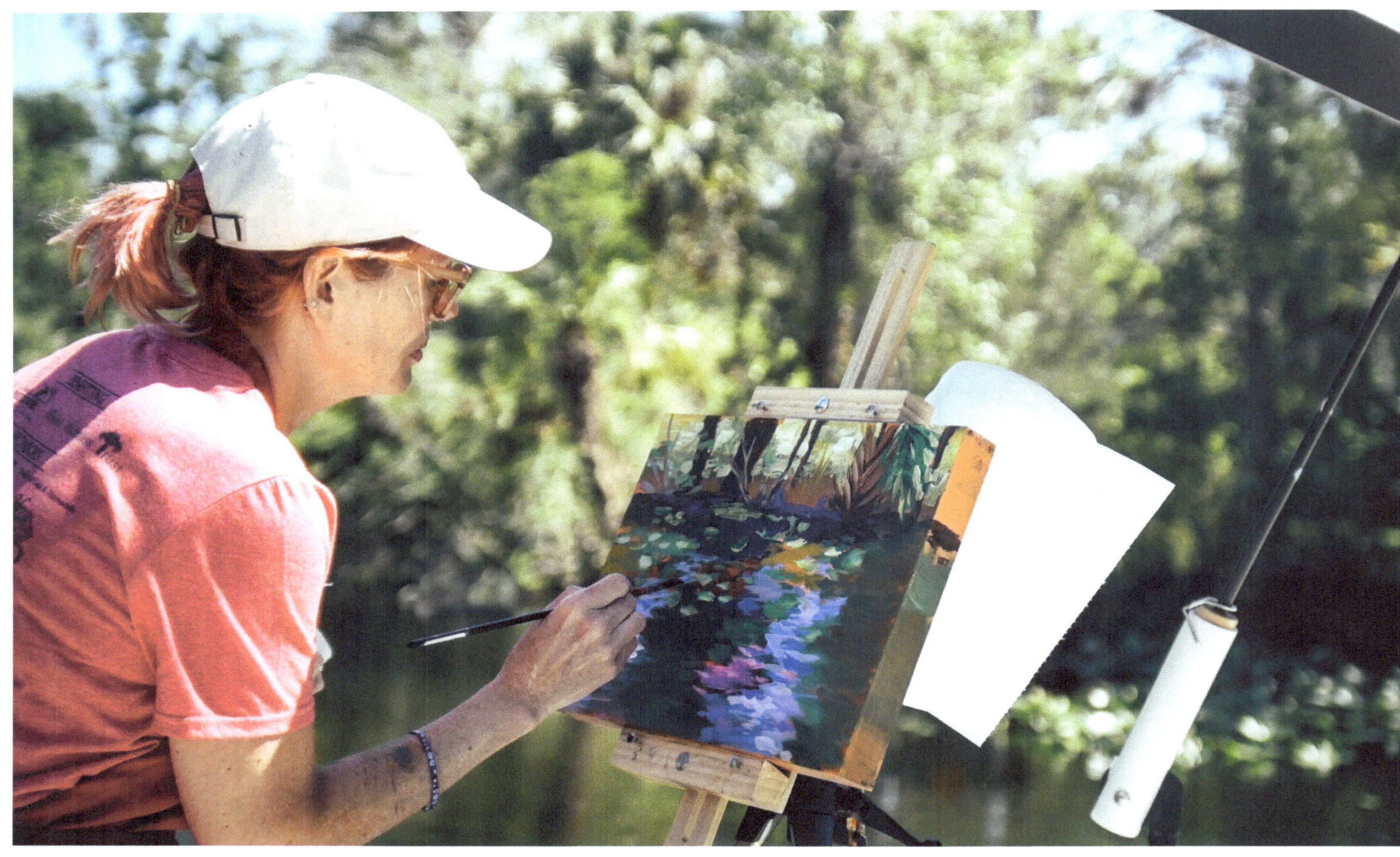

View a full portfolio of the artists work at
PaperPaintings.com

Contact the artist via email at
Elizabeth@PaperPaintings.com

The Facebook studio page offers work in progress and workshop information
Facebook.com/PaperPaintingsCollageArtwork

Follow her Tutorial Tidbits via the blog at
PaperPaintings.com

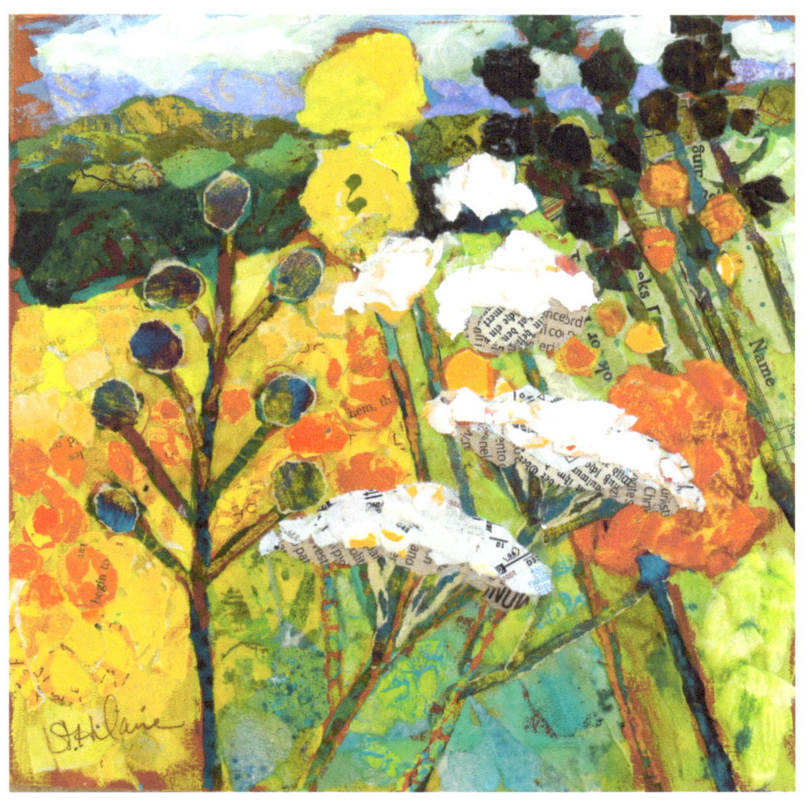

OTHER BOOKS BY ELIZABETH

Fabulous Florals!

Fashion Plate Portraits

Painterly Gel Prints

Pet and Animal Portraits

Songbirds in Collage

Mixed Media Collage Inspiration

SELF STUDY WORKSHOPS ONLINE

Building Better Backgrounds

Monoprinting for Collage Paper

Birds and Blooms

Pet and Animal Portraits

These workshops are evergreen,
always open and available to start
at any time. Visit PaperPaintings.com/onlineworkshops